Parallel Agile – faster delivery, fewer defects, lower cost

Doug Rosenberg • Barry Boehm • Matt Stephens
Charles Suscheck • Shobha Rani Dhalipathi
Bo Wang

Parallel Agile – faster delivery, fewer defects, lower cost

 Springer

Doug Rosenberg
Parallel Agile, Inc.
Santa Monica, CA, USA

Matt Stephens
SoftwareReality.com
London, UK

Shobha Rani Dhalipathi
University of Southern California
Fremont, CA, USA

Barry Boehm
Center for Systems and Software
Engineering (CSSE)
University of Southern California
Santa Monica, CA, USA

Charles Suscheck
Juniper Hill Associates
Liberty Township, OH, USA

Bo Wang
University of Southern California
Alhambra, CA, USA

Parallel Agile and Parallel Agile CodeBot are both registered trademarks of Parallel Agile, Inc.

ISBN 978-3-030-30703-5   ISBN 978-3-030-30701-1   (eBook)
https://doi.org/10.1007/978-3-030-30701-1

This Springer imprint is published by the registered company Springer Nature Switzerland AG
The registered company address is: Gewerbestrasse 11, 6330 Cham, Switzerland

Foreword

Software development has proven to be a highly problematic procedure; the data indicates that most development projects for systems or devices that contain a lot of software (and these days, that is almost everything) are significantly delayed, run over budget, and deliver far less capability than originally promised.

A number of factors—both technical and social—contribute to this depressing state of affairs:

- Most projects that contain software are awarded through a process of competitive bidding, and the desire to win the competition likely induces organizations to bid an amount that they consider the lowest credible price, with the shortest development schedule that they consider credible, too.
- Such projects are of quite amazing size and complexity; literally, in terms of the number of "pieces" involved, they are by far the largest and most complex endeavors that human beings have ever undertaken. It is routine for a system or device to have millions of lines of software code these days—BMW, for example, says that its newest cars have 200,000,000 lines of software code in them. I have seen estimates that Microsoft Windows and Microsoft Office are each about that size, too. No other human creation comes close to this level of scale and complexity.
- This is a difficult and specialized work, and unlike other human endeavors (e.g., building construction), it has proven difficult to separate the work by the various skills required, which places an additional burden on each software developer. In the building trades, no one is expected to be a master electrician, a master plumber, and a master mason, but in the software business, we often make designs that require each developer to have mastered quite a number of complex and diverse skills. This, naturally, leads to errors in the implementation.
- Such projects, due to their large size, now take very long periods of time to complete. Software development periods measured in years is a common phenomenon. These long schedules inevitably mean that particular individuals will come and go during the course of the project, and such turnover in a difficult and specialized work is an additional source of errors, delays, and cost increases.

I could go on and on, but you get the idea.

In my experience, the long development time periods are the most insidious aspect of this problem. Customers simply do not want to wait years for their new system or product, and long development time periods also increase cost—developers need to be paid every day.

What to do?

Naturally, many people have worked to solve this problem, myself included.

The collection of concepts and tools called "Agile software development" is one approach that has been offered to solve this problem. Unfortunately, Agile methods seem to work well only in a narrow set of circumstances and conditions.[1] These conditions do not seem to apply to very large systems—the ones that contain tens of millions of lines of software code. Yet these very large systems are often those that are the most important to society: automation systems for oil refineries and chemical plants, for healthcare diagnosis, for air-traffic control, for managing processing and payment of government benefits, etc.

One obvious way to shorten software development schedules is to do more of the work in parallel, that is, break the work into lots of small pieces to allow these small pieces to be built simultaneously by lots of separate teams. Often, unfortunately, the problem of selecting the set of small pieces so that they actually work the way you want when you try to put them all together after they have been built has proven to be quite difficult. Some of my own methodological improvements to the software industry are aimed at exactly this aspect of the problem (and have worked well within the industries and types of software in which I was interested). But there remain many other industries and types of software for which these problems remain unsolved.

In this book, Doug Rosenberg and my longtime friend and mentor[2] Professor Barry Boehm, together with a set of their colleagues, propound their own offering to address portions of this important—and still unsolved—problem. I believe that you will find what they have to say worthwhile.

University of Southern California,   Neil Siegel
The IBM Professor of Engineering Management;
formerly Sector Vice-President & Chief Technology Officer,
The Northrop Grumman Corporation
Rolling Hills Estates, CA, USA
July 2019

---

[1] I talk about this in my textbook *Engineering Project Management*, published by Wiley.

[2] I am fortunate also to be able to claim Professor Boehm as my own PhD advisor.

Preface: Why Can't We Develop Software in Parallel?

From the beginning of software time, people have wondered why it isn't possible to speed up software projects by simply adding staff. This is sometimes known as the "nine women can't make a baby in 1 month" problem. The most famous treatise declaring this to be impossible is Frederick Brooks' 1975 book *The Mythical Man-Month*, in which he declares that "adding more programmers to a late software project makes it later," and indeed this has proven largely true over the decades.

Two of the authors of this book, Barry and Doug, have wondered for some time about how absolute Brooks' Law might be. When he was chief scientist at TRW in the 1980s, Barry had a team that did large-scale parallel development work on Ada projects, and Doug has spent a couple of decades teaching Unified Modeling Language (UML) modeling to classes in industry organized into parallel teams for lab work. It seemed to both that, at a minimum, there must be a loophole or two somewhere.

There's Gotta Be a Loophole

This book details our attempts over the last 4 years to find those loopholes. It started innocently enough when Barry and his co-instructor Sue invited Doug to be guest lecturer in their graduate class in the University of Southern California (USC) on software engineering, CS577, in 2014. This had been a once-a-semester invitation for a couple of years, but this time was different, because Doug had a project in mind that he wanted to get developed: a mobile app that used geofencing to deliver a coupon to a user's phone when he or she gets near a business. Thinking that it might be interesting to get the students to put together a UML model of this system, he offered to grade a couple of homework assignments. When this offer was accepted, he split his problem into 47 use cases and assigned a different use case to each of the students to model.

At this point, neither Doug nor Barry knew of their mutual interest in parallel development. Barry's reaction upon learning that Doug was assigning a use case to each of his 47 students was simply a tilt of the head, a brief locking of eyes, and the comment, "That's *really* interesting."

Doug was a little unsure of what he was getting himself into, trying to critique 47 different use case designs in parallel, but he decided that if chess masters could play simultaneous games by quickly evaluating the position of pieces on the chessboard, he should be able to read class diagrams, sequence diagrams, and model-view-controller (MVC) decompositions quickly enough to make the attempt, and that however mentally taxing the effort might be, it would be worth it to get the location-based advertising system designed quickly, thus began a 4-year learning experience that resulted in this book being written.

We Learned a Few Things in Graduate School

The first lesson learned was that USC graduate students tend to do their homework between midnight and 3:00 a.m., the night before the assignment is due, and the second lesson was that most of these graduate students are really smart. The two homework assignments were called "Build the Right System" and "Build the System Right," with the first assignment covering storyboards, use cases, and MVC (robustness) diagrams and the second covering class, sequence, and data model diagrams. While grading the first homework assignment, it began to look like we were going to get a better-than-expected result, and we decided to offer an optional extra-credit assignment where the students could implement a prototype of their use case. We also decided to start tracking student time and effort expended. Twenty-nine out of the 47 students decided to try the extra-credit assignment, and that's when things got interesting.

But This Will Never Integrate, Right?

The original expectations for this exercise were that we would wind up with a fairly detailed UML model (which we did) and not much in the way of working code. The expectation of a decent UML model came from a couple of decades of ICONIX JumpStart training workshops, in which it is standard practice to work on a real industry project with multiple lab teams, with each team working on a different subsystem of the project. In those classes, we typically limit each instructor to three lab teams, so whether this approach could be stretched to 47 parallel threads of development was unknown. There was no expectation that any of the independently developed prototype code would integrate together, and the fact that it did became the first surprising result of the project.

The unavoidable fact that 29 independently developed use cases had somehow integrated into a system that hung together with a reasonable amount of cohesion seemed significant, because difficulty in integrating independently developed code has long been one of the underlying reasons why Brooks' Law has remained in effect for all of the decades since he wrote it. It also defied explanation for a while—we knew something had happened, and we knew it had something to do with NoSQL databases and REST APIs, but the underlying mechanism wasn't immediately obvious to us.

A few years later, a clear explanation seemed to have emerged: we had applied microservice architecture (the same strategy commonly used for business-to-business integration), but at a more fine-grained level, where each domain object had its own API for common database access functions, and doing this had enabled developer-to-developer integration. This design pattern was named *executable domain models* and subsequently developed into a code generator that creates a functional microservice architecture from a domain model during the inception phase of a Parallel Agile project. Executable domain models mitigate two of the underlying factors behind Brooks' Law: they improve communication across a large team, and they enable independently developed code to integrate more easily. We'll be talking a lot more about executable domain models and how they are a key enabler of the Parallel Agile process in the chapters ahead.

4 Days per Use Case × 47 Parallel Use Cases ... Is 4 Days?

The other surprising result was that we had taken a system from inception through analysis, design, and prototype implementation in about 28 hours per student total, with all of the students working in parallel. Since the students weren't working full time—this was just homework from one of several courses—the calendar time was around 5–6 weeks total. The detailed breakdown was around 8 hours for analysis, 8 hours for design, and 13 hours for prototype coding (see Fig. 1).

We thought this was a pretty fascinating result and worthy of further study. So we took the location-based advertising system through to completion and an initial commercial deployment over several semesters. We considered this first system to be a proof of concept. We subsequently took the system through a careful design

Actual time expended by 577B students was tracked and totaled 350–370 hours per assignment.

1 day on Build the Right System (requirements), average across 47 students
1 day on Build the System Right (design), average across 47 students
2 days on implementation, average across 29 students (80% of student HW worked the first time when delivered)

4 days per use case (total requirements, design, and implementation)

Actual cumulative LOE reported by students (hours)	361	358	369.5	
Hours per student (1 use case per student)	7.7	7.6	12.7	26.0
	Requirements	Design	Code/test	Total

Fig. 1 In 2014, we built a proof of concept system with a large team of developers, each working on a single use case in parallel

pass to build a minimum viable product (MVP) and then spent another semester producing a more refined version suitable for commercial release. Students for the MVP and optimization stages of the project came from a directed research program that Barry was running (CS590), where students typically worked 5–15 hours per week for course credit.

Proof of Concept, MVP, Then Release 1 in 3 Months

We followed up the original location-based advertising project with several additional projects over the next 3 years: a photo-sharing mobile app, a system for crowdsourced video reporting of traffic incidents, and a game featuring virtual reality, and augmented reality capability. We found the three-sprint pattern of proof of concept, MVP, and optimization to be a useful strategy that fits the USC semester schedule and that with part-time students and a 3-month semester, the full-time equivalent for each of these "semester sprints" was a little under 1 calendar month (see Fig. 2).

After 4 years of experimentation, data collection, and analysis, the results seemed clear and repeatable. Larger projects didn't have to take dramatically longer than smaller projects if we were able to scale the number of developers in each of our "sprints." The pattern we adopted was compatible with Barry's work on the Incremental Commitment Spiral Model (ICSM), a general-purpose roadmap for

> **Note**
> One of the noteworthy returning student exceptions was a brilliant woman named Shobha from the traffic incident reporting project (now called CarmaCam), who is also a co-author of this book.
>
> In addition, a student from the first CS577 class, Bo, is now in the PhD program at USC and is a co-author of this book. Bo developed the REST API on the original location-based advertising (LBA) project, and subsequently, he developed the code generator for executable domain models.
>
> Shobha wrote the chapter on our example project (Chap. 4), CarmaCam, and Bo co-wrote the chapter on executable domain models (Chap. 3).

reducing risk and uncertainty with a phased development effort, as will be discussed later in this book.

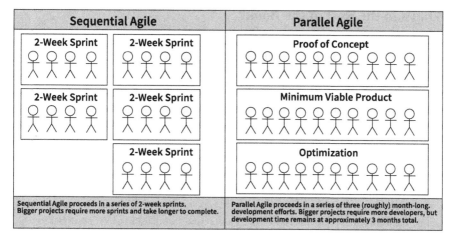

Fig. 2 Compared with a sequential Agile approach, Parallel Agile compresses schedules by leveraging the effort of large numbers of developers working in parallel

Surviving 100% Staff Turnover

There was one more noteworthy surprise: with only a couple of exceptions, we got a brand-new set of CS590 students every semester, and our projects were succeeding despite *nearly 100% staff turnover*. We were getting fairly sophisticated systems built with part-time students over three semesters, which each had a full-time equivalent of about 1 calendar month—so about 3 calendar months from inception to optimization.

So, have we repealed Brooks' Law? Probably not. But based on our experience, it does appear as though if you have properly partitioned the problem for parallel development, and if you have a good strategy for integrating the work that's been developed in parallel, you can in fact accelerate a schedule dramatically by increasing the number of developers.

Who Needs Parallel Agile?

You don't need Parallel Agile if your software development process is working perfectly, and you have no need to bring your software systems to market faster while simultaneously improving quality.

However, if you're like the rest of us mere mortals and you're developing software in an Agile environment, we hope you'll find some of our work interesting. If your feedback-driven development process is devolving into hotfix-driven development and you're not happy about it, then this book is definitely for you.

What's in the Rest of the Book?

Of course we'll reveal all of the important secrets of the universe in the remaining pages of this epic, but more specifically, you can expect to learn the following:

- Why parallel processing can speed up software development like it speeds up hardware computation
- How to be feedback driven and plan driven at the same time
- Why making domain models executable is an awesome boost to productivity and quality
- How to manage sprint plans using visual modeling
- How to do top-down scenario-based estimation and bottom-up task-based estimation
- The fundamental importance of the model-view-controller (MVC) pattern to use case-driven development
- Why acceptance testing offers greater "bang for the buck" than unit testing
- How to adapt Parallel Agile within your current scrum/Kanban management paradigm
- How all of the above topics have been put to use on the CarmaCam project
- The ways in which Parallel Agile is compatible with the Incremental Commitment Spiral Model (ICSM)
- How to scale Parallel Agile techniques to very large systems
- How to scale your projects horizontally by adding developers rather than vertically by stretching the calendar

Ready to get started? Continue to Chap. 1 for a big-picture overview of Parallel Agile concepts.

Santa Monica, CA, USA   Doug Rosenberg
                                                                          Barry Boehm

Acknowledgments

Doug would like to thank the following people for their contributions to this book:

The Greatest Copyeditor of All Time, Nicole LeClerc, for taking on this project on top of her full-time job when she really didn't have the time and for helping us create a book.

Michael Kusters who allowed us to use The Scream Guide as Appendix A.

The USC CS590 administrators: Julie Sanchez, Anandi Hira, and Elaine Venson.

And most especially Barry Boehm, for making all of this possible, and all of his USC Viterbi students (see the following list) who built CarmaCam and helped us understand parallel development by doing it.

Fall 2016 (proof of concept):

Rajat Verma, Preksha Gupta, Tapashi Talukdar, Zhongpeng Zhang, Chirayu Samarth, Ankita Aggarwal, Ankur Khemani, Parth Thakar, Longjie Li, Asmita Datar, Qingfeng Du, Maithri Purohit, Shobha Rani Dhalipathi, Seema Raman, and Sharath Mahendrath.

Spring 2017 (minimum viable product):

Shobha Rani Dhalipathi, Sharath Mahendranath, Ting Gong, Soumya Ravi, Namratha Lakshminaryan, Yuanfan Peng, Asmita Datar, Ragapriya Sivakumar, Yudan Lu, Ishwarya Iyer, Chuyuan Wang, and Jingyi Sun.

Fall 2017 (minimum viable product/optimization):

Shreyas Shankar, Akansha Aggarwal, Zhuang Tian, Yanbin Jiang, Jiayuan Shi, and Guannan Lu.

Spring 2018 (optimization):

Yue Dai, Yingzhe Zhang, Pengyu Chen, Haimeng Song, Jingwen Yin, Qifan Chen, Khushali Shah, Ying Chen, Shih-Chi Lin, Xiyan Hu, Yenju Lee, Basir Navab, Lingfei Fan, and Raksha Bysani.

Summer 2018 (optimization):

Yenju Lee, Lingfei Fan, and Haimeng Song.

Fall 2018 (optimization and machine learning proof of concept):

Akanksha Priya, Bowei Chen, Chetan Katiganare Siddaramappa, Chi-Syuan Lu, Chun-Ting Liu, Divya Jhurani, Hankun Yi, Hsuan-Hau Liu, Jienan Tang, Karan

Maheshwari, Nitika Tanwani, Pavleen Kaur, Ran He, Runyou Wang, Vaishnavi Patil, Vipin Rajan Varatharajan, Xiao Guo, Yanran Zhou, and Zilu Li.

Spring 2019 (optimization and machine learning minimum viable product):
Asmita Mitra, Chi Lin, Julius Yee, Kahlil Dozier, Kritika Patel, Luwei Ge, Nitika Tanwani, Pramod Samurdala, Shi-Chi Lin, Tiffany Kyu, Vaibhav Sarma, Zhao Yang, Zhengxi Xiao, Zilu Li, Chi-Syuan Lu, Bowei Chen, and Yanran Zhou.

Summer 2019 (optimization and machine learning minimum viable product):
Luwei Ge, Shi-Chi Lin, Zilu Li, Bowei Chen, Yanran Zhou, and Khushali Shah.

Contents

Chapter 1
Parallel Agile Concepts

Parallel Agile (PA) is a process that allows software schedules to be radically compressed by scaling the number of developers who work on a system rather than stretching the project schedule. In this chapter, we'll discuss the main concepts involved in PA, including partitioning for parallel development, planning, management and design models, risk mitigation, project management, executable domain models, process, and finally the evolution of PA from ICONIX.

1.1 Partitioning a System for Parallel Development

Parallel development requires careful partitioning of a problem into units that can be developed independently. In PA, you decompose systems along use case boundaries for this purpose. Parallelism in development is achieved by partitioning a project into its use cases. Each developer is assigned a use case and is responsible for everything from operational concept through working code for his or her assignment.

Figures 1.1 and 1.2 show the essence of how to develop software in parallel. In Fig. 1.1, the system is decomposed along scenario boundaries. Figure 1.2 shows the spiral diagram for each use case: build the right system, then build the system right, and then test what you built. To the extent that you can do these three activities in parallel, you can compress the schedule of a project.

The spirals shown in the preceding figures are basically "uncertainty reducing" or "disambiguation" spirals. To make a software system work, you have to move from a state of complete uncertainty (speculation) to executable code. PA attacks uncertainty one use case at a time using storyboards, UML models, and prototypes, as appropriate for each use case. After you set up your project for parallelism, each use case progresses along the spiral in parallel at its own pace.

Within each use case, PA follows a standard set of steps, including a complete sunny-day/rainy-day description for all use cases, as confronting rainy-day scenarios early adds resilience to software designs. Each use case is then "disambiguated"

© Springer Nature Switzerland AG 2020
D. Rosenberg et al., *Parallel Agile – faster delivery, fewer defects, lower cost*,
https://doi.org/10.1007/978-3-030-30701-1_1

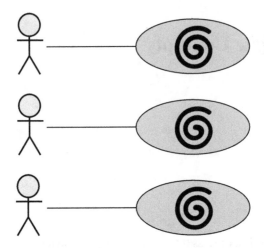

Fig. 1.1 Decomposing along use case boundaries enables parallel development

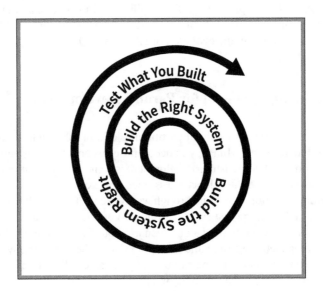

Fig. 1.2 Disambiguation spiral

using a conceptual model-view-controller (MVC) description, and then carefully designed. Typically, designs are shown on sequence diagrams; however, you could use test driven development (TDD) as an alternate detailed design process with some sacrifice of productivity. Requirements are modeled and allocated to use cases, and traceability between requirements and design is verified during design reviews, further increasing resilience of the software.

Having a small, standardized set of design steps and artifacts facilitates communication among team members who are working in parallel and also makes developers more interchangeable. One of the characteristics of student projects that run across multiple semesters is nearly 100% staff turnover every 3 months, since students typically don't take the same class over multiple semesters. Significantly, this turnover rate has not caused a problem on our student projects. Use of the UML model is a key reason that our projects have succeeded despite this turnover rate.

1.2   Just Enough Planning

Given the dramatic schedule acceleration that's possible by leveraging parallelism, and the never-ending quest to deliver software rapidly (if you're not publishing every 11 seconds, you're so last millennium), you might wonder why there haven't been more attempts to "go parallel" in software engineering. A large part of the answer relates to planning and management. Simply put, a parallel processing approach to software engineering requires careful planning and good management. But planning has been out of fashion in software engineering since the release of the Agile Manifesto, which explicitly values *responding to change over following a plan*. Since management's role often involves making sure a plan is being followed, devaluing planning simultaneously devalues management. Software processes can be rated on a formality scale ranging from *feedback-driven* (less formal) to *plan-driven* (more formal). In his book *Balancing Agility and Discipline* (Boehm and Turner 2003), Barry makes the case that for most systems the extremes on either side of this scale are expensive, and there is a cost-minimum somewhere in the middle (see Fig. 1.3).

The net effect of the Agile Manifesto has been that most Agile projects have a tendency to operate on the underplanned side of this feedback vs. planning continuum, with the classic example being the eXtreme Programming mantra of "Do the simplest thing that can possibly work" (DTSTTCPW). DTSTTCPW represents underplanning in its most eXtreme form.

In *Agile Development with ICONIX Process* (Rosenberg et al. 2005), Doug makes the case that "just enough planning" in the form of a minimalist, use case–driven approach gets close to this cost minimum and, in fact, PA has its roots in Agile/ICONIX, as we discuss later in this chapter. PA strikes a balance between plan-driven and feedback-driven development, with UML modeling used for planning and prototyping used for feedback.

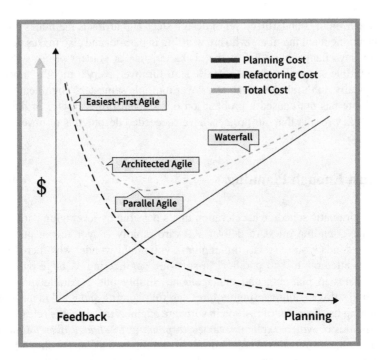

Fig. 1.3 How much planning is "just enough"?

1.3   Feedback-Driven Management, Model-Driven Design

Like most Agile methods, PA gets to code early and uses feedback from executable software to drive requirements and design. PA is feedback-driven on the management side (heavy use of prototyping) but model-driven (UML) on the design side.

PA uses technical prototyping as a risk-mitigation strategy, for user interface refinement, to help sanity-check requirements for feasibility, and to evaluate different technical architectures and technologies. PA prototypes help to discover requirements and are used to evolve the database schema, with developers prototyping various use cases in parallel against a live database.

Unlike many Agile methods, PA does not focus on design by refactoring, nor does it drive designs from unit tests. Instead, PA uses a minimalist UML-based design approach that starts out with a domain model to facilitate communication across the development team, and partitions the system along use case boundaries, which enables parallel development. PA emphasizes continuous acceptance testing (CAT) to a greater extent than unit testing.

Combining a model-driven design approach with extensive prototyping allows PA to be feedback-driven and plan-driven at the same time. Since both underplanning and overplanning are expensive, this blend of planning and feedback gets us near the cost minimum, as shown in Fig. 1.3.

The clear distinction between prototype code and production code is one of the big differentiators between PA and other agile approaches. In PA, production code is modeled, and acceptance test case scripts are generated from use case sunny/rainy day paths. This "build the right system" exercise takes a small upfront investment for each use case but results in dramatically less time spent refactoring code that was "the wrong system." By differentiating prototype code from production code, you're able to free the prototyping effort of some time-consuming tasks; notably, prototype code does not require extensive unit and regression testing.

Having a UML model allows PA to leverage automation to further accelerate development. Uniquely, PA uses UML modeling to assist with prototyping, enabling prototype code to interact with a live database by making domain models executable, using automatic code generation very early in the inception phase of the project. To be more specific, domain models are made executable by code generation of database collections, database access functions (create, read, update, delete, or CRUD, functions), and REST APIs.

Executable domain models allow developers to write prototype code against a live database in parallel sandboxes, which enables evolutionary feedback-driven database schema development. Executable domain models also assist with integration by using code generation to rapidly produce microservice architectures in the form of NoSQL databases and REST APIs at the inception of the project.

1.4 Risk Management

The Incremental Commitment Spiral Model (ICSM) provides a general-purpose risk-management strategy for software projects, where development proceeds in phases with a commitment to the next phase only after evidence has been evaluated from the previous phase. PA maps nicely to the ICSM model, where the phases are proof of concept, minimum viable product (MVP), and optimization.

Our student projects have generally applied this strategy over several semesters, where the first semester involved building a proof of concept system, the second semester involved building an MVP version of the system, and the third semester involved optimization and performance tuning, leading to an optimization.

Each of the three phases emphasizes different development techniques, as shown in Fig. 1.4. For the proof of concept sprint, we used a mix of storyboards and prototypes that connected to a live database via executable domain models. For the MVP sprint, we did rigorous use case modeling covering sunny- and rainy-day scenarios and elaborated using MVC decomposition. For the optimization sprint, we had a heavy focus on acceptance testing.

We'll talk more about the ICSM and its risk management strategies in Chap. 8.

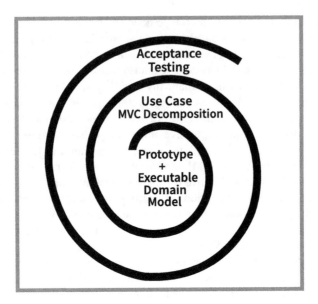

Fig. 1.4 The Parallel Agile three-phase pattern and typical techniques

1.5 Project Management

PA targets the cost minimum between "just enough planning" and "just enough feedback," and development proceeds in three roughly month-long phases as described earlier to minimize uncertainty and risk, following the ICSM guidelines. It's possible to think of each of these phases as a "sprint," although we use the term somewhat differently from the typical scrum two-week timeboxed sprint.

It has been our experience that timeboxing generally introduces numerous problems into development—typically, rushed code that's written in panic mode combined with inadequate testing. In fact, we feel strongly enough about this that we've tried to channel the spirit of Edsger Dijkstra's famous essay "Go To Statement Considered Harmful" (Dijkstra 1968).

Box 1.1: Timeboxing Considered Harmful

For a number of years, we have observed that the quality of a programmer's work is a decreasing function of the amount of time pressure the programmer is forced to work under. This we know to be a fact from the multiple decades of our lives we have spent programming for a living. Later we discovered that the industry trend of test-first development led to an over reliance on unit tests as an indicator of software quality. When the Agile development methods were only popular for quickly putting up websites, these observations (which we published in Extreme Programming Refactored) were not widely perceived to be of too much importance; however, with the increasing amount of safety-critical software being produced, particularly in the context of software-intensive systems (which characterization now describes virtually all systems), we now submit that our considerations are of significant concern.

Our first remark is that, inevitably, excessive time pressure leads to shoddy workmanship. An environment of continual "sprinting" towards getting the software out the door does in fact get software out the door, but that software is often of dubious quality. Our intellectual powers are better geared to finding solutions to complex problems when there is adequate time to consider the problem at hand, rather than grasping for the simplest solution that comes to mind as an expedient to move on to the next problem. Software constructed from a codebase that has been developed with routine focus on finding the quickest path to getting the release out the door behaves as if it were slapped together in a hurry, because, in fact, it was slapped together in a hurry.

On our student projects the "timebox" is the end of the semester, which generally comes with final projects, final exams, and job interviews for the students, and most of the quality issues we've had to deal with on these projects have involved students running out of time to complete their assignments.

With that off our chests, since the scrum/sprint management paradigm has become so ubiquitous in industry, we think it's advantageous to use the scrum terminology of *epic*, *user story*, and *task* as the management paradigm for PA projects.

You can perform sprint planning at various levels of formality depending on the scope of the work being undertaken in the sprint, the experience level of the manager, and so on. While informal sprint plans can be effective for a small scope of work that fits within a two-week timebox, in our experience when managing the output of more than 25 developers working in parallel, a well-organized sprint plan becomes a necessity rather than a luxury.

PA uses UML to model sprint plans, so they can be kept in the same model with the requirements and with the technical design of the software. Visual modeling of sprint plans involves a UML profile that stereotypes elements as epic, user story, and task, where the epic describes the goal of a related set of user stories, and each story is decomposed into its tasks. These sprint plans can be used for bottom-up cost estimation on a task-by-task basis. An example fragment of a sprint plan model is shown in Fig. 1.5.

We'll go into more detail about visual modeling of sprint plans in Chap. 5.

1.6 Executable Domain Models

Domain modeling has long been one of the keys to success when following a use case–driven process. Writing the use cases in a common vocabulary defined by the domain model is essential to smooth collaboration when multiple developers are

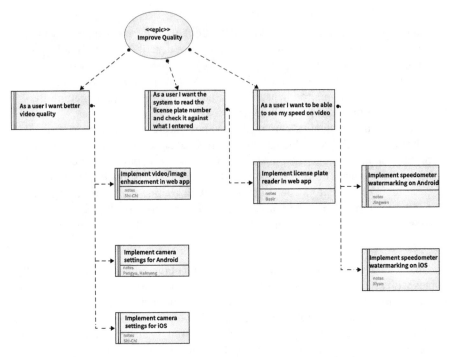

Fig. 1.5 Parallel Agile uses visual models to show epics, user stories, and tasks

implementing use cases in parallel. This has been true for many years and is independent of any particular database technology because it relates to "building the right system" (i.e., getting the behavior requirements straight).

Executable domain models in the form of NoSQL collections and REST APIs that implement database access functions offer even greater advantages when it comes to developers working in parallel sandboxes and later integrating their work into a cohesive whole. The first advantage is that if you can think of something that belongs in the problem domain, you can immediately make it live in the database. In essence, as a developer you can simply start calling methods to create and manipulate conceptual entities.

A second advantage is that when multiple use cases share the same domain object (e.g., a BadDriverReport object), it's not necessary to predefine all of the attributes for that object. This is helpful because it's common for different use cases to need different attributes. Each developer can start building immediately with the attributes needed and worry about integration later. Developers must ensure they use the correct name of the domain object.

In our first location-based advertising PA test project, we developed a design pattern where students could rapidly "clone" some sample database code that implemented the database CRUD functions. To access the database from both Android and iOS code, we then wrapped the database functions in a REST API.

Bo, one of the students on the location-based advertising project, decided to pursue automating this design pattern as part of his PhD research. He built a code generator that takes a domain model and generates a NoSQL collection for each class, creates the database access functions, and wraps them in a REST API. We piloted the code generator on the CarmaCam project with excellent results, and we are continuing to use it on other projects.

Benefits of using executable domain models include

- Less time writing database access code
- Absence of bugs in database access code
- Less time developing APIs
- Absence of bugs in the API code
- Evolutionary database schema development from prototypes developed in parallel

We'll go into more detail on executable domain models in Chap. 3.

1.7   Parallel Agile Process

PA includes an inception phase that sets up for parallel development, followed by developing use cases in parallel, as shown in Fig. 1.6.

We'll present the detailed process roadmap in Chap. 2, but at the highest level Fig. 1.6 shows how it's done. You're developing a set of use cases in parallel, most

Fig. 1.6 Set up for parallelism in the inception phase, and then develop use cases in parallel

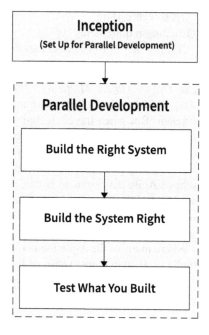

of the time with one developer working a single use case from requirements through code that passes acceptance testing.

The inception phase consists of the following:

- Building a domain model (and making it executable)
- Identifying use cases on use case diagrams
- Developing a sprint plan that shows epics, user stories, and tasks

Making the domain model executable has multiple benefits:

- Ensures that domain modeling isn't skipped
- Establishes a common vocabulary for use cases that will be developed in parallel
- Enables prototype-driven requirements exploration where the prototypes connect to a live database
- Puts a fully functional microservice architecture in place so that independently developed use cases can communicate easily

Visually modeling the "sprint plan" includes allocation of resources (developers, testers, and user experience [UX] designers) to specific user stories and tasks. For large projects, more use cases are developed in parallel, and mapping out the epics, user stories, and tasks becomes increasingly important. If you are attempting only 5 or 10 use cases in parallel, you can perform this step informally, but when you get to 25–50 use cases on a large system, creating the task plan becomes absolutely essential.

"Building the right system" involves a variety of techniques:

- Prototyping
- UX storyboarding
- Eliciting requirements
- Crafting first-draft use case narratives

For low-risk, common use cases, model-driven techniques as described in *Use Case Driven Object Modeling: Theory and Practice* (Rosenberg and Stephens 2008)—UX storyboarding, requirements elicitation, use case narratives) are often sufficient. But when there's technical risk, new technologies are being evaluated, there are performance-sensitive use cases, or the database schema is not fully understood, prototyping plays a valuable role.

Prototyping puts a lot of the "Agile" in Parallel Agile. One of the fundamental truths of Agile development is that you learn a lot from having an executable system. Most of the time you learn more from interacting with live software than you can from diagrams and documents. However, it's a huge mistake to throw diagrams and documents away completely.

Where many of the Agile methods get it wrong is in shipping the prototype code, usually (at least in theory) after adding a "feel good" layer of unit tests and building a regression test environment, and then in replacing forward-thinking design with refactoring.

Test-driven design (TDD) is a lot like spell check–driven writing. To paraphrase the old saying, a thousand monkeys armed with spell-checkers aren't going to turn out Shakespeare. In a similar way, a thousand Java programmers armed with JUnit aren't likely to turn out a well-architected system, and the pain from refactoring is likely to be eXtreme.

The fundamental truth about unit testing in general is that a million green bars don't guarantee a working system. In fact, green bars don't guarantee anything. A tragic example demonstrating that unit testing is not a good indicator of reliability occurred in 2018 when a self-driving car in Phoenix, Arizona, ran over a pedestrian. As it turns out, the car's vision system had detected the pedestrian a full six seconds before running the person over, but someone had disabled the autobraking function because it was causing erratic start-and-stop behavior while driving (Bomey 2018). No amount of unit testing could have prevented this tragedy because unit testing catches bugs only where the programmer has committed a coding error (errors of commission). By and large these are the easiest bugs to catch in a software system. It's *errors of omission* ("Whoops! We forgot that user story: as a pedestrian I'd like the emergency braking system to always be enabled . . .") that cause most of the trouble in software projects. Because green bars don't guarantee anything, the presumption that it's okay to ship a system after the regression tests all turn green is a dangerous one, especially where safety-critical systems are involved.

"Building the system right" is where all of the diagrams and documents pay off. With prototyping against a live database having moved you down the cost curve from the feedback-driven side, you can use some tried and tested UML techniques, including the following, to make sure the design of each use case is complete:

- Full descriptions of both sunny-day and rainy-day cases for all each use case
- Use case decomposition at the conceptual level along an MVC pattern
- Requirements traceability (mapping requirements to use cases)
- Detailed design at the sequence diagram/state machine level

Use of these techniques moves you down the cost curve from the less refactoring required (plan-driven) side.

"Testing what you built" can certainly include unit testing, but more important, it includes a thorough and robust acceptance testing phase where each requirement is tested independently and all paths through all use cases are fully exercised. Similar to how you use code generation to make domain models executable, you use test case generation (Rosenberg and Stephens 2010) to expand sunny- and rainy-day paths for each use case into fleshed-out acceptance test scripts.

1.8   Scalability and Evolution of Parallel Agile from ICONIX Process

PA starts with a highly scalable process, ICONIX Process, and then extends it. ICONIX Process has been used in a wide range of industries on project sizes from very small to extremely large for a couple of decades. The areas where PA extends ICONIX Process all serve to increase flexibility and make it more scalable. As a result, we have every reason to expect that PA will be highly scalable.

Table 1.1 compares ICONIX Process to PA and summarizes the benefits provided by PA.

Essentially, ICONIX Process focuses on analysis, design, and testing but is agnostic with respect to implementation. That's one reason it has been used in such a diverse set of industries, including aerospace, banking, pharmaceuticals, and telecom.

PA builds on the ICONIX techniques but offers significant amounts of automation for projects that can use a cloud-hosted database with access functions provided by a REST API. This general category of project includes mobile development and web app development as we've demonstrated with student projects, but since REST APIs are callable from virtually any environment, these types of projects don't define a limiting set.

Table 1.1 Comparison of ICONIX Process and PA, and Benefits Provided by PA

ICONIX Process	Parallel Agile	Parallel Agile Benefits
Storyboards, use cases, MVC	Storyboards, use cases, MVC, prototypes	Facilitates clear communication between developer and stakeholder
Domain model	Executable domain model	Reduces time spent implementing database access functions and microservice architecture, improves reliability of database layer
Deduce database schema from analysis	Evolve database schema from prototyping	Supports feedback-driven development as well as plan-driven development
Design by sequence diagram and state machine	Supports model-driven design and test-driven design (TDD)	Compatible with "standard Agile practices"
Design-driven testing (DDT)	Supports both DDT and TDD	Autogenerated requirement tests and use case thread tests helpful to independent verification and validation (IV&V)
Database agnostic	NoSQL database default for code generator	Scales to large data volumes, cloud hosting with no additional effort, flexible schema supports feedback-driven development
Architecture agnostic	Microservice/REST API autogenerated	Eliminates integration issues with parallel development, supports cross-platform development, highly flexible
Management process agnostic	Supports both massively parallel and scrum/Kanban backlog-driven	Leverages parallelism for schedule compression but still compatible with "standard Agile practices"

1.9 Summary

Let's briefly review the key concepts that define PA:

- Scaling a system by adding developers requires careful partitioning of the system along use case boundaries.
- Combining feedback-driven management (early prototyping is used extensively to help define requirements, resolve uncertainty, and reduce risk) with model-driven design (where corner cases and exceptions are considered carefully before the design phase is considered complete) hits the cost-minimum that exists at "just enough planning."
- Projects progress in three phases, each roughly a month long, to minimize overall risk. Each phase is driven by specific techniques:
  - Proof of concept: Prototype-driven requirements discovery
  - Minimum viable product (MVP): Model-driven design
  - Optimization: Acceptance test–driven release strategy
- Agile project management follows the paradigm of epics, user stories, and tasks. However, "sprints" are flexible, with a nominal length of about a month.
- The inception phase sets a project up for parallel development, and involves executable domain models, use case diagramming, and visual modeling of epics, user stories, and tasks.
- Executable domain models provide a number of advantages, including feedback-driven database schema development, elimination of manual coding for database access functions and API development, high reliability of generated code, and easier integration of independently developed use cases.
- Parallel development proceeds with a developer assigned to each use case across all three phases (proof of concept, MVP, optimization).
- PA is a highly scalable process that starts with proven model-driven design techniques (ICONIX Process) and risk management techniques (ICSM). PA then adds in automation in the form of code generation for executable domain models, test case generation for requirement and scenario testing.

We'll take you through all of these topics in detail in the rest of the book. The next chapter presents the PA process roadmap. If you'd like a really quick overview of PA, we suggest you check out "Fundamentals of Parallel Agile in 3 Minutes" at: http://bit.ly/pa-in-3-minutes.

References

Boehm, B., and R. Turner. 2003. *Balancing agility and discipline: A guide for the perplexed.* Boston: Addison-Wesley.

Bomey, N. 2018. Uber self-driving car crash: Vehicle detected Arizona pedestrian 6 seconds before accident. USA Today. https://www.usatoday.com/story/money/cars/2018/05/24/uber-self-driving-car-crash-ntsb-investigation/640123002/. Accessed 18 July 2019.

Dijkstra, E. 1968. Go to statement considered harmful. *Communications of the ACM* 11 (3): 147–148.

Rosenberg, D., and M. Stephens. 2008. *Use case driven object modeling with UML: Theory and practice.* Berkeley: Apress.

———. 2010. *Design driven testing.* Berkeley: Apress.

Rosenberg, D., M. Stephens, and M. Collins-Cope. 2005. *Agile development with ICONIX process: People, process, and pragmatism.* Berkeley: Apress.

Chapter 2
Inside Parallel Agile

Plans are good, and feedback is good. However—just like in politics—when one side gains too much control and drowns out the other side, problems quickly begin to creep in. A project that's entirely plan-driven ends up too rigid, with the team unable to respond to changes, while a project that's entirely feedback-driven can get stuck in refactoring hell, meandering aimlessly. Parallel Agile (PA) strikes a balance between plan-driven and feedback-driven to get the best from both without pushing the project to either extreme (see Fig. 2.1).

2.1 Code First, Design Later

Agile practitioners correctly believe that it shouldn't take a long time to get to code because you learn a lot from working with executable software. As a consequence, some are fond of disparaging anything they don't like as "Oh, that's just waterfall," with *waterfall* defined as "taking too long to get to executable code." In contrast to waterfall, PA "gets to code early" and uses feedback from executable software to drive requirements and design. PA is feedback-driven on the management side (e.g., heavy use of prototyping to determine feasibility of new technologies), but model-driven (UML) on the design side. PA facilitates communication across the development team (and radically accelerates your development) by starting out with an executable domain model, and enables parallel development by partitioning the system along use case boundaries.

© Springer Nature Switzerland AG 2020
D. Rosenberg et al., *Parallel Agile – faster delivery, fewer defects, lower cost*,
https://doi.org/10.1007/978-3-030-30701-1_2

Fig. 2.1 A balance of
model-driven and
feedback-driven

2.2 Prototyping as Requirements Exploration

It's hard to write good requirements for software in the abstract, without having some working software to play with. It's easier to identify requirements following an "I'll know what I want when I see it" approach. Uniquely, PA uses UML modeling to assist with prototyping, enabling prototype code to interact with a live database by making domain models executable, using automatic code generation in the inception phase of the project. This enables you to see an initial working system early in the project life cycle, which can be a powerful catalyst—the "light bulb moment" (or, more accurately, a series of light bulb moments)—while exploring the business requirements. Prototyping helps you to build the right system; design helps you to build the system right. As an added bonus, prototyping provides early insight into the design, especially important for high-risk use cases. Both prototyping and design are necessary, and both can be done in parallel.

PA also uses a concurrent test team working in parallel with the developers and generates acceptance test scripts from use cases following the design-driven testing approach.

2.3 Overview of the Parallel Agile Process

In Chap. 1, we provided a simple overview of the PA process; Fig. 2.2 shows a more detailed overview. PA encourages parallel development with an elastic staffing approach, as described in Chap. 7. However, since elastic staffing is not always a realistic option, it's possible to leverage other features of PA with a sequential (scrum) implementation phase. We describe how to use PA with scrum in Chap. 5.

PA projects start out with an *inception* phase, where the project is set up for parallel development. Inception is followed by a focused effort to make sure you're

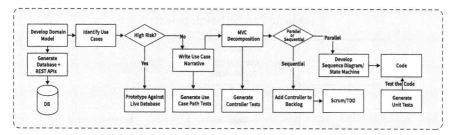

Fig. 2.2 Overview of Parallel Agile, including a sequential (scrum) option for small teams

building the right system (analysis) using a combination of prototyping and use case modeling, then by an effort to make sure you're *building the system right* (design). Finally, the *testing what you built* stage involves an effort to drive rigorous testing from the design (design-driven testing).

It's worth repeating that PA blends feedback-driven development (you make extensive use of prototyping during the build the right system phase, where you're figuring out the requirements) with model-driven design and testing.

We discuss each of these phases in the remainder of this chapter.

2.4 Inception

During inception, you set up your project so that the team can work in parallel. Since you're going to be assigning an independent developer to each use case, it's necessary to partition the system into use cases. One use case per developer is a default partitioning—you can split up complex use cases later if needed. And since each developer will be working against a domain-driven microservice architecture, you need to put that executable framework in place early (see Fig. 2.3).

The steps in Fig. 2.3 (Model the Problem Domain, Identify Use Cases, and Organize Use Cases into Packages) are illustrated by example in Chap. 4, where we describe the design of CarmaCam. Generate Code and API from the Domain Model is described in detail in Chap. 3, and Assign Developers to Use Cases is covered in Chap. 7.

If you'd like an in-depth tutorial on domain modeling and use case modeling, Doug and Matt describe them in the book *Use Case Driven Object Modeling with UML: Theory and Practice* (Rosenberg and Stephens 2008).

2.4.1 Evolving Database Schemas

Domain modeling has long been one of the keys to success when following a use case–driven process, but we've introduced a new twist by using it to enable prototyping. Writing use cases in a common vocabulary defined by the domain model is

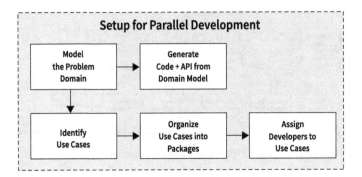

Fig. 2.3 Project inception gets you ready to develop in parallel

essential to smooth collaboration when multiple developers are implementing use cases in parallel. This has been true for many years and is independent of any particular database technology.

Executable domain models in the form of NoSQL collections and REST APIs that implement database access functions offer even greater advantages when it comes to developers working in parallel sandboxes and later integrating their work into a cohesive whole. NoSQL databases are flexible with respect to schema, and thus are well-suited for "sandbox" development. Parallel development can then proceed in the sandbox, and when it reaches maturity, the database schema can be unified and promoted out of the sandbox into a production instance of the database.

When attempting schedule compression via massively parallel development, flexibility is key. The database schema changes frequently because individual developers are working in sandbox mode and may require different attributes on the database collections. Of course, you must merge attributes when moving out of the sandbox into a production system. Because flexibility is so important, our initial research has focused on NoSQL databases, with all scripts and generated code written in JavaScript (but callable from any language). Recently we've been focusing on making the code generator re-targetable, with work underway on both mySQL and Firebase.

2.4.2 Enabling Integration Between Developers

Microservice architecture has become increasingly popular in today's software development. You can access services via URL using RESTful APIs. Microservices are generally useful in business to business (B2B) integration, allowing multiple applications to communicate easily and with great flexibility. PA uses microservices to enable developer to developer (D2D) integration, by virtue of code generation that creates NoSQL collections for all domain objects, with database access (CRUD) functions generated and wrapped in a REST API.

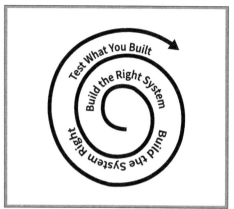

Fig. 2.4 Essential Parallel Agile: the three phases

2.5   Parallel Development Proceeds in Three Phases After Inception

After inception, PA follows a three-phase approach to development that's a simplified version of the Incremental Commitment Spiral Model (ICSM). Your project starts with a proof of concept phase, where you'll make extensive use of prototyping to help discover requirements. The prototyping phase is enabled by having database access functions code-generated and made available via an API. For the most part, prototyping focuses on building out sunny-day scenarios, which enables you to prototype quickly. (See Fig. 2.4.)

Once the concept has been proven, you proceed to a carefully designed minimum viable product (MVP), where you add in the corner-case analysis by doing some proper use case modeling. After the MVP is complete, you move into acceptance testing (which may uncover performance and UX issues) and optimization. You'll find an overview of ICSM in Chap. 8.

2.6   Proof of Concept (Building the Right System)

Writing production code tends to go a lot more smoothly when the developers have a clear understanding of the requirements they are coding against.

The wisdom of Agile methods is that it's extraordinarily difficult to determine requirements in the absence of an executable system. So, in PA, you make extensive use of prototyping, get to code early, and give the users a functional system to play with.

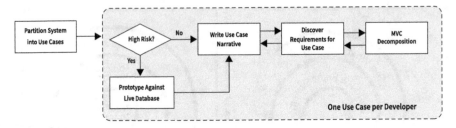

Fig. 2.5 Figuring out requirements requires a mix of prototyping and modeling

The mistake made by many Agile methods is to throw the baby out with the bathwater, skip any kind of modeling, and deliver production code by constant refactoring of prototype code. This approach tends to be slow, painful, and expensive.

Parallelism in development is achieved by partitioning a project into its use cases and assigning each developer a use case, with each developer responsible for everything from operational concept through working code for the assigned use case. For situations where a use case involves front-end (e.g., Angular JS) code interacting with complex server-side logic (beyond generated database functions), you would simply split the server-side logic out into a separate use case.

PA's hybrid approach (see Fig. 2.5) involves creating technical prototypes for high-risk use cases and proceeding for all use cases with storyboarding, requirements discovery, writing sunny/rainy-day narratives, and MVC decomposition. Prototyping against a live database enables evolutionary, feedback-driven development, while adequate planning is assured by developing use case narratives and MVC decomposition.

See Chap. 4 for some real-world examples and Chap. 3 for a tutorial.

Since you're mixing prototyping and modeling together, it's helpful to have some guidance on when to prototype and when to model. This guidance is simple: if the use case involves technical risk (e.g., voice recognition in a noisy environment or power-safe geofencing), prototype it. If it's straightforward, model it. (See Fig. 2.6.)

On the CarmaCam project, we made extensive use of technical prototyping to test voice recognition toolkits (ultimately deciding that ambient noise in the car couldn't get us the accuracy we needed); to test different strategies for watermarking speedometer data onto videos; to test video file size, resolution, and upload time; and for numerous other purposes.

2.7   Minimum Viable Product (Building the System Right)

In theory, use case–driven development is straightforward, yet in practice developers often struggle with these techniques. A few decades of teaching people how to write good use cases pinpoints a common factor that generally leads to success (or

Fig. 2.6 Parallel Agile
uses prototyping as a
risk-mitigation technique

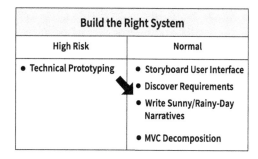

failure, when it's not well understood). That factor, originally proposed in the land-mark book *Object Oriented Software Engineering* (Jacobson 1992), is the decom-position of a use case along conceptual model-view-controller (MVC) boundaries.

2.7.1   Using MVC Decomposition to Make Your Use Cases Less Ambiguous

MVC decomposition addresses the biggest problem with use cases, which is ambig-uous use of language, by forcing explicit naming of screens, data (or database col-lections), and logic.

One way to understand the benefits of decomposing use cases along MVC boundaries is to consider the "cone of uncertainty" presented in Barry's book (Boehm et al. 2014), and shown in Fig. 2.7. Analyzing each use case in detail pinches the cone of uncertainty earlier in the life cycle. You can do the majority of refinement at this level rather than by constant refactoring after programming.

An MVC decomposition for a web application would explain a use case in terms of its JavaScript pages (the view), NoSQL database collections (the model), API calls to access the model, and logic that makes the JavaScript pages function (the controllers).

2.7.2   Using Parts of Parallel Agile with Scrum

Although it doesn't fully leverage the benefits of parallel development, using other parts of PA (executable domain models, MVC decomposition, test case generation) is possible with a more common Agile/scrum implementation team. In other words, PA is not an all-or-nothing process. Scrum is widely accepted in industry, and we have no expectation that it will disappear overnight. Instead, PA assumes a flexible posture with respect to implementation strategy. Figure 2.8 illustrates the sequential vs. parallel decision. If you have a small team and want to use scrum, see Chap. 5. To work in parallel, see Chap. 7.

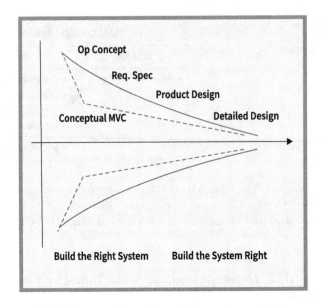

Fig. 2.7 Conceptual MVC decomposition pinches the "cone of uncertainty"

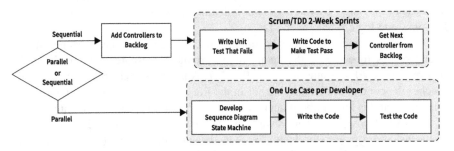

Fig. 2.8 Some parts of Parallel Agile are useful with a sequential implementation phase

Not surprisingly, we think parallelism has a lot going for it, especially if you're trying to compress your schedule and shorten time to market. One developer working a use case all the way through has many advantages.

2.7.3 Adding Controllers to the Scrum Backlog

If you're proceeding with a typical Scrum approach, once you've decomposed a use case along MVC boundaries, it's easy enough to add the controllers (and sometimes the views) to the backlog. The model is already in place because it's been code generated.

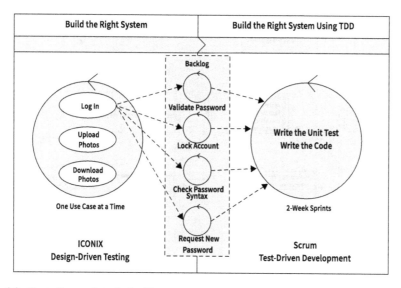

Fig. 2.9 Controllers go into the backlog

Figure 2.9 shows controllers being added to the backlog for a project that has chosen a traditional scrum/test-driven design (TDD) implementation approach rather than going massively parallel.

2.7.4 Tracking Agile Projects by Epic, User Story, and Task

Parallel Agile is agile on the management side and model driven on the development side. If you are doing sprint planning using epics, tasks, and user stories, you'll have no trouble understanding a PA project plan. Our preference is to keep the management artifacts in the same UML model with the design, which is easily accomplished using a UML profile for scrum. Figure 2.10 shows an epic from CarmaCam with a goal of improving video quality, decomposed into user stories and tasks.

An important management aspect of PA is support for accurate cost estimation. Modeling use cases provides a good basis for estimation. We introduce a bottom-up task-based estimation strategy in Chap. 7.

2.8 Optimization and Acceptance Testing

While PA does not dispute the usefulness of unit testing and automated regression testing frameworks, it places an even higher value on acceptance testing and providing automated support for generating acceptance tests from use case and requirement models. Figure 2.11 shows PA's testing strategy, adapted from *Design-Driven Testing* (Rosenberg and Stephens 2010). We discuss testing in depth in Chap. 6.

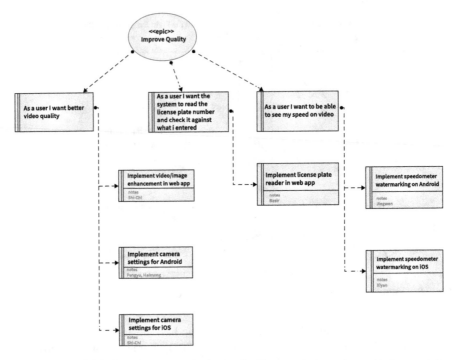

Fig. 2.10 Parallel Agile projects are tracked using familiar user stories, epics, and tasks

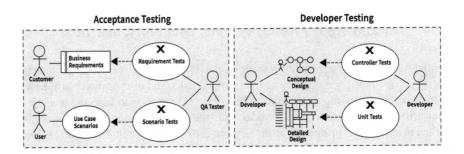

Fig. 2.11 Parallel Agile drives acceptance tests from designs

Of particular importance is the automated expansion of use cases into *thread tests* that exercise all sunny- and rainy-day paths through a use case.

2.9 Balancing Agility and Discipline

Figure 2.12 shows that both underplanning and overplanning are expensive. Overplanning leads to analysis paralysis, while underplanning leads to constant refactoring and a steady stream of hotfixes.

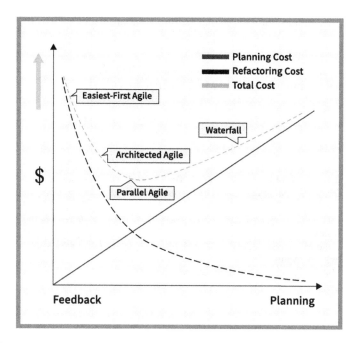

Fig. 2.12   Parallel Agile balances agility (feedback) and discipline (planning)

PA is feedback-driven, with great emphasis placed on getting to code early and discovering requirements from interacting with prototype, proof-of-concept working systems. However, PA differentiates between prototype code and production code, and benefits from careful modeling of use cases, MVC decompositions, and automated test case generation. PA's balance between feedback and planning targets the "just enough planning" cost minimum shown.

2.10   Summary

PA is a flexible process that supports large-team parallel development; by default, you assign a developer to each use case and adjust assignments as needed. If you don't have a large team, you can still benefit from using some parts of PA with a scrum/Kanban backlog approach. PA is a feedback-driven (Agile) process that gets to code quickly and uses prototyping to drive requirements discovery. You model sunny-day and rainy-day behavior during the MVP phase, and you focus acceptance testing on the corner cases during the optimization phase.

In this chapter, we presented a high-level overview of Parallel Agile, and provided pointers to later chapters in the book where you can get more detail.

In the chapters that follow, we cover

- Executable domain models (Chap. 3)
- Illustrated examples for the CarmaCam project (Chap. 4)

- Support for a small team sequential (scrum/Kanban, backlog-driven) approach (Chap. 5)
- Continuous acceptance testing (Chap. 6)
- Strategies for managing parallel development (Chap. 7)
- Incremental Commitment Spiral Model (Chap. 8)

References

Boehm, B., J. Lane, S. Koolmanojwong, and R. Turner. 2014. *The incremental commitment spiral model: Principles and practices for successful systems and software.* Upper Saddle River: Pearson.

Jacobson, I. 1992. *Object oriented software engineering: A use case driven approach.* Boston: Addison-Wesley.

Rosenberg, D., and M. Stephens. 2008. *Use case driven object modeling with UML: Theory and practice.* Berkeley: Apress.

———. 2010. *Design driven testing.* Berkeley: Apress.

Chapter 3
CodeBots: From Domain Model to Executable Architecture

Box 3.1

Doug explains how being able to instantly make a domain model executable is like waving a magic wand for a project manager.

Bo Wang started developing a code generator that produced NoSQL database access code and Node.js APIs a couple of semesters before we started the CarmaCam project, but that was the first place that we put it to use. The effect was startling.

The first student team to work on CarmaCam (originally called Bad Driver Reporting) consisted of 15 students. When I got the student team assembled, I went up to the whiteboard and sketched the domain model, which I pretty much had in my head after a couple of months of thinking about the problem. It had objects like Video, Video Metadata, and Bad Driver Report. We knew the reports had to be reviewed, so there was also a Review object, and we needed Accounts. Bo came to class with the code generator on his laptop and generated all of the Mongo database collections, the database access functions, and a Node.js API to access them.

The students watched wide-eyed with astonishment as, a few seconds after generating all this code, Bo had it deployed on a server and started testing the API. The magic wand had been waved.

I proceeded to assign a developer to fill out the reports, a developer to work on crowdsourced reviews, and a couple of mobile app developers to upload videos and metadata, and our proof of concept system had begun. The domain model serves as a "software backplane" that all of the use cases can plug into as they are being independently developed. We had few issues with integrating the individually developed prototypes.

A semester or two later we decided that we needed to provide an incentive for people to participate in our crowdsourced review process, so we developed a reward point system. This required some extensions to our database, and Bo came in a waved the magic wand again. Then we decided to take on emergency alert reporting and needed some additional database functionality. With a wave of the magic wand, the database was built and an API made available for testing.

At the time of this writing, we're developing machine learning capability to have AI models automatically check the videos that get uploaded to try to

© Springer Nature Switzerland AG 2020

D. Rosenberg et al., *Parallel Agile – faster delivery, fewer defects, lower cost*,
https://doi.org/10.1007/978-3-030-30701-1_3

filter out false reports. We built a special webpage that allows us to capture still images from the start and end of an incident, and then annotate them in a way that the AI models can understand (e.g., draw a box around a traffic light and label it "traffic light"). We waved the magic wand one more time and created that database and API, and I immediately assigned the webpage to a developer.

Executable architectures are a magic wand for developers, too—especially for developers who like to focus on the user side of a use case rather than on the database access layer. Database access is obviously necessary, but if you have to do a lot of it, it can get repetitive, and you start wishing you didn't have to write that code by hand. If you're developing REST APIs on top of your database layer, you have a second level of repetitive code. If you're a tester, you can spend a lot less time testing whether the database (and API) is working or not, because the autogenerated database code is generally bug-free.

Finally, from a project manager's perspective, going from zero to a cloud-hosted database and API in 15 seconds tends to generate a lot of enthusiasm and positive momentum among the other developers, and it's never too early to start getting victories on a project.

In this chapter, Bo explains how his code generator fits into the overall Parallel Agile (PA) process, and Matt explains how he turned Bo's code generator into the PA CodeBot.

3.1   Solving Problems to Enable Parallelism

To effectively leverage parallelism in development, you must solve a number of problems, the three biggest of which follow:

- *Communication among a team of developers who are each working a separate part of a project can be challenging.* This issue has plagued use case–driven development for decades due to the difficulty of sharing knowledge. Increasingly, teams turn to domain-driven design to help solve this problem. Establishing a common domain model at the inception of the project creates a common vocabulary that you can then use consistently across use case narratives, requirement descriptions, software designs at both conceptual and detailed levels of abstraction, and even into the code.
- *It's difficult to predetermine a precise and complete data schema required by independently developed use cases.* Different use cases often require different

attributes, and changes can happen at any time due to the revision (either enhancement or replacement) of requirements. It is a general weakness of plan-driven development and is most efficiently addressed by Agile feedback-driven techniques. PA uses prototyping against a live database with a flexible schema during the proof of concept phase to resolve as many of these issues as possible before a minimum viable product (MVP) is attempted. During this phase, the significant advantages in the NoSQL database allow developers to specify a partial data schema during prototyping at a relatively early stage and worry about the unification later.

- *Integration of code produced by developers working in parallel is tricky.* Code integration is usually an intractable problem for Agile development because of the challenges arising from frequent updates, stamp coupling of modules, and so forth. However, the emergence of REST APIs and microservice architectures is valuable in providing a set of loosely coupled services to guarantee the continuous delivery and integration.

PA uses code generation to address all three of these problems simultaneously, by generating a NoSQL database and a set of REST APIs from a domain model at the inception of the project. Executable domain models are fundamentally important to setting up for parallelism because PA projects start prototyping use cases in parallel with a flexible-schema database in place, database access functions already working and addressable via a set of APIs.

3.1.1 Parallel Agile Versus Agile/ICONIX

The biggest difference between PA and Agile/ICONIX is the existence of a code generator that makes domain models executable. In addition to addressing the three major issues of communication, feedback-driven database design, and integration, this code generator shortens development time by eliminating manual coding and configuration of the back-end, improves reliability because all of the generated code is bug-free, and reduces the time spent on unit testing.

Our experience has been that the generated code tends to make up about one-third of a typical application, so these time savings have been significant, as reflected in the overall cost and schedule improvements we have gained with PA.

From a process standpoint, our CodeBot code generator allows prototyping against a live database to begin immediately at project inception, resulting in a rapid discovery of requirements. Prototyping against a live database versus user interface (UI) storyboarding enables a much deeper exploration of requirements. (See the "Why Prototype at All?" sidebar later in this chapter.)

3.1.2   Cost Benefits

Historically, code generation has suffered from the problem of requiring a lot of upfront work creating models, which offsets its benefits on saving coding effort. As a general example, the source code of a set of classes with specified attributes and behaviors is usually generated from a detailed design. This requires a procedure to be rigorously considered and formally presented so that it can be converted into executable code.

We suggest making the design executable at an early stage, while developers have the conceptual models in mind. To be precise, CodeBot creates an executable architecture from your domain model and lets you start prototyping against it. Upfront analysis time to determine a precise design class and database schema is replaced by evolutionary development. Later, whenever domain updates happen, CodeBot can immediately generate and deploy a new back-end. In this way, the front-end code can always interact with live services.

We use a microservices architecture to reduce the risks from frequent changes and continuous delivery and integration. It fits the process when we decompose a large system into use cases, each with a separate component and independent capability.

Moreover, once you give CodeBot a domain model as the input, it can automatically generate and deploy a microservice, so ideally developers don't need to worry about the infrastructure of the back-end. This approach also reduces the potential technical learning curve and deployment effort.

3.1.3   Origin of Executable Architectures

The origin of executable architectures can be traced back to our location-based advertising (LBA) project. The initial implementation team who developed the billing system requested to work in PHP/MySQL because they had more experience with that technology. Our success in other parts of the system using NoSQL was good enough that in the following iteration we re-created this part of the system using Cassandra and JavaScript (JQuery Mobile), so that we had a unified code baseline.

During this exercise, we developed a design pattern where developers could rapidly "clone" some sample code that implemented the database create, read, update, delete (CRUD) functions. To access the resource from both Android and iOS, we wrapped the database functions in a collection of REST APIs.

We decided to pursue automating this pattern and built a code generator that works with domain models. We then kept working on enhancements to this code generator, as well as an independent software as a service (SaaS) to support more general usage. We piloted the code generator on the CarmaCam project with excellent results, and we're continuing to use it on additional projects.

3.1.4   Developer to Developer Integration

In Appendix B, you can find some example project architectures illustrating how the generated components can fit into your project, so that the UI and other code can interface with the evolving model and its API (spoiler alert: microservices). But for now, it's worth a quick jaunt into the thinking and intent behind parallel integration of work done in this way.

Business to business (B2B) integration is routinely accomplished using microservices and REST APIs. Separate business entities can work independently and in parallel to accomplish a common goal. Each business publishes its own API, and federations of businesses can get stuff done. An example might be "login using Facebook"; many independent app developers use Facebook's API to handle account management.

PA applies this philosophy to integrating the work of a large number of developers working independently to accomplish a common goal (let's call it *developer to developer*, or D2D, integration). But there's a key difference between B2B and D2D integration using APIs. With D2D integration, each developer does not publish his or her own API. Instead, *the problem domain publishes an API* (more precisely, a domain-driven API is generated via CodeBot) and *all developers participating in solving the problem described by this problem domain use that common API,* which allows business objects to be created and manipulated via a service.

3.1.5   Resilience to Staff Turnover

Bus number is an Agile term describing the number of people on your team it would take to be run over by a bus for the project to fail. Having an executable architecture based on the project domain increases the bus number. It helps you create a more resilient project because all the developers understand the problem domain and can access it via a common API.

As mentioned previously, PA originated on student projects that had close to 100 percent staff turnover every semester, as we'll demonstrate in the book's main example project, CarmaCam, in the next chapter. Because PA uses a standard set of visual notations to describe a use case, we were able to continue work across semester boundaries and push the project forward to a successful conclusion. The simplified Incremental Commitment Spiral Model (ICSM) spiral of "proof of concept, MVP, optimize" was also useful in this regard, as we generally started each new phase with a new team of developers.

For the rest of this chapter, we'll walk through how to use CodeBot on your own project, so you can benefit from domain-driven prototyping (which, as you now know, forms a major portion of the PA process).

3.2 Domain-Driven Prototyping

In this section, you'll learn how to create an executable architecture using CodeBot, a cloud-based automation tool (see Fig. 3.1), and how to tie in the tool with rapid prototyping of the model.

But first let's set the scene.

Imagine you have a project that's just getting started, with multiple developers (perhaps even multiple teams) set to work on different parts of the new system. You need a way for everyone involved to work in parallel with as little communication overhead as possible.

As you learned in previous chapters, to enable teams to work in parallel you allocate a self-contained deliverable (ideally a single use case) to each developer. During prototyping, developers use CodeBot to help prototype their use case's sunny-day scenario. (The all-important rainy-day scenarios will be explored in the next phase.) Each developer has a month to prototype a two-paragraph use case—so the nature of the prototype changes from "Here's what the graphical user interface is going to look like" to "Here it is, working."

Fig. 3.1 CodeBot turns your UML domain model into a complete executable architecture

Note 3.1

Before CodeBot, prototyping would generally involve making the basic database access work and connecting it to the screens. Now the database access is (almost) free, so in a month you can prototype the whole sunny-day functionality, spending much of that time walking through updates with the stakeholder and discovering new requirements.

The glue that enables these separately developed use cases to bind together cohesively is the *domain model*, the ubiquitous language with which everything in the project is designed and written. The idea is to create a model that accurately represents the stakeholder's business domain, and to create this as early in the project as possible.

Note 3.2

In domain-driven design (DDD), *domain model* or *executable domain model* refers to the active code implementation of the domain concepts, behavior, and business rules, captured from whiteboard sketches. While coding the domain model is usually a manual process, PA uses CodeBot to instantly make the domain model executable. This is referred to as the *executable architecture*.

You can then use the executable architecture to create an early prototype, and evolve it through successive rapid iterations, all the while placing the prototype UI in front of stakeholders to record their feedback.

In other words, here's the process:

1. Hold a quick workshop to create the domain model (it's fine for this to be *really* quick because you'll discover missing domain objects and further details while prototyping).
2. Generate an API and database from the domain model.
3. Create a prototype (UI, business logic) of your use case using the generated API.
4. Put the prototype in front of the stakeholders.
5. Hold up a net and catch all the change requests that the stakeholders start shouting out. These are the requirements.

Clearly, then, the key is being able to create a working prototype as early as possible. In this chapter, you'll learn how to use CodeBot to do that *very* early, like on day one of the project after an hour or two of domain modeling.

Before you do anything else at all, though, get set up so that you can follow along and create a domain model, which you will then turn into an executable architecture.

3.2.1   Introducing CodeBot

There are, of course, many ways to automate software development. The approach we'll look at here is especially optimized toward code generation of working prototypes. We've been developing cloud-based software to support the process described in this book, so we'll spend some time here walking through what we have. Note that you don't have to use our cloud-based system to adopt the PA process on your own project, but we hope you'll agree that this system will make your life as a software developer much easier.

With that disclaimer out of the way, let's talk about CodeBot. In a nutshell, CodeBot is a cloud-based architecture creation tool. You hand it a Unified Modeling Language (UML) domain model, and within seconds CodeBot will create a complete REST API with a database schema, client libraries in various languages, Swagger API documentation, plus various useful extras such as JSON Schema definitions for each domain object. As an added bonus, CodeBot automatically deploys your new prototype API to the cloud (complete with its own live MongoDB database), where you can test it via a secure access token.

Once you've created an account at https://parallelagile.net and logged in, you should see a page similar to the one in Fig. 3.2.

At the top right is a button to download the CodeBot add-in for Enterprise Architect (EA). This free add-in enables you to run the generator on your domain model from within EA. The add-in also has many other useful features that we'll cover later in the book.

Note 3.3
If you can't use EA for any reason, as long as you can export your model as an XMI file, you'll still be able to do everything we cover in this chapter. It won't be quite as convenient, but it will still be doable.

We'll return to CodeBot later in this chapter for a full walk-through. For now, you should be all set up ready to create a domain model in EA and turn it into an executable architecture using our EA add-in. This is the mechanism by which you'll develop your prototype system through a rapid series of feedback-driven iterations.

First, though, since prototyping is a key part of this process, let's explore it in more detail.

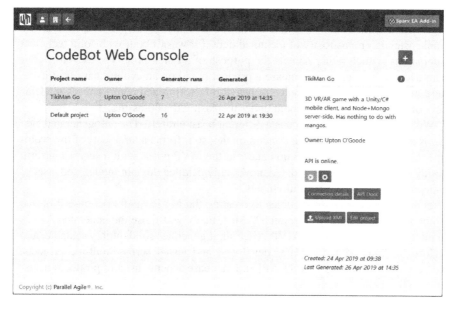

Fig. 3.2 CodeBot web console

3.2.2 What Is Prototyping?

Typically, developers create their software prototypes early in the project life cycle, to explore various aspects of the new system before development begins in earnest. The developers explore technical aspects of the design, while the stakeholder, product manager, business analysts, and user experience (UX) designer get to view a working (or, more likely, semiworking) UI. Only part of the system is prototyped—enough to give a flavor of what's required.

There are many approaches to prototyping, and often one project will involve a number of small-scale prototypes. From the perspective of eliciting feedback from the stakeholder as early as possible, however, there are typically two approaches:

- *Throwaway prototyping:* A quickly bashed-together system is paraded in front of the project stakeholders, then immediately wheeled away and dismantled. The production system is written from scratch, although certain parts of the prototype might be carried over, along with the lessons learned from the prototype (may it rest in pieces).
- *Evolutionary prototyping:* The quickly bashed-together system is developed gradually into a production system. Automated tests are retrofitted, and the design is refactored and reworked as the developers' understanding of the system they're building grows, and as requirements are updated based on the prototype itself.

Each approach has advantages and disadvantages. The throwaway prototype might seem like wasted work, and the evolutionary prototype can turn into a Frankensteinian monstrosity of technical debt if it wasn't built with solid technical foundations (which rather defeats the purpose of a quick prototype). Even if your team eventually manages to release a product based on an evolutionary prototype, there will be scar tissue: evidence of heavy refactoring and compromises made as parts of the code are hacked about under increasing time pressure.

With PA, the early prototype is a different beast entirely. The autogenerated system is driven directly from the domain model, so it forms a large part of the prototype itself, and development starts anew in the MVP phase with a server platform freshly generated from the updated, now richly detailed domain model, and a set of in-depth, well-understood requirements.

You might ask, "When it comes to creating the MVP, should we base it on the prototype, or start over from scratch?" Most likely you'll use the generated API as an integral component of the MVP. After all, it generates solid, highly scalable, and performant code from templates developed and tested across multiple projects. We've seen the generated REST API and database schema used in production systems with excellent results.

However, there might be certain rare situations where it isn't possible to use the generated API (e.g., the production system will use a different architecture, or there's a company-wide mandate about which third-party libraries can be used). Even in this case, the prototype phase gives your project a flying start, though there are definitely more benefits to be gained if you can continue to use the generated API.

As for the handwritten code that was created to complete the prototype, keep in mind it was all quickly written sunny-day code with no error handling. Do keep it around as a reference, but MVP development should definitely start afresh with thoughts of rainy-day scenarios foremost in the developers' minds, and with a rigorous requirements-driven testing process (see Chap. 6).

Back to the proof of concept phase.

3.2.3 CarmaCam Domain Modeling Workshop

Right at the start of a project, you'll hold a short domain modeling workshop from which you'll generate the first iteration of the working prototype. The workshop should involve all the project stakeholders: customer, business analyst, architect, UX designer, and at least one of the senior developers. Spend an hour or two modeling the problem domain on a whiteboard and then 15 minutes capturing the output in your favorite graphical model/design tool (we highly recommend EA).

It might seem like you can't get the whole domain model done at a detailed level in 2 hours, and that's correct: there won't be much detail yet. Details such as exact relationships—aggregation versus composition, multiplicity, and so on—are the wrong things to focus on during the early stages of prototyping. However, these details will become important later, and you will want to have them pinned down by the time you start the MVP phase. The relationships *become* significant as they directly affect what gets generated, as you'll see later in this chapter.

The domain model will evolve all through the prototyping phase; however, we've found that version 1 of the model typically has the majority of pieces already in place. After that, discovery tends to be in the form of individual fields, data types, and so forth.

In the remainder of the prototyping phase, you invite the stakeholder to try out the prototype, which leads to more requirements discovery.

3.2.3.1 Extending the CarmaCam Domain Model to Support Machine Learning

To illustrate how domain driven prototyping works, let's look at an extension of the CarmaCam domain model to support machine learning training. As the CarmaCam project evolved, the team recognized the need for sanity checking incident reports using machine learning. They decided to build a webpage that allows videos to be annotated for the purpose of training AI models.

This exercise had two important objectives:

- Since the machine learning classifiers analyze each frame of a video, the team wanted to cut down the video size by cropping it to show only the actual incident. Since they were using 20-second videos and a typical incident might be over within 2 seconds, reducing the number of frames in the video or eliminating useless frames from the video is a large computational saving.
- The machine learning training process requires video keyframes to be annotated. For example, you can draw a box around a vehicle and label it "vehicle," as shown in Fig. 3.3.

Fig. 3.3 Incident start and incident stop images for TensorFlow model training

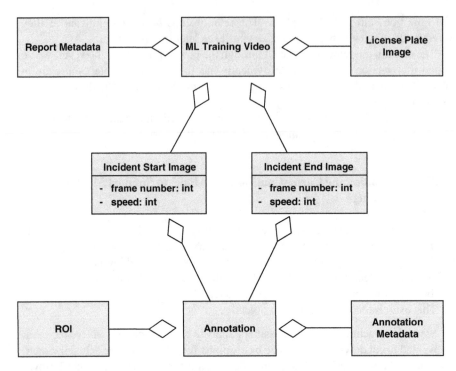

Fig. 3.4 A more refined CarmaCam incident reports domain model

These extensions resulted in a whiteboard sketch, which we quickly transposed into a class diagram. We updated the CarmaCam domain model to show that machine learning training videos have start-incident and stop-incident images, and that those images can be annotated, as shown in Fig. 3.4.

As soon as the team ran CodeBot again, Doug was able to assign a developer to immediately start prototyping the video trimmer/annotator, because the database access code had been generated and was accessible via an API.

3.2.3.2 Running CodeBot Again

When you run CodeBot, at a broad level it creates two things:

- A zip file containing all of the project source code, API documentation, and so forth
- A secure, deployed copy of the API up in the cloud, which you can start testing immediately

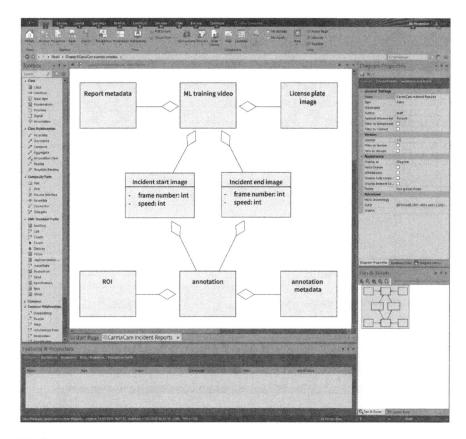

Fig. 3.5 Load the domain model in Enterprise Architect

Load your copy of EA and open your domain model (see Fig. 3.5).[1] Right-click the package or within the diagram, and choose Specialize | Parallel Agile | Generate Project. CodeBot kicks into action (see Fig. 3.6).

Once CodeBot has finished, you'll see the All Done screen, similar to Fig. 3.7 (click the Get Token button to see the connection details).

The details shown in Fig. 3.7 enable you to connect to your new cloud-hosted API. All of the connection details that you see on the screen are also available on the website (more on that shortly).

As you can see, the add-in has also downloaded and saved the zip file containing your generated project. Click the Open Folder button and extract the files. Figure 3.8 shows a subset of what's been created. (Please note that the Server folder, which contains the Node Express API code, isn't available with the free license; however,

---

[1] If you can't use either Enterprise Architect or the Parallel Agile add-in for any reason, as a fallback you can export your model as an XMI file and then run CodeBot via the Upload XMI button shown in Figure 3.2.

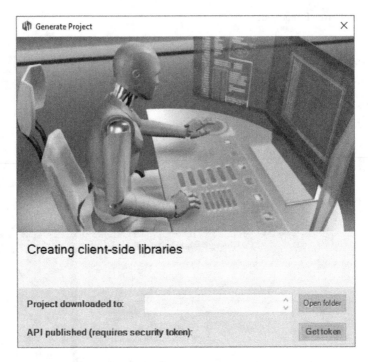

Fig. 3.6 CodeBot in action

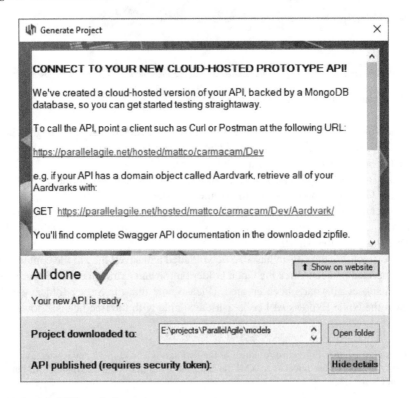

Fig. 3.7 Your API is ready for testing

Fig. 3.8   CodeBot creates server-side code, client-side code, and API documentation

```
 1
 2  // If your API service is running locally, replace this with:  http://127.0.0.1:2000/carmacam/
 3  var url = "https://parallelagile.net/hosted/mattco/carmacam/Dev/"
 4
 5  // If the access token has expired, create a new token at https://parallelagile.net
 6  // (click the Connection Details button for your project):
 7  var accessToken = "2f8abc90-aa3f-40b0-a56b-84d69339f6c9"
 8
 9  var DBAdapter = {};
10
11  DBAdapter.create = function(collection, data, successCB, errorCB) {
12      if (is_defined(collection) && is_defined(data) && (is_array(data) || is_object(data))) {
13          ajaxCall(collection, "POST", "", data, successCB, errorCB);
14      } else {
15          errorCB("Error: " + "Invalid Parameters");
16      }
17  };
18
19  DBAdapter.get = function(collection, param, successCB, errorCB) {
20      if (is_defined(collection) && is_defined(param)) {
21          var data = "/" + param;
22          ajaxCall(collection, "GET", data, null, successCB, errorCB);
23      } else {
24          errorCB("Error: " + "Invalid Parameters");
25      }
26  };
27
```

Fig. 3.9   Client-side code is automatically configured to point at the cloud server

you do still get a free, cloud-hosted deployment of the API that you can test, plus all the generated client code for connecting to the hosted API.)

Figure 3.9 shows the top of JavaScript/Adapter.js. This bit of code is part of the JavaScript-based REST client, which you can use in your own client code to access the generated API. As you can see, the database adapter is already set up to call the hosted API directly. An access token has been generated and placed in the generated file. To keep the API secure, this token lasts for 24 hours; a new one can be generated any time via the web console.

The server code is set up so that you can run it as a Node Express REST service. You can also deploy it without modification as a "serverless" AWS Lambda function (it achieves this via the open source serverless-http library, https://github.com/dougmoscrop/serverless-http); in fact, Lambda and serverless-http are what we're using behind the scenes to automatically create and deploy the cloud-hosted APIs. A discussion of the possibilities opened up by having a serverless deployment target is beyond the scope of this chapter, but it is a good example of how you can use CodeBot to generate a completely different deployment target, a different database, or even a different architecture, based on the same domain model. (For an in-depth blueprint of CodeBot-driven architectures, see Appendix B.)

Now that you've generated the project, let's flip back to the CodeBot web console and see what's new (see Fig. 3.10).

We have lift-off! CodeBot has automatically deployed your new API into a cloud-hosted environment for testing. If you want to use Postman (or Curl, or some other REST client) to try out the hosted API, click Connection Details. Alternatively, you can test the API directly from the web console, courtesy of the generated Swagger documentation. Click API Docs to bring up the complete Swagger documentation for your API (see Fig. 3.11).

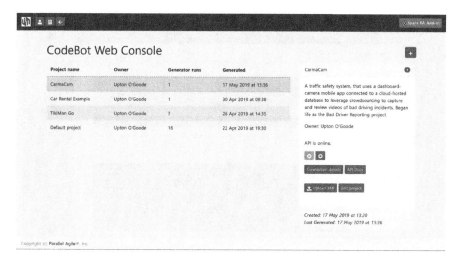

Fig. 3.10 Your API is already in a private online sandbox—time to start testing

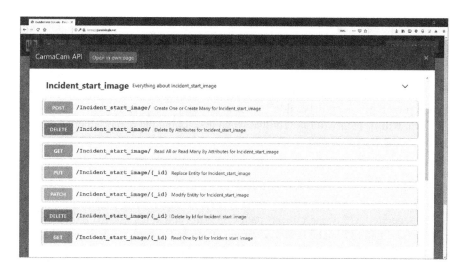

Fig. 3.11 REST API endpoints available for the Incident_start_image domain object

To test creating a database record via the API, open one of the domain objects (in the image, we chose Incident_start_image). Then open the POST endpoint at the top, click Try It Now, fill in some data (or use the generated defaults), scroll down, and click Execute.

The first time the hosted API is called, it takes a few seconds, as it's running from a cold start. Subsequent calls should be quicker; after a period of inactivity, it goes back to sleep until the next time it's prodded awake.

Fig. 3.12 One record created

You should see a result similar to the one shown in Fig. 3.12: one new domain record created in the cloud. You can then run search queries and retrieve any data you've created via the GET endpoint.

Once you have a REST API up and running, you can start to create a prototype UI and any other accompanying code. Keep in mind that this prototype is exactly that—a prototype—so you wouldn't want to spend time perfecting the code or the UI. There will be plenty of time for that when developing the real production-ready system during the MVP phase.

Note 3.4
The generated API doesn't do any data validation unless it's told to (validation and other features can be switched on or off). For prototyping this is great, as it means you can evolve the data structures on the fly—to add a new field or change a data type, either modify the JSON data in your client code, or directly modify the BSON (Binary JSON) data in the database. Just be sure to feed the changes back into your modeling/design tool, so that they survive when you next need to run the generator.

At this stage, the customer, business analyst, product manager, and UX designer should have a clear idea of how their business domain translates into a technical solution.

A cynic might ask, "What's so great about having a working prototype that's generated on the first day of the project and evolves as the team's understanding of the requirements and the subtle complexities of the business domain evolves?" See the sidebar for our response.

3.2.4 The Prototyping Is Done—What's Next?

That pretty much wraps it up for domain driven prototyping. You've seen that prototyping is a straightforward process, and a highly effective way to discover the requirements and help the stakeholder (and business analyst, subject matter experts, etc.) turn their "I'll know it when I see it" reaction into "That's great, but can it be more like this?"

CodeBot isn't only useful during prototyping. The generated system can also be carried through to the production system. This brings with it a whole separate set of considerations, which we explore in the next section.

Box 3.2: Why Prototype at All?

Customers and stakeholders generally are experts in their business domain, but not in software, UX design, or data modeling. Asking them to define software requirements in a room where someone is scribbling data diagrams on the whiteboard or tabbing through mocked-up user UIs can be suboptimal, to say the least. Often, all the stakeholder can manage is, "I'll know it when I see it," which sounds like a cop-out—but it's true. The stakeholder is being asked to make a decision based on incomplete data. So the analyst and the development team must often compensate or fill in the gaps, essentially guessing the requirements and hoping that what they produce matches what the business needs.

This cognitive barrier is why stakeholders' brains will often light up when they finally see the "finished" software. Suddenly they understand how it all ties together—how the business domain that they carry in their heads maps to software—and they start asking for changes. In reality, the unstoppable stream of changes they're suddenly asking for are the real requirements.

There's a moment of richness. Given "I'll know it when I see it," they've just seen it. Of course, on some projects this "singularity of singular clarity" arrives much too late: the budget's spent, the product's about to be shipped, the key developers are already moving on to new projects. It's a shame, as ironically the stakeholder is now ready to sit down and say exactly what they need from this new system. That was one expensive epiphany.

Traditionally on Agile projects, the "I'll know it when I see it" issue has been addressed by chopping the iterations down into very fine releases. These may not be releases into production; rather, they are new slices of working software that the stakeholder can check out. This process works to an extent, but it's an evolutionary design approach that introduces its own set of problems. One disadvantage is that it's quite a zoomed-in, myopic way of working—it's like 3D printing an elephant.

Another disadvantage is that the first slice of working software may not be ready to show to the stakeholder until the first two-week sprint has finished.

The approach that you're able to take with PA is to show the stakeholder working software on the first day of the project, to give them that "I've just seen it" moment of clarity right away. Based on the stakeholder's feedback, you can update the domain model and generate a new prototype within moments. This is about as iterative a development process as it gets: "So let's change those fields . . . Hit Generate . . . There, is that more of what you had in mind?"

Of course, the *entire* project can't be fully code-generated, although we're making great strides in that direction. The idea is that when you show stakeholders working software, they immediately understand what's going to be possible and, trying out the prototype in front of them, they'll produce a stream of change requests: "That's great, but could it work more like this?" and "About that screen . . . No, nothing like that, it should be more like this . . ."

In this way, the project doesn't need to go through months of iterations and evolving designs as stakeholders keep "inexplicably" changing their minds. Instead, that stream of change requests based on the early prototype—the *real requirements*—are pinned down early in the project, before any production code has been written.

3.3   Using CodeBot During the MVP Phase

With the prototype done, and a fully crystallized domain model plus a solid set of requirements in place and agreed-on, your team will embark on the MVP phase, creating the first version of the production system, with some well-deserved confidence.[2]

---

[2] It's possible for different parts of a project to be in different phases simultaneously. In the video trimmer example, mainstream CarmaCam was in an optimization phase but machine learning was in proof of concept.

Up until now, the team would have been prototyping the sunny-day part of their respective use cases, and refining the prototypes based on stakeholder feedback. During the MVP sprint, they'll flesh out the corner cases and develop the scenario descriptions needed for the acceptance testing phase.

At this stage, certain details start to matter. The idea is to contain as much relevant detail as possible in the domain model. The richer it is, the more precisely it represents the business domain, and the more details CodeBot has to chew on. Additionally, you'll be pinning down the architecture details—in particular, how the generated APIs will fit into the overall system being delivered.

We'll examine these concerns in this section, starting with the importance of specifying the correct UML relationships. The exact relationship types virtually didn't matter during prototyping, but they're certainly important for the MVP phase.

3.3.1 What to Expect from Your UML Relationships

Note 3.5
Although putting relationships in a table like this can make it all seem very formal with lots of caveats, you should find that these effects are intuitive and do exactly what you might expect.

When you generate the model with CodeBot, certain relationships affect what gets generated, while others are deliberately ignored, so that they can be used to model business abstractions that might not make sense in the generated code. Even these "ignored" (as in, nonsemantic) relationships might still be picked up and used in the API documentation, though.

3.3.1.1 Choosing a Different Relationship Type Affects What's Generated

Table 3.1 shows what to expect when you hand your UML model to CodeBot, going from the strongest relationship type to the weakest.

You should find the composition relationship useful for creating nested JSON structures, something that particularly lends itself to MongoDB collections, where the recommended best practice is that child elements with a strong ownership relationship are nested within each parent element, rather than put into separate collections.

All other relationship types—dependency, realization, responsibility, and so forth (*ad infinitum*)—are treated as nonsemantic by CodeBot, so you can safely use them to define more abstract concepts that document the model rather than drive it.

Table 3.1 How relationships in your UML model affect generated code and database schema

Relationship type		How it affects the generated client code	How it affects the database schema
	Generalization	StartImage and EndImage will be subclasses of IncidentImage. If IncidentImage is abstract in the model, it will also be created as an abstract class.	Separate StartImage and EndImage collections will be created. StartImage and EndImage will also include all the attributes that are defined in IncidentImage. If IncidentImage is abstract, an IncidentImage collection/table isn't created.
	Composition	Annotation, AnnotationMetadata, and TrackingDetails are all created as separate classes. Annotation contains both AnnotationMetadata and TrackingDetails objects, as either a single reference or a list, depending on the multiplicity defined in the relationship.	AnnotationMetadata and TrackingDetails are nested objects within the Annotation collection.
	Aggregation	Same as for composition.	MlTrainingVideo, ReportMetadata, and LicensePlateImage are all created as separate collections/tables. They're linked via ID relationships in MongoDB, or as foreign keys in relational databases. Where the database supports it, relational integrity and cascading deletes will also be enforced.
	Association	The Annotation class will include an roi_id field, which can be used to look up an ROI as a separate query.	Aside from the roi_id field, there's no real relationship between the two collections. Relational integrity isn't enforced.

3.3.1.2 Multiplicity Affects What's Generated

If you define multiplicity in the relationships (e.g., 0..1, 1..*), CodeBot uses these wherever possible for validation checks. If you don't define the multiplicity, it defaults to either 0..1 or 1, depending on the context.

Multiplicity also affects whether fields are generated as a single item or a list of items. Additionally, in languages that support optional types (e.g., Option in Scala, or Optional in Java), a multiplicity of 0..1 will be generated as an optional type.

Table 3.2 illustrates how multiplicity affects your API, with some brief code examples.

To round off the chapter, let's have a look at how a domain-driven generated API can fit into your project, regardless of its architecture.

3.4 Deployment Architecture Blueprints (Preview)

We're fully aware that the generated API won't exist by itself—it will need to fit in with an overall project, part of which will include handwritten business logic, systems that interface with other systems, and so forth.

In Appendix B, we explore a variety of possible architectures to illustrate how the generated API can fit into your project.

The most straightforward architecture is simply to run the express.js API and web server on the same server, with the API connecting to a database somewhere. It's likely you'll use a setup like this while prototyping, to keep things simple so that the focus is on requirements discovery. For the production system, things will become more complex, as the emphasis and needs will differ. The easiest (and intended) way to use the API is to treat it like any other microservice with a REST interface. We would expect the majority of projects to be set up in this way.

In a surprise twist, it's also possible to deploy the API as an integral part of a so-called monolith server, while still enabling your team to develop software in parallel. Both the microservice and monolith approaches have their advantages and disadvantages, which we explore in detail in Appendix B.

3.5 Summary

In this chapter, we walked through a domain modeling example for CarmaCam machine learning, and combined this with PA's rapid, iterative, feedback driven prototyping process using the cloud-based CodeBot automation platform[3] and Enterprise Architect add-in.

---

[3] CodeBot is evolving rapidly, so by the time you read this chapter, a whole host of new capabilities will be available for you to try out on your projects for free at https://parallelagile.net.

Table 3.2 How multiplicity assignments affect your API

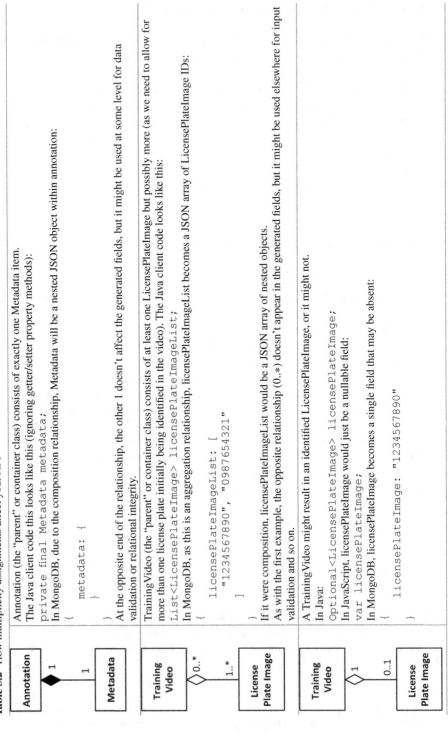

Annotation ◆ 1 — 1 **Metadata**	Annotation (the "parent" or container class) consists of exactly one Metadata item. The Java client code this looks like this (ignoring getter/setter property methods):
	
	`private final Metadata metadata;`
	
	In MongoDB, due to the composition relationship, Metadata will be a nested JSON object within annotation:
	
	<pre>{
	  metadata: {
	  }
	}</pre>
	At the opposite end of the relationship, the other 1 doesn't affect the generated fields, but it might be used at some level for data validation or relational integrity.

Training Video 0..* ◇ 1..* **License Plate Image**	TrainingVideo (the "parent" or container class) consists of at least one LicensePlateImage but possibly more (as we need to allow for more than one license plate initially being identified in the video). The Java client code looks like this:
	
	`List<LicensePlateImage> licensePlateImageList;`
	
	In MongoDB, as this is an aggregation relationship, licensePlateImageList becomes a JSON array of LicensePlateImage IDs:
	
	<pre>{
	  licensePlateImageList: [
	    "1234567890", "0987654321"
	  ]
	}</pre>
	If it were composition, licensePlateImageList would be a JSON array of nested objects.
	As with the first example, the opposite relationship (0..*) doesn't appear in the generated fields, but it might be used elsewhere for input validation and so on.

Training Video ◇ 0..1 **License Plate Image**	A TrainingVideo might result in an identified LicensePlateImage, or it might not.
	In Java:
	
	`Optional<LicensePlateImage> licensePlateImage;`
	
	In JavaScript, licensePlateImage would just be a nullable field:
	
	`var licensePlateImage;`
	
	In MongoDB, licensePlateImage becomes a single field that may be absent:
	
	<pre>{
	  licensePlateImage: "1234567890"
	}</pre>

You've seen how executable architectures improve communication across a large team of developers, how you can rapidly evolve the database schema to meet new requirements, and how CodeBot enables immediate prototyping against a live database.

In the next chapter, we'll illustrate PA by example, by exploring CarmaCam in depth.

Chapter 4
Parallel Agile by Example: CarmaCam

Box 4.1

Doug explains the history of CarmaCam and the role of the author of this chapter, Shobha, on the project.

In 2015 we were working on our second Parallel Agile test project on the University of Southern California (USC) campus. For fun I was mentoring a team of students who were building a photo-sharing application called PicShare (with a couple of students who had just been admitted to the PhD program), and for work I was consulting at a large satellite TV company located near the Los Angeles airport (LAX). My consulting assignment involved working on a service that handled communication between the set-top box and the broadcast center, which had to handle hundreds of millions of messages per day, and on a project to modernize the set-top box user interface. Both of these projects were built with NoSQL databases and REST APIs, the same technologies we were targeting with executable domain models.

My daily commute to LAX was littered with fender-bender accidents that frequently turned my 20-minute commute into an hour-long ordeal that raised my blood pressure and stress levels. As the months wore on, my grumpiness about bad driving slowly simmered to a boil. One morning I was about to make a left turn onto the Santa Monica Freeway—the left arrow light turned green, and my foot hit the gas pedal—when suddenly a car that was two lanes to my right made a U-turn in the intersection right in front of me. Thanks to the two cups of coffee I had just consumed, my foot was fast enough to jam on the brakes and avoid an accident. Having grown up in New York, my reaction was quite naturally to swear a bloody blue streak at the driver who had nearly caused me to have an accident. But even as I was doing my best NYC cab driver impression, my mind was thinking that if there was any justice in the world, that driver's insurance company would see a video of what just happened and his insurance rates would go up, while mine would go down for avoiding the accident.

And then I thought, if we had a mobile app similar to PicShare that uploaded videos instead of photos, we could view the video and scroll back to the point where the bad driver's license plate number was visible. As I continued dodging traffic on the way to work, I started flipping the problem around in my mind. Of course, we'd need video of the incident, metadata associated with the video such as the time and location, a description of the incident, and the other car's license plate number.

© Springer Nature Switzerland AG 2020

D. Rosenberg et al., *Parallel Agile – faster delivery, fewer defects, lower cost*,
https://doi.org/10.1007/978-3-030-30701-1_4

At this point, Bo had been working on the code generator for nearly a year, and it was demonstrable in an early form. Which led me to think, we need to test this executable domain model code generator and gather some more project data anyway, so why don't we just go ahead and build it?

We could create a database and sell access to it to insurance companies—surely they would pay to be able to identify their high-risk drivers before they got tickets and caused accidents. By the time I got to my consulting job, I had the design concept in my head and had decided to do it. I recruited a team of students for the next semester, and we started working on what we originally called Bad Driver Reporting (BDR), now CarmaCam.

The first two students to sign up were Shobha and her friend Asmita. Asmita had been in a car accident and was still recovering, and Shobha recruited her roommate to join the project as well. Shobha's first assignment was to work on storing videos in MongoDB and helping to build this large file capability into the code generator. Next she built the "glue" between our mobile app and our web application, some server-side code that looked up the account information of the person uploading the video and sent them an email with a link to the video in it, so that they could get the license plate number. Asmita worked on the web application page. We spent a lot of time that first semester prototyping; we prototyped our circular video buffer and we spent a lot of energy prototyping voice command activation because I was intent on the system being voice activated. We got voice activation working, but not reliably.

I was happy when both Shobha and Asmita (along with another student named Sharath) decided to take a second semester of Directed Research and work some more on the BDR project. For the second semester Shobha became the Android team lead (after that team had been struggling early in the semester), and Asmita took charge of the web application, while Sharath worked on crowdsourced reviews both semesters. Those three students were the only exceptions to 100 percent staff turnover on the project. We tried for most of the semester to make voice activation reliable enough to use with ambient noise in the car, but in the end we were feedback-driven and backed off to a one-touch user interface that is both simple and reliable.

By the end of the semester, Shobha was mostly managing the project for me, and that's how she became the author of the chapter you're now reading.

This chapter introduces you to one of our example projects, CarmaCam (formerly called Bad Driver Reporting), and how we used Parallel Agile to create CarmaCam.

CarmaCam is a traffic safety system that uses a dashboard-camera mobile app connected to a cloud-hosted database to leverage crowdsourcing to capture and review videos of bad driving incidents (see Fig. 4.1). For this experiment in Parallel Agile, we were pushing the boundaries to see how the three sprints would progress

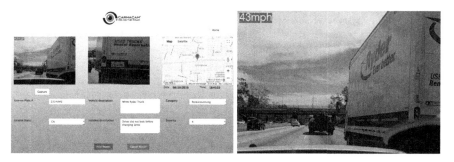

Fig. 4.1 CarmaCam

with part-time students as developers, and with a new batch of students for each sprint.

The CarmaCam project itself provides a mechanism to identify bad-driving hotspots, help insurance companies to find bad drivers, and presents numerous possibilities for actionable data analysis. In this chapter, we present the CarmaCam architecture and design, then focus on how we progressed through the three sprints, and wrap up with next steps for the project.

4.1 CarmaCam Architecture

The architecture represents a high-level abstraction of the software system you're going to design and implement. It consists of a collection of computational components, linked together by connectors that represent how these components interact. Architecture plays an important role in Parallel Agile, as it determines which use cases can be developed in parallel, and which use cases are dependent on each other.

The high-level architecture of the CarmaCam project is shown in Fig. 4.2. The three main components of the system are the mobile apps, the web apps, and the MongoDB database hosted in the cloud (and accessed by Node.js APIs).

As shown in Fig. 4.2, the idea is that a user (good driver) has the dashboard camera mobile app up and running, and it's recording a video saved in a circular buffer. When the user witnesses a bad driving incident, the user issues the upload command, which will upload the last 20 seconds of video clip to the cloud. The user then receives an email with a link to a bad driving report, which contains the uploaded video along with other metadata information. The user can then add comments and post the report. This posted report will be independently reviewed to establish its validity. If a report has been reviewed and accepted by three reviewers, it is then moved to the insurance database, which is available for querying by insurance companies. The goal is to hold bad drivers accountable, leading to a reduction in bad driving incidents.

Architectural design decisions are never completely set in stone. As we started developing and prototyping use cases, some of the initial architectural design decisions had to be modified or dropped in order to support the product's core needs.

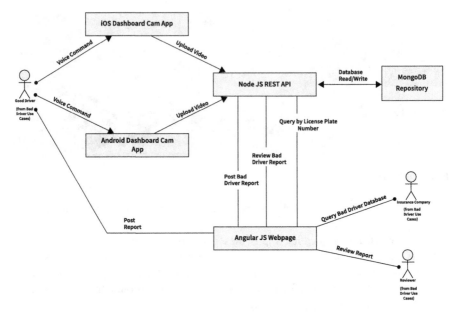

Fig. 4.2 CarmaCam architecture

One such decision was dropping voice activation from the mobile app, as Doug explained previously in the sidebar, and instead having users trigger the video upload from the app by tapping the screen.

Now that you have a general understanding of the system architecture, let's dive into the details of how we actually built the project.

4.2   Sprint 1: Proof of Concept

The first sprint was the proof of concept, to demonstrate that we were building the right system. We started off by establishing and agreeing upon business requirements, which are basically a list of "As a user what I want is . . ." statements. We investigated these from the point of view of each of the end users: driver, reviewer, and insurance company. We then used visual modeling to collect and organize these "what" statements into a sprint plan. Having a well-defined sprint plan to help organize all tasks was important to leverage parallelism with multiple developers.

Figure 4.3 illustrates our sprint plan for the proof of concept phase. We used epics to describe the goals we were trying to achieve in that sprint. Each epic is realized by one or more user stories, and each user story is accomplished by a set of tasks. Also, each task or group of tasks corresponds to a use case, and partitioning

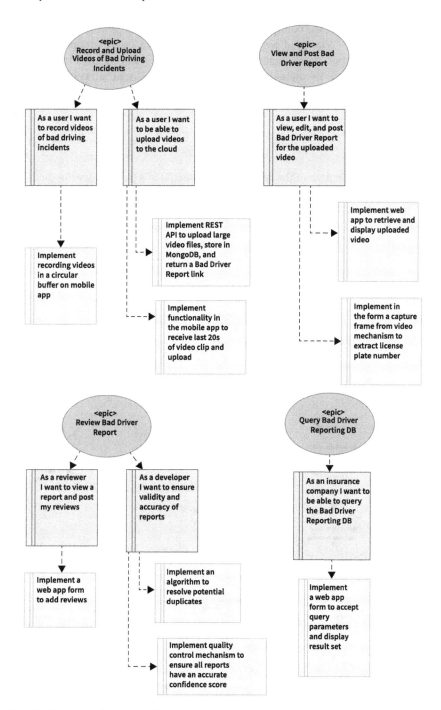

Fig. 4.3   Sprint plan for the proof of concept phase

the system along use case boundaries enabled parallel development. For example, the tasks under the "View and post bad driver report" epic were grouped into the "Post bad driver report to insurance DB" use case, which was handled by one student developer. Figure 4.4 shows all the use cases for the CarmaCam system that we derived from the sprint plan tasks.

> **Note 4.1**
> A visual representation of the sprint plan is essential in a parallel development environment. It's easy for everyone on the project to understand, and having all the tasks captured allows you to do bottom-up estimation on a task-by-task basis.

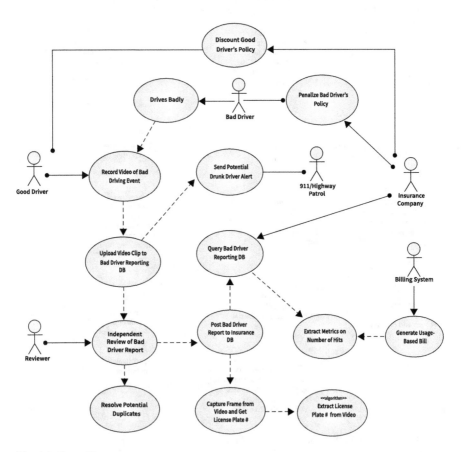

Fig. 4.4 CarmaCam use cases

4.2.1   Executable Domain Model

Once we had our use cases defined, it was time to breathe life into the prototype via an executable domain model. Figure 4.5 illustrates the first draft of the domain model for the CarmaCam project. We created this during the first couple of collaborative brainstorming sessions involving all the student developers. We started off by identifying the required classes/entities based on the user stories, and then we established the relationships between the entities and how the create, read, update, delete (CRUD) functions would be triggered. We added most of the attributes for the entities based on the business requirements that we had gathered so far. This model evolved, as each developer started adding attributes that were required for his or her respective use case. Figure 4.6 shows the evolved domain model that we designed by the end of this sprint.

We were able to be flexible with the design of our domain model due to the code generator, which is what made this model truly executable. We used it to automatically generate the NoSQL database collections, using the domain model as the schema, along with Node.js REST APIs for the CRUD functions. Doing so enabled us to start working on use cases that required prototyping during the requirements gathering stage, like the voice command activation module in the mobile app, where we had to play around with multiple rounds of prototyping to check the feasibility of the different speech toolkits available.

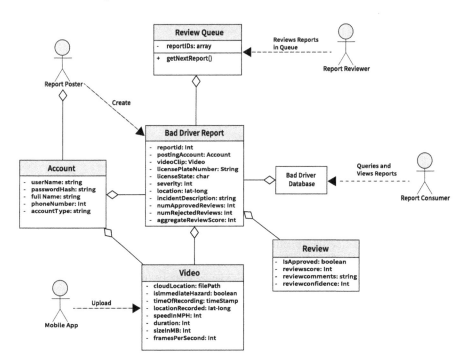

Fig. 4.5 CarmaCam's initial domain model

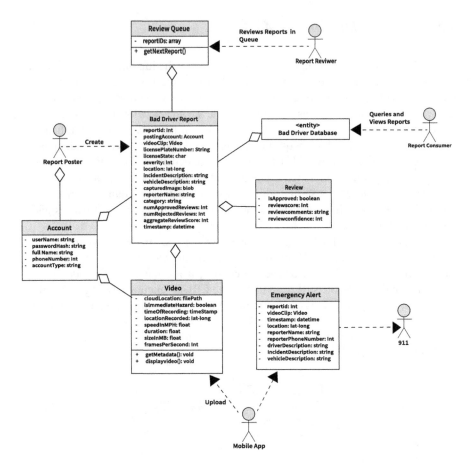

Fig. 4.6 CarmaCam's evolved domain model

4.2.2 Use Cases and Storyboards

Once we had identified and assigned all the use cases, we began writing the *use case narratives*. Think of the narrative of a use case as its user manual. When you write out a use case, the text gives you a holistic view of the use case, with all of its scenarios (basic course and alternate courses) together in one place. This format helps you discover and define the functional requirements for your use case, and in turn for the entire system. Defining functional requirements for your system also helps during acceptance testing. Generating acceptance tests from a use case's basic and alternate courses, and testing them against the complete list of requirements results in improved coverage.

We added both the sunny- and rainy-day scenarios in our narratives, to ensure our design covered all the edge cases. The following is the narrative for the "Post bad driver report" use case.

Case 4.1: Basic Course
System displays recorded video clip.
System fills the location, time, and date from video metadata into noneditable
   fields on the report screen.
Reporter enters vehicle details (license plate number, state, etc.).
Reporter enters incident details (category, severity, etc.).
Reporter clicks capture.
Invoke Capture Frame from Video.
Reporter clicks Post Report button.
System posts report to Bad Driver Reports Queue.
System closes report screen.
System displays success message.
Alternate Courses
Cannot identify license plate number:
Reporter clicks Cancel Report button.
System deletes video clip and report from database.
System closes the report screen.
License plate number is empty when user clicks Post Report:
System displays error message popup asking for license plate number.
User clicks OK button.
System closes popup and goes back to report screen.
Extracted license plate number is incorrect:
User clicks Cancel on popup.
System closes popup.

The next step in the requirements gathering stage was to storyboard the Post
Bad Driver Report web app form, creating screenshots of how the finished product
could look. Figure 4.7 shows the storyboard our student developer drafted for this
use case.

We discovered missing requirements during these storyboarding sessions. For
example, while storyboarding the Post Bad Driver Report form, we determined that
the report needed to have an image that identified the bad driver's license plate. This
led us to create the "Capture frame from video" use case, which is invoked from the
Post Bad Driver Report form. We added this use case to enable the user to play the
uploaded video clip, pause at a frame where the bad driver's license plate is recog-
nizable, and take a screenshot of it using a selection tool.

During these sessions, we also discovered and identified the attributes of the
domain model objects that were required for our respective use cases. We started
adding these to the evolving domain model without worrying about the integration,
since the code generator was used to regenerate the database collections as and
when needed, along with the CRUD functions.

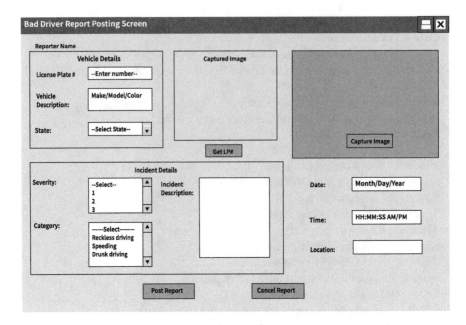

Fig. 4.7 Storyboard for the Post Bad Driver Report form

Figure 4.8 shows the final view of the "Post bad driver report" use case.

4.2.3   Prototypes

We used prototyping heavily in the CarmaCam project to derive requirements, perform a sanity-check on the feasibility of those requirements, refine the user interface, and evaluate different technologies. We developed these prototypes against a live database that was created by the code generator. We spent most of the first sprint prototyping, and the sections that follow cover a few of those prototypes.

4.2.3.1   Upload Large Video Files to MongoDB

For the "Upload video to cloud" use case, we needed to first build a REST API to upload large files and store them in MongoDB. The earlier version of the code generator that was available at this stage could create CRUD functions for regular types of data, but not for large blobs. It was important to have APIs that we could use to store video files along with metadata information and retrieve them across the system. This code would later become a part of the code generator.

The first step in the development of this use case was, of course, creating the narrative, the first draft of which is below.

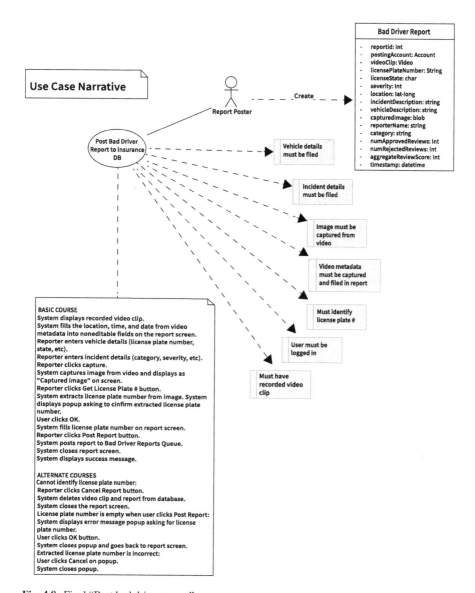

Fig. 4.8 Final "Post bad driver report" use case

It took a couple of brainstorming sessions with the team to arrive at the flow described in the use case. When we first started breaking down use cases, we had not decided on how the uploaded video would be notified or sent to the end user/ uploader. We just knew that users needed to have access to the web app link where they could view the video and post the bad driver report. Since the mobile app was going through prototyping sessions of its own, we could not send a notification to it,

Case 4.2: Basic Course

From the mobile app, on the "Upload video" voice command, you invoke the send request.

In the send request, you prepare the HTTP request with the video file and metadata information as payload, and send it to the server.

You receive the request at the Node.js server, in /api/fileupload. Here you prepare the video file to be written onto the DB.

You write the video file as chunks onto the Video collection of MongoDB, along with the video metadata.

Send a response to the mobile app, which contains a unique ObjectID (or link to the bad driver report for the newly uploaded video).

On receiving the response at the mobile app, you send an email to the user with the link to the bad driver report.

You then display a small toast message on the screen, saying upload was successful.

Alternate Courses

Request cannot be sent to server:

After some timeout, retry sending the HTTP request.

If the send fails again, then display a toast on the screen saying "Server cannot be reached."

Save the video file with a new name, or ensure that it is not overwritten by another video.

Server sends error response:

Save the video file again with a new name, to ensure that it is not overwritten, and user can try uploading from a web UI.

Display the error as a toast on the screen of the mobile app.

User gives another "Upload video" command while current request is in progress:

There should be a mechanism to continue recording and save the current clip with a different name, so that no video clips are lost during back-to-back uploads.

so we instead decided to send an email notification on a successful video upload. This email would contain the link to the Post Bad Driver Report form.

Before we could start coding, we needed to think through a detailed design. This meant gathering all the nitty-gritty implementation details, which is where sequence diagrams came into the picture. We started designing sequence diagrams early for this use case, since we needed a visual aid to show the event/response flow through the objects at runtime, and figure out all the components that would be needed to implement it. Figure 4.9 shows the sequence diagram for "Upload video." The process of designing the sequence diagram was helpful, as once the flow was broken down into a sequence of functions, all we needed to do was implement the code for the individual functions and tie them together through invocation and response handling.

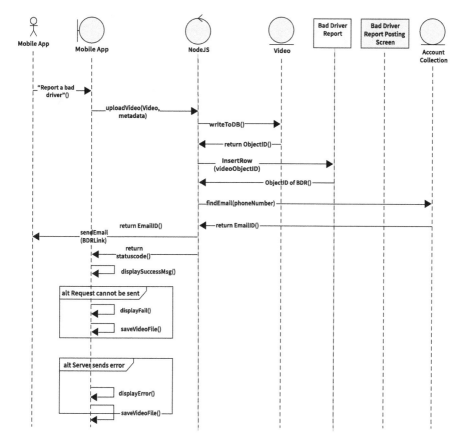

Fig. 4.9 "Upload video" sequence diagram

The next step was coding. We started playing around with Node.js, MongoDB, and GridFS, and learned that we could store the video file in chunks on MongoDB. After a series of prototyping rounds, we had the following:

- A simple Android app that records a video, and sends an HTTP request with the video as payload to the server.
- A Node.js server that stores the video file in chunks, inserts a row in the BadDriverReport collection, and returns a link with that report ID in an email.
- A simple GET API that retrieves the report and video, which can be viewed in a browser.

As we started building out the rest of the system, the server-side prototype logic eventually became a part of the production code. We started improving upon it to handle a large number of video upload requests, along with security features, as you will see in the next two sprints.

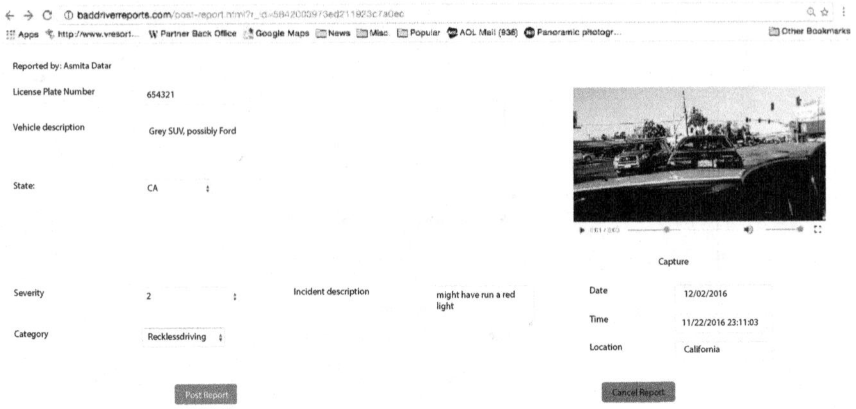

Fig. 4.10 Post Bad Driver Report form prototype

4.2.3.2   Web App

Once we had storyboarded all the web app use cases, we started developing prototypes for the user interface. The user interface went through stages of refinement as
we figured out a good arrangement of label fields and boxes, decided on font param-
eters to optimize readability, and made the web pages responsive for viewing on
different devices. Once the API for downloading video was available, we started
prototyping the web page video player, along with determining the ideal video resolution across different browsers.

Figure 4.10 is a screenshot of the first working prototype of the Post Bad Driver
Report form. Toward the end of the final sprint, you will see how this design evolved.

4.2.3.3   Mobile App Circular Video Buffer

Prototyping the mobile app was important since we did not have many experienced
Android/iOS student developers for the first sprint. In addition, the idea of storing
video clips in a circular buffer to have the app in a continuous recording state
sounded good in theory, but we needed to ensure that we could build it with the
available resources. Most important, the video buffer was the core of our mobile app.

We decided at this point that the uploaded video clips needed to be 15 seconds
long, so we implemented a circular buffer with six video clips/elements, each clip
5 seconds long. When the buffer was at full capacity, it would contain 30 seconds
worth of video. And when the upload command was issued from the app, we would
extract the last three clips and concatenate them together. This prototype went
through a series of iterations and revisions as we started running into bugs and

issues, demonstrating one of the significant benefits of prototyping: issues were caught early on and could be factored into the design for the production version if needed. We also started acceptance testing for this use case early, by taking the app on drives and checking if the uploaded clip was long enough to capture a bad driving incident and ensure the requirements were met.

4.2.3.4 Mobile App Voice Command Activation

As mentioned previously, our initial design for the mobile app included voice activation, a feature that would make the app hands-free for the road. This was a technical risk area in our project, so we wanted to start coding exploratory prototypes.

Three members of the mobile app team were dedicated to researching different speech toolkits that could be used on both Android and iOS devices. The goal was to find a toolkit we could use to build our own speech recognition model for commands like "Record video," "Upload video," "Emergency alert," and so on. We found two candidates: Yandex SpeechKit and PocketSphinx, from the CMU Sphinx toolkit.

First, with the Yandex toolkit, we built a prototype app that listened to the voice commands listed previously. However, after extensive testing we found that the app triggered many false positives. While trying to improve the voice model, Yandex informed us that support of voice models was suspended for all languages except Russian.

In our search for another compatible speech recognition toolkit, we discovered PocketSphinx. PocketSphinx seemed like an ideal replacement for Yandex, since it was an open source, lightweight, continuous-speech recognition system. However, it was still in the early stages of development and was not accurate enough.

We ended up with two prototypes, one for each toolkit, and we started comparing test results to see which was suitable for and compatible with our mobile app. We noticed issues with both prototypes: many false positives, sensitivity to ambient noise, and a degradation of app performance when we tried to integrate into other prototype modules, such as the speedometer.

With the available resources at this point in the sprint, we could not build a reliable prototype that included the voice activation feature. We made a decision, almost toward the end of the semester, to shelve this feature and instead keep things simple by using button-click events. This approach worked out great, since it not only got rid of all the performance issues we noticed with the voice commands, but also was quite easy to use while driving. Granted, the app was not actually hands-free in the end, but when it was mounted on the dashboard, users could operate it as easily as turning a car radio on and off.

By the end of sprint 1, we had our proof of concept. We had built an end-to-end prototype system with the mobile apps, in Android and iOS, that could record and upload videos to the server. The server would send an email containing the link to the Post Bad Driver Report web form to the user. The video could be viewed on the web app form, and the user could provide more details on the bad driving incident and post them back to the server.

4.3 Sprint 2: Minimum Viable Product

We had identified and established a list of functional requirements covering the entire system and allocated them to different use cases by the end of the first sprint. The second sprint involved taking the system through a more careful design pass to build a minimum viable product (MVP) that met all the requirements. The initial challenge with the second sprint was working with a new team of student developers, with the exception of three students who had carried over from the first sprint. This meant nearly 100 percent staff turnover. We were now a team of 13 students, and the use cases had to be reassigned to the new student developers.

We spent the first couple of meeting sessions getting our new teammates up to speed on the progress made in the previous sprint, and helping familiarize them with the prototype code that was built. We also discussed new functional capabilities to make the product more user-friendly, such as accelerometer-based reporting (i.e., auto-upload on slamming of brakes or collision), map-video dual display, and audio feedback notification for the mobile app.

Figure 4.11 shows the task plan we designed for this sprint.

4.3.1 MVC Decomposition

All the use cases we described in the previous sprint had to now undergo a thorough implementation design. We elaborated on the use case models using model-view-controller (MVC) decomposition. We designed robustness diagrams for each use case to illustrate the controllers to be invoked and the data the use case touches. A *robustness diagram* is a pictorial version of a use case, with individual software behaviors (controllers) linked up and represented on the diagram.

Figure 4.12 shows the robustness diagram for the "Post bad driver report" use case. Drawing robustness diagrams was useful during development and integration of the web app, as it helped us visualize how each field or box of the web page would be populated, and which controller would trigger the next use case. For example, the Capture Image button on the Post Bad Driver Report page triggers the "Capture frame from video" use case, which is a different web page where the user can view the video, pause it, capture the frame image, crop the image, and zoom to enhance the license plate. Robustness diagrams also helped us gain a sense of the work we needed to do to implement the use case and further derive the detailed design through the sequence diagrams.

As a next step in the MVC decomposition, we created sequence diagrams. As discussed in the "Upload video" use case, sequence diagrams capture the implementation details, before we begin coding. Figure 4.13 shows the sequence diagram for "Post bad driver report," derived from the robustness diagram in Fig. 4.12. The sequence diagram defines the names of the methods (or controllers) and what those methods need to do. All we needed to do next was code the logic for each of those methods and bring them all together.

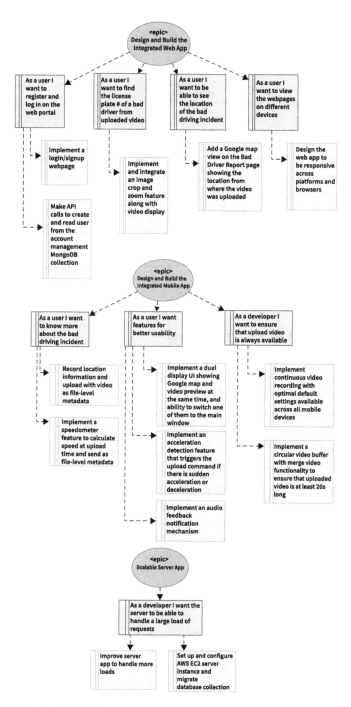

Fig. 4.11 Sprint plan for MVP

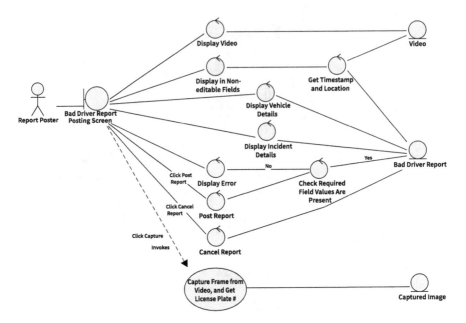

Fig. 4.12 "Post bad driver report" robustness diagram

4.3.2   State Transition Diagram

We had prototyped the individual use cases for the mobile app, and we now had to integrate them to ensure that the end-to-end functionality met our list of requirements. Integration of the mobile app was tricky since there were multiple events to handle, and those events had to be triggered in a specific sequence. At this point, we brainstormed and designed a state transition model for the mobile app.

Figure 4.14 shows the state transition model for the mobile app UI. This diagram helped us build a cleaner integration, as everyone on the team could follow a common model for event handling. It was also useful for the testing team, who had to ensure that the app behaved as expected during the acceptance tests; the diagram was used as the reference point for all of those tests.

4.3.3   Testing

We unit tested the individual components of the system at all stages. As much importance—if not more—was given to acceptance testing since there were a lot of moving parts involved. We needed to ensure that these parts worked effectively and efficiently when integrated together.

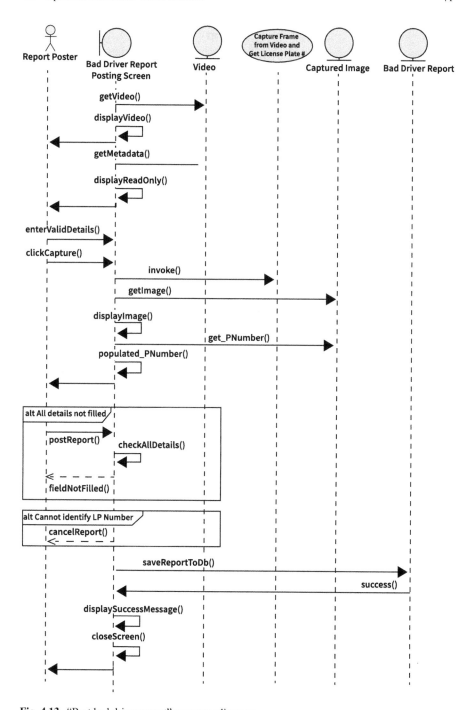

Fig. 4.13 "Post bad driver report" sequence diagram

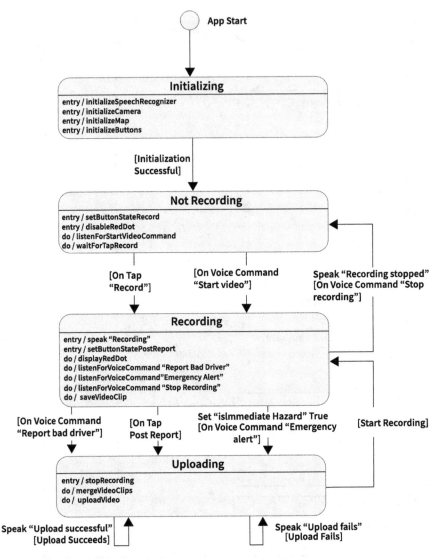

Fig. 4.14 State transition diagram for the mobile app user interface

4.3.3.1   Acceptance Testing

In this sprint, we also started testing the code against all the functional requirements of the system. Our testing team was equipped with the API documentation for the CRUD functions, along with all the source code. We used the ICONIX/DDT add-in for the Enterprise Architect tool to automate our test plan. The goal was to ensure that the system met the requirements that we had established. We wanted to get as

close as possible to 100 percent test coverage, and testing against our list of requirements was one way to achieve it. We used the add-in to generate test cases from the
requirements, and then we wrote scenarios for each of those test cases, including
both the default (sunny day) and the alternate (rainy day) scenarios. Once we
described the scenarios, we specified the input data sets along with expected results.
With a comprehensive test plan in place, writing the actual test code was pretty
straightforward.

4.3.3.2   Mobile App Testing

Many of our testing resources during this sprint were allocated to the mobile app.
This was necessary to ensure that the mobile app integration was moving along as
expected, which meant rerunning tests as more code was added, to ensure we didn't
break anything that was already written. As mentioned previously, we started user
acceptance testing of the mobile app quite early. Doug and a couple of student
developers took the app out for drives to check the ease of use, audio feedback notification and, most important, the quality of the video clip that was uploaded. We
captured a good number of real-world bad driving incidents during these tests, and
each of those reports was a validation that the system worked.

Another aspect of the mobile app testing was device compatibility testing. We
used the Android Studio emulator to test the user interface layout, especially the
dual-display component. However, we needed to do manual testing on different
devices for the uploaded video quality, since certain default camera settings on a
device could affect the video quality. After trial and error on different devices, we
decided to implement digital zoom and set it to 40 percent of the maximum available on a device. Our tests indicated that this zoom value provided a clear view of
the license plate of a vehicle, without creating any out-of-frame issues. We would
later improve this code by providing a setting to allow the user to manually set the
zoom value.

4.3.3.3   User Experience Testing

As with any web app user interface, we tested the compatibility and responsive
behavior of the web app against different browsers and devices. One component that
we tested exhaustively was the behavior of the video player control on different
browsers. In addition to displaying a good quality video, scrolling on the video
player had to be seamless so that the user could stop at any timestamp and invoke
the "Capture frame from video" use case. The captured frame would be used to crop
and select the image of the license plate, which had to be as clear and sharp as
possible.

4.3.3.4 Server Load Testing

The goal in this case was to ensure that the server was capable of handling multiple concurrent requests, along with collecting load test data that would be used to select an optimal Amazon Web Services (AWS) Elastic Compute Cloud (EC2) instance type. We had written a script to make a specified number of concurrent upload video requests to the server. We collected results for an incremental number of requests per second and increased video file sizes for uploads. The results included the server response time and request limits that overloaded the server. These tests helped us discover a couple of rainy-day courses that were not being handled properly. Fixing them involved adding proper error-handling code and returned different response codes for different failures to let the client-side applications throw more relevant error messages to the user. These small fixes made a substantial improvement to the server code.

The load tests also helped us confirm that the performance bottleneck was at the database. There were quite a few out-of-memory database crashes, and sometimes having an optimized server application will not resolve the issue if the available memory is simply not sufficient to handle a specific load. We were constrained by the hardware specs of our development server, and it was time for an upgrade.

4.3.4 Server Migration to AWS

Another goal for this sprint was to have a scalable server application by migrating to AWS EC2. With the result set that we had collected from the server load tests, we determined the CPU and memory requirements for the AWS EC2 instance, along with how much of the memory was to be allocated to the database. We started the migration around halfway into the sprint, when we had an improved, optimized, and more stable server application. The migration was a milestone in our project, as the application was now hosted in the cloud and we were one step closer to establishing a production server.

By the end of sprint 2, we had our MVP.

4.4 Sprint 3: Optimization

The third sprint was the optimization of the product. Again, there was nearly 100 percent staff turnover, with a new batch of student developers taking over the project. The initial challenge for the new team was, of course, to understand code that had gone through two sprints of work. The implementation diagrams we designed earlier were useful in onboarding the new team, to help them get a good sense of the system architecture, and understand what had already been built and what still needed to be developed. For this sprint, we focused on improving the system to

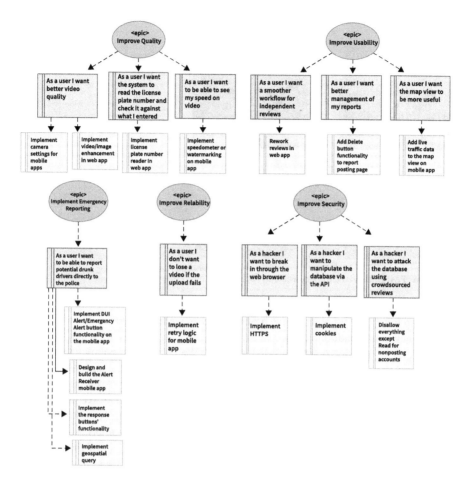

Fig. 4.15 Sprint plan for optimization

make it industry ready, with a lot of user acceptance testing. Most of the resources were allocated for optimization, performance tuning, and adding new features to improve the product's usability. Figure 4.15 shows the sprint plan for this phase.

We made significant improvements across the system during this sprint. Let's take a look at these enhancements through the different components.

4.4.1 Web App

Before the start of this sprint, we renamed the project to "CarmaCam" from "Bad Driver Reporting." Doug coined the name CarmaCam after he told a friend about the sheer satisfaction of uploading a video of someone making an illegal U-turn—like instant karma. The friend suggested spelling *karma* with a *C*, and a product

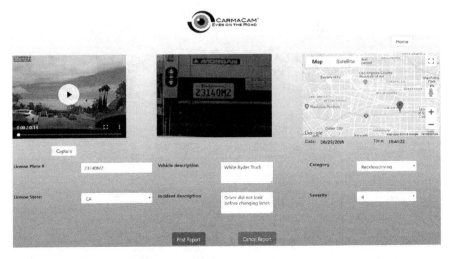

Fig. 4.16 Post Bad Driver Report web app form

name and logo were born. This new branding meant we had to redesign our website, add the new name and logo to the pages, modify the color palette to match the logo design, and adjust the layout for easier viewing. We enhanced a couple of existing features, such as in the "Capture frame from video" use case. We integrated a third-party JavaScript framework to support options for adjusting image brightness, exposure, and contrast, to improve the quality of the license plate image. We also added a few new features to the web app: delete report functionality on the user homepage, the image of the captured license plate as the thumbnail for a report, and a reset password option. The overall goal was to polish the look and feel of the app and improve the user experience. Figure 4.16 shows the new Post Bad Driver Report web page, which evolved from the prototype design shown in Fig. 4.10.

4.4.2 Mobile App

We made major progress during this sprint on the mobile app, with our most significant accomplishment being the design and development of the Emergency Alert Receiver app, which we discuss in the next section. The goals for the mobile app team were to optimize existing features and continue some of the work carried over from the previous sprint. We made several improvements to the quality and performance of the app:

- To improve video quality under low-light conditions, we added three different mode settings on the app: sunny (day) mode, cloudy mode, and night (moon) mode. Each mode has a custom ISO value set, and the user can toggle between them to control the exposure.

- We built functionality to show live traffic data on the Google map view of the dual-display, including a zoom in/out feature. To ease the drive for a user, we wanted to ensure that the map view provided more than just an update of the current location. Enabling traffic data brought us one step closer to making this a hands-free user experience, where the user need not toggle between the CarmaCam app and a navigation app.
- Continuing the work on the speedometer prototype that we built in the previous sprint, we wanted to watermark the real-time speed data onto the video to give a sense of how fast the bad driver was driving in comparison to the user's speed. We used FFmpeg library to watermark sections of the video clip in parallel using multithreading and then upload the watermarked video to the cloud.
- A rainy-day scenario with the "Upload video to cloud" use case that we needed to handle was failed uploads. We implemented retry logic to handle this case, where we save the last five videos that could not be uploaded onto the SD card or into phone memory, and then resume uploading them when the user restarts the app with an internet connection.

We had to integrate all of these enhancements built in parallel into the baseline code of the app. Our mobile app team lead for the sprint took charge of the baseline integration and worked with each member to merge the code and resolve any merge conflicts. This was an iterative process since each update to the baseline code was followed by a round of acceptance testing. As in the previous sprint, the acceptance testing for the mobile app included using the app out on drives to get real-world input and feedback.

4.4.3 Emergency Alert Receiver App

A new feature that we added to the dual-display of the mobile app was the DUI Alert or Emergency Alert button. In addition to creating a bad driver report, this feature sends higher-priority video clips to a new collection in the database, aptly named the Emergency Alert collection. The Emergency Alert collection retains these high-priority alerts for only 30 minutes, and it's accessible via a geospatial (location-based) query. Our goal with this system is to "broadcast" video showing reckless driving behavior or possible drunk driving to patrol cars within a desired radius, making law enforcement aware of these reckless/possibly drunk drivers in near-real time.

We designed and built a dedicated Emergency Alert Receiver prototype app for first responders. The app queries and pulls data from the CarmaCam Emergency Alert collection on a timer (every 5 minutes), displays locations of Alert videos within the desired radius on a map, and allows first responders to view the video in a patrol car by tapping the location icon on the map. It also provides options to "respond," "reject," or "resolve" an alert. First responders can update the tactical status of an incident by rejecting an alert report, indicating that they will respond, or

Fig. 4.17 Emergency Alert Receiver app

signaling that the incident has been resolved. To avoid the abuse of the emergency reporting system, we built in logic to automatically mute accounts that upload multiple rejected reports. Figure 4.17 shows screenshots of the app, where spatially relevant alerts can be viewed in real time from a situation map, along with the video associated with the alert.

The executable domain model code generator again proved to be a useful tool in our project, since we were able to create and integrate the new Emergency Alert collection, along with its CRUD functions, in almost no time. With the back-end code ready, we could then focus on building the geospatial database operation to query the alerts and the front-end app to display them. With one student developer assigned as the dedicated resource to this use case, we were able to handle it smoothly along with the rest of the tasks on our plan.

4.4.4 Server App

Our goal with the server was to make it production ready, which meant lots of security enhancements and more performance tuning for scalability. The first step was to set up a dedicated test environment. The existing server was assigned as the new test environment to ensure all ongoing work progressed without interruptions. We set up a new AWS EC2 instance as the production server, with an upgraded version of Node.js and MongoDB. We installed and configured Nginx to enable HTTPS, and to be used as a load balancer for better scaling in the future. We also redesigned the REST APIs to handle only authenticated requests.

At the beginning of this sprint, we were mostly working on the client side of the system. We changed direction mid-sprint when database and API security issues arose. A task force of developers who had completed their initial tasks early managed the change.

4.5 What's Next?

We have big plans for CarmaCam. In addition to the product's immediate value of getting dangerous drivers off the roads faster and more effectively—avoiding injuries, damages, and even loss of life—we feel there is intrinsic value to building a database of driving under the influence (DUI) videos.

In the near term, once a database of location-tagged, time-stamped DUI videos exists, it's straightforward to develop analytics that show hotspots of drunk/intoxicated driving; Esri mapping software has sophisticated capabilities in this area. Future research will develop this analytic capability so that law enforcement can use the data to better target sobriety checkpoints in both location and time.

In the longer term, machine learning can be used to build an AI system to automatically identify dangerous driving and post videos to the CarmaCam emergency alert database. These AI systems could even be deployed in autonomous vehicles patrolling the roads in areas with high incidences of DUI-related accidents as a preventative measure.

The team is exploring all of the above options, specifically using machine learning to make the system more accurate and efficient. You will read more about this in Chap. 9.

4.6   Summary

In this chapter, we introduced the CarmaCam project and walked through its first three sprints. We discussed the task plan for each sprint and how we went about implementing these plans using PA concepts. We also discussed some of the lessons learned and certain design decision changes that we were able to make along the way.

The key takeaway from this experience was that as each semester rolled around along with a new class of students, somehow the project was able to take nearly 100 percent staff turnover in stride, thanks to Parallel Agile.

Chapter 5
Taking the Scream Out of Scrum

Box 5.1

On the surface, it might seem that scrum and Parallel Agile (PA) are diametrically opposed to one another, and it may be puzzling to find a chapter on scrum in this book. Doug explains that while in theory elastic staffing eliminates a lot of complexity in project management (see Chap. 7), in practice not all organizations are going to be able to staff their projects elastically, so we need to explain how to leverage other PA strategies (e.g., the use of CodeBots) in a small team environment—which brings us back to scrum.

One of my favorite quotes about Agile goes like this: "Agile is great if you do it right, but unfortunately most people do it wrong."[1] With the pervasiveness of Agile (and particularly Agile/scrum) in industry, the "most people do it wrong" issue creates a lot of problems out in the field.

There are many misconceptions about Agile in general and about scrum specifically. The top two (in my book) being the common interpretations of the Agile Manifesto as devaluing planning and of timeboxes as a mechanism used by management to force development teams to work under continuous time pressure so as to squeeze more work out of them.

We called on one of the world's leading Agile/scrum experts, Dr. Chuck Suscheck, to write this chapter. Chuck understands Agile as it's supposed to work, and he is intimately familiar with a wide range of Agile failure modes, since he makes his living by correcting them.

---

[1] Credit for this quote goes to Daniel Litvak, one of Doug's former DirecTV co-workers.

© Springer Nature Switzerland AG 2020
D. Rosenberg et al., *Parallel Agile – faster delivery, fewer defects, lower cost*,
https://doi.org/10.1007/978-3-030-30701-1_5

In this chapter, we'll examine what the Agile mindset is—and isn't—and explore some of the ramifications of misinterpreting the Agile mindset. We'll discuss whether Parallel Agile is "truly" Agile, and contrast it to another approach at scaling agility, the Scaled Agile Framework (SAFe). We'll look at how scrum is intended to work, and cover a number of failure modes that can make your development team scream (see Appendix A for some satirical detail on Scream). Finally, we'll wrap up the chapter by imagining what part of the CarmaCam project would have looked like if a large team had not been available and it had been developed with scrum rather than PA.

5.1 Agile Mindset

Agile is not something you *do*, it's a *mindset* you follow. It's the idea that you're going to learn about your product as you evolve it, so you need a way to incorporate what you learn. In order to understand any Agile process, you need to understand the Agile mindset.

Ralph Stacey created a marvelous model for understanding work effort based on complexity, as shown in Fig. 5.1. He divided how work was done (in this case, technology) and what was being done (requirements) along an axis and categorized work efforts from known to unknown/uncertain.

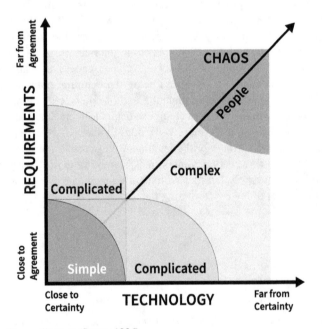

Fig. 5.1 The Stacey diagram (Stacey 1996)

David Snowden and Mary Boone extended the Stacey diagram by describing the different approaches for leadership in each quadrant (Snowden and Boone 2007). In this model, there are four quadrants for the state of a particular work effort: simple, complicated, complex, and chaotic.

The first quadrant, simple, is where most everything is known: the process as well as the product. It's typically the realm of low innovation (a non-novel product being created) and rote execution. Manufacturing and command-and-control approaches to management work well here.

As the process for the work effort or the end product become less certain, you move to the second quadrant: complicated. In this quadrant are a lot of knowns but enough unknowns that it's difficult for nonexperts to determine a direction or next steps in a work effort. This type of work effort requires experts with experience to detect patterns of process and provide advice on how to move forward. This is where industry best practices can be reviewed and melded to work with the current way of doing work. The way of going about a work effort must be managed with more flexibility than the command-and-control approach. A "good enough" practice is used and then flexed when needed.

If there are even more unknowns—in fact, more unknowns than knowns—the work effort is considered complex, for both the process and the product. This is often the world of innovation and creativity. There are so many unknowns that much will be leaned as the work effort progresses. You must have a feedback mechanism to take advantage of what is learned in order to correct or perfect the work. A learning mechanism is critical. In this area, any process for going about work must be flexed, and even the experts don't know the details since there are so many unknowns.

The fourth quadrant, chaotic, is where very little is known. Neither the expected outcome nor the way of going about moving in a particular direction is understood. Snowden and Boone state that this particular environment requires a leadership role that acts in an almost dictatorial manner to drive down certain assumptions so that the organization can move forward based on assumptions.

Agile is built for the complex world, where feedback is a key to creating world-class, innovative products. Here you need a way to inspect and adapt, which is the heart of the Agile process. It's inspecting and adapting not only the product, but also the schedule.

Do you remember the good old days in high school when you took physics, chemistry, or biology science classes? Do you remember the scientific method? You created a hypothesis and then an experiment to prove or disprove the hypothesis. You analyzed the results of the experiment, and from those results you either adjusted or extended the hypothesis and went through the scientific method once more, as shown in Fig. 5.2. This empirical approach uncovers knowledge that may not been discoverable or knowable beforehand. This tried-and-true method is the same approach that Agile is based upon. You're applying the empirical approach to project management or product development with a plan–do–inspect–adapt approach.

You get a hypothesis of what you'll build and how you'll build it. You then execute against the hypothesis (your experiment per se). Finally, you inspect or analyze

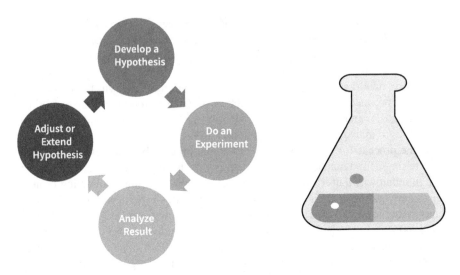

Fig. 5.2 The scientific method: planning out a small work effort is equivalent to the hypothesis

the results of how you worked, as well as what you produced. You then use the results of your analysis to adjust your hypothesis for the next experiment, which consists of what you are going to build, how you should go about building it, and your capacity for the time period.

In this way, Agile is a mindset, not a methodology. It's a way of approaching a problem from the perspective that you don't know everything up front, and you're going to discover things as you progress on the work effort. It's not a bunch of hipster guys sitting around a big table, hacking code with no plan or direction; rather, it's a controlled, formulated approach *if done correctly.*

Box 5.2: Agile as Curling

A good way to explain the Agile approach is through a sports analogy. The traditional predictive process is like archery: you have a target at which to shoot, you pull back the bow, and you let fly the arrow. If you've taken everything into consideration, you have a good shot and hit the target right where you expected—but that is really tough.

The Agile approach is more like curling, where the player slides a stone on ice toward a target. As the stone progresses down the ice, people walk alongside with a broom and steer the throw, sweeping the stone toward the goal or, if the throw was quite bad, sweeping the stone toward a completely different goal.

The important part is that Agile has a goal, but the trajectory of your work effort is steered toward the target as you learn more. The inference is that Agile without a goal is not Agile, it's just hacking. Without a goal, you're not doing Agile—you're just writing code or attempting to create a product.

5.1.1 General Agile Mindset Misconceptions

If you read much of this book, you'll see that there are many misapplications and misunderstandings of Agile. Some glaring examples are as follows:

- Using an Agile approach as a command-and-control effort, telling people when something will be done and how much will be done, and then constraining it into too-short sprints
- Using timeboxes as pressure boxes rather than measures of progress at periodic intervals
- Assuming that since you're using Agile, there is no planning needed, only experimentation
- Using Agile as an excuse to remove all documentation
- Thinking that Agile is a magic bullet to get the same amount of work out as any other process, except faster and cheaper
- Using Agile when you believe that you can specify everything upfront and then locking down the requirements and schedule without any chance to take learnings back into the plan
- Thinking that a two-week sprint results in released software every time. It results in an inspectable increment that is *potentially* releasable

In the next few sections, we're going to address some of these misapplications and show how proper Agile, implemented with scrum and PA, can all work together for more effective product development.

5.1.2 The Sweet Spot of Parallel Agile in the Agile Mindset

Scrum can take advantage of PA, in particular the domain-driven executable architecture part and the prototype–design–optimize approach. PA augments and supports many of the properties of scrum and the Agile mindset.

PA scales via elastic staffing, which is possible with truly well-designed architecture (see Fig. 5.3). PA helps you to follow good engineering practices (minimizing coupling, maximizing cohesion, and making dependencies visible) so that large teams have a good basis for collaboration. Domain-driven APIs are particularly helpful in this regard. The enabler for PA lies in solid design and technology. PA would have barely been possible a few short years ago. Microservice architectures, NoSQL databases, code generation from domain models and interaction diagrams, and modern architectural tools all created a confluence where technical dependencies can be minimized through tightly cohesive software design with well-defined interfaces. The current state of technology makes an elastic staffing approach.

In PA, projects progress in three phases, each roughly a month long, to minimize overall risk. Each phase is feedback-driven towards specific targets:

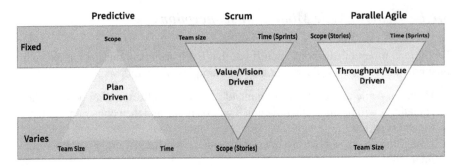

Fig. 5.3 Unlike scrum, the flex in Parallel Agile is not scope, but team size

- Proof of concept: Prototype-driven requirements discovery
- Minimum viable product (MVP): Model-driven design
- Optimization: Acceptance test–driven release strategy

PA sets a project up for parallel development, and involves executable domain models, use case diagramming, and visual modeling of epics, user stories, and tasks.

Executable domain models provide a number of advantages, including feedback-driven database schema development, elimination of manual coding for database access and API development, high reliability of autogenerated database access functions and API code, and early microservice architecture to facilitate integration of independently developed use cases.

Parallel development proceeds with a developer assigned to each use case as build the right system (prototype-driven), build the system right (design-driven), and test what you built (acceptance test–driven).

5.1.3 Scaled Agile Framework and Parallel Agile

Many companies decide to use Scaled Agile Framework (SAFe) for their Agile framework. SAFe is like a sharp samurai sword: in the right hands, it can be a powerful tool, but if you try to pick it up as a novice, you're going to get a bad cut. SAFe deals with program and portfolio management and uses lean concepts along with scrum concepts. The good part is that SAFe has a lot of information about organizing Agile efforts overall, but it can be a bolt-on process with lots of bureaucracy and little real agility. Using SAFe requires a mature Agile mindset that understands the unpredictable nature of software development. SAFe isn't bad—it's just easy to apply the mechanics and not get many benefits.

PA approaches scaling Agile projects using a technical approach, reducing problems with *integrating the work of large teams working in parallel* using executable architectures that are generated from domain models. PA doesn't add more layers of management as a solution to scalability, whereas SAFe frequently implements many layers.

SAFe and scrum are fundamentally different in that SAFe organizes work around the project, while scrum emphasizes organizing around products. SAFe can lead to an excessive emphasis on time, scope, and budget over product value. Scrum focuses on producing high value for a product, a longer-term view of work. PA also focuses on value but scales via larger teams. PA achieves schedule compression without using timeboxes as a sledgehammer by leveraging parallelism in development.

> **Box 5.3: But What About Projects?**
> Glad you asked. In traditional scrum, it's all about product development—evolving the product and releasing new versions of the product when there is enough business value to be useful. A project is a temporary endeavor that affects the functionality in the product (or multiple products). In other words, a *project* has a start and an end, but a *product* may last for years, continually evolving.
>
> In scrum, you can think of a sprint as a mini project that delivers an increment of new product functionality. That functionality may or may not be released, depending on the value that is added to the product. You can also think of a project as a number of changes to multiple products, but those products are evolved using scrum.
>
> Talking about a project in a scrum environment doesn't always make a lot of sense. It's like talking about lighting a match underwater.

5.2   Scrum as It Should Be: A Quick Overview

Scrum (see Fig. 5.4) is an excellent way of implementing the Agile mindset. You can be Agile and not use scrum—there are certainly other techniques that you can use. Conversely, you can use scrum and not be Agile as well—you won't get the benefits

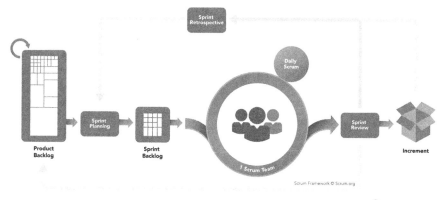

Fig. 5.4 The Scrum Framework (Scrum.org 2016)

of a scrum approach. Scrum provides a structured framework for managing work that uses an empirical approach of inspect and adapt.

Remember the good old days when a process was described in multiple volumes of books and hundreds of pages? Every problem you ever needed to solve was addressed in those books; it's the compilation of all needs, so it's large. Your job as a process engineer was to remove the parts of this process that you didn't really need—a subtractive process. Unfortunately, it's hard to figure out what you don't need, so the end result is a large process with many parts, just in case you need them.

Scrum is the intersection of all needs—an additive process. The root of scrum is the Scrum Guide (ScrumGuides.org 2017), the canonical reference for discovering the essence of scrum. Scrum is a lightweight framework with three roles, three artifacts, and five events all described in the Scrum Guide in a little over 16 pages. Many people tend to add other practices to scrum in order to make the process more effective in their particular organization. For example, user stories are not required in order to use scrum. Neither are story points, burn-down charts, estimating with planning poker, pair programming, and other practices. What you *do* needed as a minimum is listed in the Scrum Guide.

The root of scrum consists of the following elements: a product owner with the authority over the product, a scrum master who can help the team understand the scrum process, and a development team that is self-organizing, cross-functional, and reasonably sized. Additionally, you need a product backlog, a sprint backlog, and a product that you're developing, also known as an *increment*. For the events in scrum, you will need a sprint, sprint planning, a daily scrum, a sprint review, and a retrospective. That is the framework.

Figure 5.5 shows the terminology we'll use for the remainder of the chapter. Note that product backlogs can contain epics and (unplanned) user stories, while the sprint backlog contains (planned) user stories and their tasks.

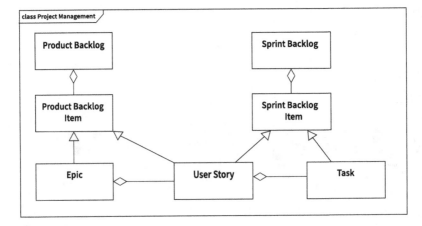

Fig. 5.5 Scrum terminology

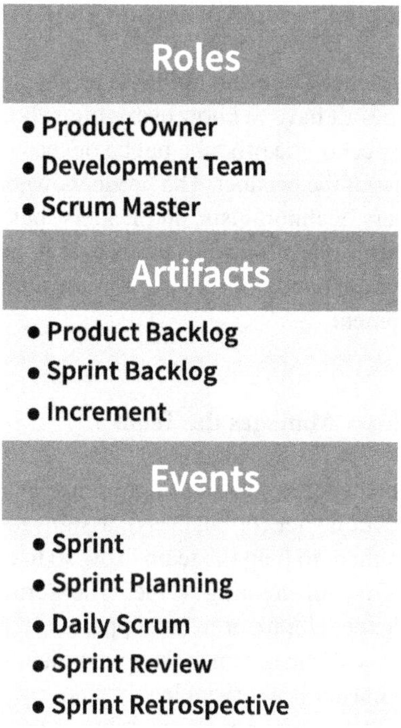

Roles

- Product Owner
- Development Team
- Scrum Master

Artifacts

- Product Backlog
- Sprint Backlog
- Increment

Events

- Sprint
- Sprint Planning
- Daily Scrum
- Sprint Review
- Sprint Retrospective

Fig. 5.6 Scrum roles, artifacts, and events

There is a big difference between practicing scrum and practicing scrum well. Companies can adopt scrum without understanding the philosophy of Agile, leading to mechanical scrum and introducing difficulties that outweigh the benefits.

In the next three sections we'll discuss common misconceptions about roles, artifacts and events that might cause developers to scream or be screamed at by an ignorant leader. Figure 5.6 lists the three roles, three artifacts, and five events described in the Scrum Guide. You'll also get a little therapy from Appendix A (The Scream Guide), a satirical look at how things can go off the rails.

5.2.1   Misconceptions About Scrum Roles

Scrum requires three roles: product owner, scrum master, and development team (member). They must be filled by at different people (i.e., a product owner cannot be a scrum master or a development team member) and are most effective when these people are on the project full time and are consistent. Let's explore the misconceptions of these roles.

5.2.1.1 You Have Multiple Product Owners on Your Product

To practice scrum well, you need one and only one product owner for a given product. The product owner doesn't have to know everything about the product, nor have all authority over every aspect of the product, but he or she is the ultimate tiebreaker, decision-maker, and owner of the product. The product owner needs to be collaborative with other stakeholders, technologists, and leaders, but must have the ultimate authority on the product. This doesn't always happen, as companies sometimes have product owners who either are hands-off or have limited authority, leading to lots of churn on product development.

5.2.1.2 The Scrum Master Manages the Team

A scrum master is not a manager in the traditional sense. A manager often acts as a go-between with the product owner (or business), assigns tasks, or facilitates meetings. The scrum master is there to help the team grow so that they can be even more self-organizing and effective in creating value. The scrum master supports the development team and the development team supports the product owner. It is not the product owner dealing with the scrum master who manages the team and acts as a go-between. The scrum master is a servant leader who tries to work him- or herself out of the position of facilitator or controller and into the role of coach or mentor.

5.2.1.3 You Reform the Development Team Every Sprint

The development team should be a team, not a collection of individuals. Consistent membership and a small team size (three to nine people) help quite a bit with becoming a performing team rather than a collection of people. If people are constantly moved in and out of the development team, teamwork—especially the trust needed for self-organization—is negatively affected. It's not unusual for organizations to make the misstep of pulling people in and out of development teams based on niche skill sets, rather than taking the time to build a truly cross-functional team. The thought is that moving people around is an efficient use of resources, when in fact establishing good team cohesion is more effective when building innovative products.

5.2.2 Misconceptions About Scrum Events

Let's look at some scrum events: sprint planning, sprint review, retrospective, daily scrum, and the sprint itself.

5.2.2.1   Sprint Timeboxes Are Used to Squeeze More Work Out of Developers

Sprints are based on increments of time, not feature completion. The development team picks the amount of work they feel they can commit to during the timebox. The amount they pick is based on their capacity, which may mean part of a feature, not all of it, is developed during that timebox. It's important to make short sprints and break the work into small chunks (often user stories) that the team can choose. If the team gets ahead during the sprint, they will go to the product owner and ask for more, but if they get behind, they have (hopefully) a good reason and the product owner should collaborate on what they can complete. You hire the best and brightest now, don't you?

5.2.2.2   The Length of Sprints Changes All the Time

Sprints are timeboxes—consistent segments of time. Sprints must be a consistent length in order to gain any sort of predictability or repeatability; a fixed-length sprint is key. If sprint lengths vary, it is almost impossible to figure out how much work can be absorbed within a sprint. Once set, the length of a sprint should not be changed unless there is a really good reason, such as a need to coordinate with external groups or a major change in risk. It should be like moving to a new home: you don't want to do it unless there's a good reason since it's painfully disruptive, and once you move, you should stay there for quite a while.

5.2.2.3   Sprints Are Long, So You Can Get More Work Done

How do you figure out how long a sprint should be when starting up a work effort? It should be based on the appetite for risk, not the amount of work. Generally speaking, a riskier piece of work should be inspected more frequently, leading to setting a shorter sprint at the beginning of a work effort. Shorter sprints are easier to estimate and manage. If you're not getting what you committed to done during a sprint, it's not that you need a longer sprint, it's that you need to stop overcommitting.

5.2.2.4   You Do All Estimating and Refinement During Sprint Planning

As the first step in the sprint, the development team and the product owner need to plan what is going to be created during the sprint. Sprint planning shouldn't be about discovering new work, it should be about planning what is going to be worked on during the rest of the sprint. During sprint planning, requirements and details are discovered, but the purpose is to figure out what to do during the remainder of the sprint, not to brainstorm new functionality.

5.2.2.5   During the Daily Standup, You Justify Your Existence

Once the work has been determined for the sprint, a daily rhythm begins. Part of that rhythm is the daily scrum. The purpose of the daily scrum is to coordinate dependencies and create a plan for the next 24 hours. It is not a status or progress check; rather, it is a coordination session for the development team. Since this meeting is held every day, it is timeboxed at 15 minutes by setting a hard stop time. The hard stop forces people to learn how to plan in a short amount of time. Since development teams consist of three to nine people, 15 minutes is achievable.

The daily scrum isn't about "What did you do yesterday, what will you do today, and are there any blockers?" It's about coordinating: "What did you complete *that we can start using*, what will you complete *that we should be using (testing, integrating)*, and are there any things that may hinder you *that we can help with?*"

5.2.2.6   The Sprint Ends with a Demo (aka Dog and Pony Show)

As the last part of a sprint, scrum teams inspect the product they are creating and the process they used to create it. These are the sprint review and retrospective, respectively. The sprint review is an opportunity for the scrum team (product owner, scrum master, and development team) to inspect the increment of product and reflect on how to improve it by adding to, refining, or reordering the product backlog. It's also a chance for the product owner, with the counsel of key stakeholders and the development team, to decide if the increment should be deployed. Many companies misinterpret the sprint review as a demo or some sort of a rehearsed show. While it may be reasonable to execute the product during this period, the intent is not to promote the product to stakeholders; it is a chance to look holistically at the increment and make sure the work effort is heading in the right direction.

5.2.2.7   Retrospective Time: Let's Complain About What Went Wrong

As the sprint review is a chance to inspect the increment, the retrospective is an opportunity for the team to reflect on their way of doing work and look for efficiency improvements. The retrospective is not something that can be skipped; it is process improvement focus time. The retrospective covers not only technical improvements, but also people and relationships, relationships with groups outside of the team, and organizational impediments to becoming more agile.

From the traditional development approach, the retrospective is much like a lessons learned session or project postmortem with a couple of key differences: the retrospective is done in small increments (every sprint), and immediately following the retrospective the next sprint begins. This leads to a powerful opportunity to try experiments in process improvement and adjust the team's effectiveness incrementally.

5.2.3 Misconceptions About Scrum Artifacts

The three artifacts of scrum are product backlog, sprint backlog, and increment. Let's discuss each of these in turn.

5.2.3.1 User Stories Are the Only Thing You Can Put in a Product Backlog, or User Stories Are Required to Be Agile

The product backlog contains all of the desired changes to the product and it is sequenced in the order of execution. These changes are called product backlog items (PBIs) since they can be written in any format, although they are often expressed as user stories. You can express your requirements as use cases, Gherkin scenarios, or free-form text. You can add defect corrections to a backlog, too. Many Agile shops find value in user stories since they focus on business need.

5.2.3.2 The Product Backlog Is Ordered by Priority . . . and We Have 50 Priority 1 PBIs

One important nuance with the product backlog is that it is sequenced (ordered) in the order of execution, not necessarily by priority. A high-priority PBI may not be at the top since there are dependencies before it can be developed. For example, the top priority of your work may be to charge the customer's credit card, but that may not be possible until some low priority work, such as connecting to the bank and setting up a customer profile, have been completed. In such a case, priority 1 may be sequenced lower in the product backlog.

Each piece of work within the product backlog has varying degrees of detail. Items at the top that would be selected soon need to be broken down to a point where multiple items can be selected for an upcoming sprint. Items further down the list are left less detailed so that these items are not prematurely detailed, thereby increasing the flexibility with the product backlog.

5.2.3.3 Detail Your Product Backlog Completely (or as Much as Possible)

Oftentimes organizations try to flesh out a great deal of the product backlog well before sprint planning, which can lead to rework as more information is discovered. Only roughly two sprints worth of PBIs should be "planning ready." If you put too much detail in a user story up front and you're going to learn something, you may have to rework based on what you learn. So you should leave enough looseness as to reduce rework. Think of refining the product backlog as a rolling wave: each PBI is enriched through four or five refinement sessions before being planned.

Note 5.1
User stories are requirements written from a user/business perspective.

The big difference between a user story and other types of requirements is that it is a business need, not a system functionality. The functionality that fulfills the need is the development team's job—that's design. Expressing what a user needs is the product owner's job. In requirements-speak, the system requirements that your developers will build to are derived from the user stories (business requirements).

Epics are a categorization that is described inconsistently in the Agile community. Sometimes epics are containers of user stories; other times, epics are containers of features, which contain user stories; and still other times, epics are a type of story that needs to be broken down. For this book, we'll consider an epic a container of user stories, and an epic can contain other epics, which in turn contain user stories.

5.2.3.4 Preplan Sprints Before the Sprint Planning Meeting

The sprint backlog is simply the subset of the product backlog selected by the development team during sprint planning. The sprint backlog and associated items in the sprint backlog are owned by the development team. The sprint backlog is created during sprint planning and ceases to exist after the sprint review. This is an important nuance: sprint backlog items that are not completed are moved to the product backlog as part of the sprint review and are resequenced by the product owner as he or she sees fit. Incomplete items are not necessarily carried over to the next sprint since the sprint review may come up with more important PBIs or a better direction for the product based on what is learned during the sprint review.

5.2.3.5 Every Sprint Release Is an Increment to Production

The ultimate output of a sprint is the product increment: a *potentially* releasable product. Contrary to one of the most common misunderstandings about scrum, actual deployment of the product may not occur at this point. The product is potentially releasable in that everything that the development group can do to bring the product into a releasable state has been done—for example, user documentation, testing at various levels, deployment documents and readiness, code refactoring for quality, and more. It may, though, not be possible to release (deploy) at the end of every sprint. Consider software for embedded medical devices, nuclear missile guidance systems, or driver assist software in a car. You wouldn't want new versions of these items deployed every few weeks, but the increment can be as close to releasable as possible by testing through simulations, evolving the field test script, or even preparing part of the compliance documents.

Note 5.2

People understand the term minimal viable product (MVP) in a variety of ways, most commonly as a product that is ready to be deployed and used by the customer. We would like to add more to this definition: generally, an MVP is something that provides enough value for the customer to warrant a deployment. With this distinction, a sprint may create something that is potentially deployable, but requires more functionality in subsequent sprints to warrant a release. "Potentially" means that the increment of product created in the sprint must be tested, integrated, documented, and prepared for deployment to the highest degree plausible by the end of the sprint, and it needs another round of more work before it is deployed as the MVP.

5.3   Example: Parallel Agile with Backlogs and a Small Team

PA flexes people. If you need speed, PA allows you to add more people by making each piece of functionality highly cohesive and radically decoupled (each use case is developed independently and each domain object has its own API). What if you have a scrum shop where flexing people isn't an option? PA still offers plenty of benefits.

At first blush, PA may be seen as a misapplication of Agile: a "wagile" approach where waterfall-wrapped Agile process with big requirements and design up front (BDUF) are followed by development using multiple sprints, and finally a large test effort. We agree that such a process doesn't get much of the Agile benefit and in fact may not be Agile at all.

In PA, requirements and design become feeders to the technology, not as a hand-off to the development team, but it infuses the requirement as a technology through executable design. Requirements are elaborated as use cases, and the design is initially created as an executable domain model.

Let's walk through a typical example with the CarmaCam project from Chap. 4 and a typical scrum shop:

- We'll assume they've been using scrum for some time and there isn't a lot of bad scrum behavior.
- They hold a fixed-length sprint of 2 weeks—small enough to adjust and big enough to produce something significant.
- They have a cross-functional, self-organized development team of eight members.
- They have one product owner and one scrum master.

Keep in mind, this example is based on how typical Agile work efforts evolve, not as a set of command-and-control steps. The purpose of this example is to show that PA can be used to good benefit with scrum.

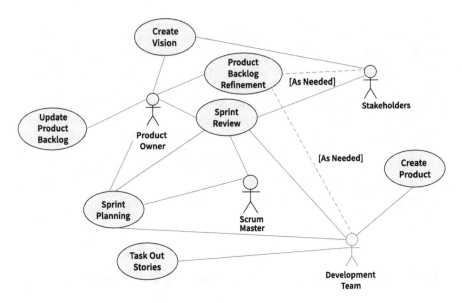

Fig. 5.7 Scrum-based activities and role involvement

5.3.1   From Product Vision to Product Delivery

Figure 5.7 shows how stakeholders are involved in review, initial product backlog creation, product backlog refinement, and visioning. The product owner is refining the product backlog during the sprint, while the development team creates the product. The diagram also points out that the development team, product owner, and stakeholders review the product at the sprint review for the purpose of adjusting and updating the product backlog—all standard operating procedures for a well-oiled scrum team.

5.3.2   Preparing the Product Backlog

First, the product owner has to have an idea of what the product is. In this case, CarmaCam is a cloud-connected dashboard camera app that keeps a continuous video recording and uploads segments of the video when requested. The video product is purposed toward traffic incidents. The big challenge is to have a video recording continuously running, and when an upload is requested, the last 20 seconds of recording is uploaded. Continuous recording is a complex requirement to build in a short sprint, so balancing that with keeping only what's important will be a challenge.

The product owner comes up with a vision statement for the product in conjunction with sponsors and other stakeholders.

Vision:
- Record and build a crowd sourced database of bad driving incidents so that bad drivers are motivated to change their behavior.

The product owner will have to work alone and with stakeholders to come up with a rough idea of what should go into the product backlog. The product owner, in conjunction with the stakeholders, decides that the main areas of focus, expressed as epics, will be as follows.

Epics:
- Continuously record video and, when signaled by the driver, upload the last few seconds of video to the cloud
- Create a Bad Driver Report (BDR) from a segment of recorded video
- Allow special reviewers to check BDRs
- Allow insurance companies to access BDRs
- Enhance reviewer and insurance company access
- Enhance the app's mobile experience

The PBIs are sequenced in a way that seems reasonable for the product owner and the stakeholders. The top few epics are fleshed out with more detailed requirements expressed as rough user stories. Notice that epics and user stories are in the same list. The main epic on video capture has been replaced by a more detailed set of stories:

- As a driver records videos
- As a driver uploads videos
- As a driver creates a BDR
- As a driver saves a BDR to the repository
- As a driver edits a BDR
- Allow reviewers to check BDR
- Allow insurance companies access to BDRs
- Enhance reviewer and insurance company access
- Enhance the app's mobile experience

You can use a task board to visualize the product backlog, as shown in Fig. 5.8.

From here it's time to start to flesh out the top epics so you can more easily manage the manage the work (see Fig. 5.9).

The product owner brings this work to one of the software architects and with a bit of collaboration comes up with an initial architectural diagram and a quick domain model. (See Chap. 4 for the domain model.)

Product Backlog	Ready for Planning	Sprint Backlog	In Process	Complete
Record Videos				
Upload Videos				
Create Report				
Save Report				
Edit Report				
Review Report				
Insurance Company				
Enhance Mobile				

Fig. 5.8 Task board prior to sprint planning

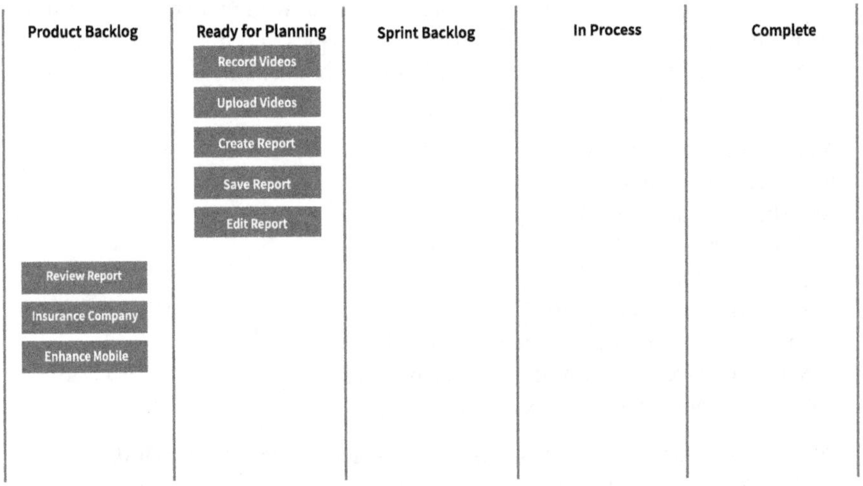

Product Backlog	Ready for Planning	Sprint Backlog	In Process	Complete
	Record Videos			
	Upload Videos			
	Create Report			
	Save Report			
	Edit Report			
Review Report				
Insurance Company				
Enhance Mobile				

Fig. 5.9 The stakeholders, technical specialists, and product owner refine the product backlog

5.3.3   Sprint Planning

Now it's time to plan out a sprint. The product owner and development team get together to run a sprint planning session to figure out what they're going to do during the sprint and how to go about it. Since this is a first sprint, the product owner identifies a number of risks:

- Are we building the right thing?
- Can we build it in a reasonable amount of time?

- What features and functionality are being used by the customer?
- How can we maximize acceptance of the product by the market?
- Do we know how to build the product with the right technology?

During sprint planning, the development team advises the product owner that a few items should be sequenced in the product backlog and attacked early, to mitigate technological risks.

This being the first sprint, the development team picks what they feel they can complete during the sprint. The team decides to make sure they don't select too much work, as the details of what the product should do are not clear.

The sprint backlog consists of the following subset of the product backlog. The development team selects the following:

- As a driver records videos
- As a driver uploads videos
- As a driver creates a BDR
- As a driver saves a BDR to the repository
- As a driver edits a BDR

They begin to detail out some of these stories, sequencing them with the product owner in a way that meets both technical and business needs.

Notice that the Android functionality is attacked first to reduce technological risk. iOS functionality is still in the product backlog but Android is sequenced first. If the team gets ahead during the sprint, they will probably choose the iOS work. Also notice that some of the product backlog items are reordered and changed as they are added to the sprint backlog. This is a natural progression of sprint planning. Figure 5.10 shows the state of the sprint backlog at this point.

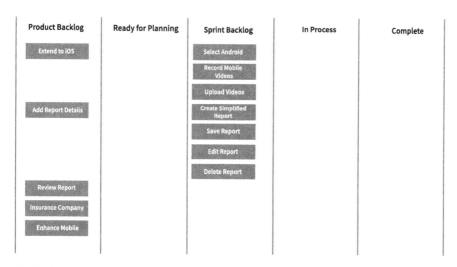

Fig. 5.10 Items are planned for the sprint and refined

Sprint backlog items (SBIs):
- Pick a technology that will support video on Android
- Use a mobile device to capture the videos
- Upload a video
- Create a highly simplified BDR
- Save a BDR to the repository
- Delete a BDR
- Edit a BDR

Note 5.3

At first blush, the sprint backlog and product backlog might be hard to differentiate. The product backlog has all the work that seems like it should be done to the product. The sprint backlog is a subset of PBIs selected from the product backlog during sprint planning that the development team expects to complete during the sprint. Items in the sprint backlog (SBIs) are often detailed out to one degree or another during sprint planning, but that's not a hard-and-fast rule. It's important that the sprint backlog is created by the development team by pulling work from the product backlog, not work that is pushed by management.

Also note that the sprint backlog is owned by the development team, and the product backlog is owned by the product owner. Once the development team picks an item from the product (PBI) and puts it in the sprint backlog (SBI), the development team owns how to go about creating the product.

Sprint planning consists of selecting the work to go into a sprint backlog, creating a sprint goal, and determining a plan for how to modify the increment to meet the intent of the SBIs (the forecast).

In the example case, it looks like the sprint should be able to support continuous video capture and create a simple BDR report. That becomes the sprint goal.

The team also crafts some nonfunctional requirements and adds them to the definition of done. The ramification is that no SBI is complete until it is in compliance with the definition of done. For example, the following original product backlog item:

- Upload must be real-time and fast

becomes an item in the definition of done similar to this:

- Video upload must be continuous with a latency time of 5 seconds

During the remainder of the sprint planning, the SBIs are broken down further by the development team into a plan on fulfilling each of the SBIs. They decide to use tasks (see Fig. 5.11).

Fig. 5.11 Part 2 of the sprint planning: adding tasks and detailed technical approach to the SBIs

Before the end of the sprint planning session, the development team decides to elaborate the domain model a bit more and then generate the code from the domain model.

- Pick a technology that will support video on Android
- Investigate available technologies
- Use a mobile device to capture the videos
- Investigate circular buffer technology
- Pick a strategy for buffering
- Implement a strategy for circular buffer
- Wireframe the app GUI
- Implement an initial app GUI
- Mark a segment of video as "saved" when the driver specifies
- Create a highly simplified BDR
- Create a repository for BDRs
- Save a BDR to the repository
- Delete a BDR
- Determine a way to select a BDR
- Delete a BDR from the repository when selected
- Edit a BDR
- Determine which fields are editable
- Allow editing without constraints
- Add constraints on fields

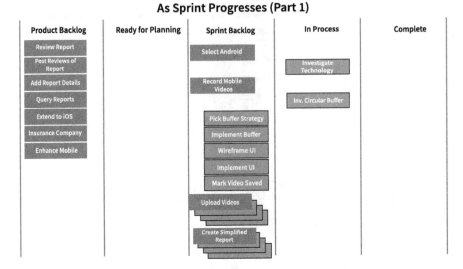

Fig. 5.12 Snapshot of progress a couple of days into the sprint

5.3.4 Sprint

During the sprint, each sprint backlog item (SBI) is elaborated with a combination of domain model updates, use case diagram and text updates, sequence diagrams, and robustness diagrams as needed. Exploration is part of every SBI and is accomplished using tools that make coding visual.

Using the PA approach, the CodeBot takes care of a surprising amount of the work providing database access and an API. It's almost like the development team has a hyperproductive member who gives everyone a running start at the code. Figure 5.12 shows a snapshot of work progressing during the early part of the sprint.

During the sprint, the product owner is helping to describe the intent of the stories and giving the team input on the product details as new learning emerges.

The product owner also has an important job during the sprint: to refine the product backlog. The product owner continues to work with stakeholders, technical staff, and others as needed. The product owner may also need to work with technologists to detail the architecture and domain model. Using the PA approach, the product owner has a mindset of creating a prototype that will primarily mitigate risks and secondarily be deliverable for inspection by a select set of users (or their representatives). Organizing and detailing the product backlog like this directly relates to creating a PA proof of concept.

The sprint progresses as shown in Fig. 5.13.

During our example sprint, the development team begins to get ahead of schedule and may finish the sprint backlog early. The CodeBot is increasing productivity more than expected because it's so easy for the mobile app and web app to access the database. We know that sprints are timeboxes; they can't be shortened or length-

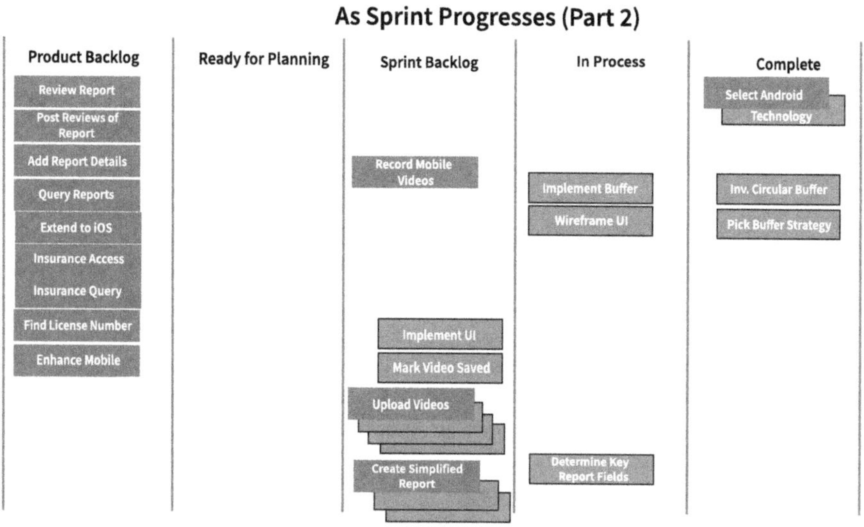

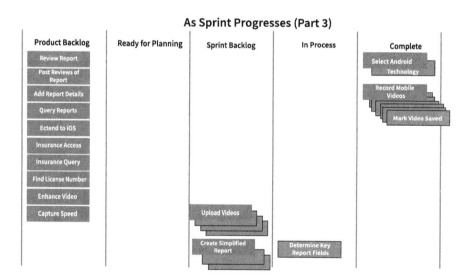

Fig. 5.13 Snapshot of progress about halfway into the sprint

Fig. 5.14 Snapshot of progress near the end of the sprint

ened. If the development team gets behind, they will work with the product owner to simplify or remove work. If the development team gets ahead, they should collaborate with the product owner to select items from the product backlog—preferably ones that will augment the sprint goal (see Fig. 5.14).

After discussions with the product owner, it seems that moving on to setting up functionality for BDR reviewers is going in a different direction than the sprint goal. They decide to add iOS support to the product. Fortunately, the team learned how to upload videos to the cloud using the CodeBot-generated REST API, and building the iOS app goes quickly.

5.3.5 Sprint Review

On the last day of the sprint, it's time for the sprint review and retrospective. For the purposes of this example, we're going to skip the retrospective since it is not affected by PA. During the review, on the other hand, PA inspects not only the increment, but also the various diagrams for the purpose of determining the right direction for product development. It is quite possible that during the sprint review, new discoveries are made that affect not only the product backlog, but also the domain model and use case models. SBIs that are not started or only partially completed are added back to the product backlog to be sequenced against the remaining PBIs. While it's likely that those items will be selected for the upcoming sprint, it's possible they no longer hold as much value as other work in the product backlog and therefore should be reconsidered in the next sprint planning (see Fig. 5.15).

During sprint review the product owner updates the product backlog to incorporate feedback from working with the early builds of the mobile apps and web app. Working with running software early alerts the team to problems with video quality in poor lighting situations, making it difficult to obtain license plate numbers. This feedback provides direction for upcoming sprints. Notice that some of the epics are replaced with more detailed stories.

Product backlog PBIs (version 3) as augmented by the sprint review:
- As a driver, need more data in a BDR
- As a driver, increase video quality

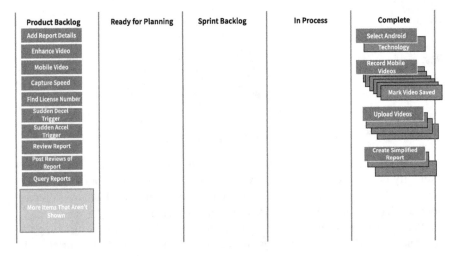

Fig. 5.15 Snapshot just before sprint review

- As a driver, use mobile device video to its best ability
- As a driver, capture speed
- As a driver, find the license plate number of the offender
- As a driver, automatically capture videos during sudden deceleration
- As a driver, automatically capture videos during sudden acceleration
- As a reviewer, view BDRs
- As a reviewer, post reviews of a BDR
- As a reviewer, query the BDR repository
- Allow insurance companies access to BDRs
- As a driver, see a map and video simultaneously
- As a driver, use additional mobile devices
- As a reviewer, the system must respond quickly (near real time)

From this point, the development team has a better idea of what the CodeBot can do for them. The scrum team holds a retrospective and identifies process improvement action items. The primary item identified is to update the domain model with additional attributes after working with the initial build, then use the CodeBot to re-generate the database and API. The next item after the retrospective is sprint planning for the subsequent sprint.

5.4   Summary

At this point, you can see that using PA enhances the capability of the development team to quickly create a product that can be inspected during the sprint. The documentation created in PA helps the team communicate from technical and business perspectives. Because the database and API are generated from a visual model, everyone has a shared understanding and database access is readily available to a wide range of clients.

Using PA with scrum has many advantages:

- PA tightens collaboration with the product owner and technologists through visual models that are not just models, but are used to produce code.
- Sprints in PA move from developing a workable prototype, to augmenting the prototype, to focusing on perfecting the prototype. This helps to keep the scrum effort from being an all-too-common hackathon.
- Requirements in the form of use cases can be divided among team members in such a way that interdependencies are reduced.
- The combination of technology tooling reduces technical dependencies within the code. Looser coupling and higher cohesion in code offers a serious design.
- The CodeBot works as an additional, hyperproductive team member, creating code from documentation so quickly that the team will almost certainly underestimate capacity in the first few sprints.

PA must be adjusted when using a classic scrum approach in a few minor ways:

- The three phases of PA will probably not each be completed in 1 month. With smaller teams it might take longer, which suggests that a series of shorter sprints can help with schedule risk.
- PA emphasizes having many developers working in parallel. Classic scrum keeps a team size and competition stable, necessitating flex by the number of sprints rather than people.
- PA looks to reduce dependencies of requirements so that an individual team member can complete a requirement in near isolation. Scrum emphasizes whole-team ownership of requirements. Team members typically swarm on requirements rather than divide them among members.

Scrum is a management framework that's tailored for small development teams. You can scale by having multiple small teams - in this case you'd probably assign an Epic to each team, with the various Epics glued together by the domain driven API. In Chap. 7, we'll discuss how to manage a software project when you have a large team available and you want to work in parallel without using short sprints and backlogs.

References

Scrum.org. 2016. Scrum framework. https://s3.amazonaws.com/scrumorg-website-prod/drupal/2016-06/ScrumFramework_17x11.pdf. Accessed 18 July 2019.

ScrumGuides.org. 2017. The Scrum Guide. https://www.scrumguides.org/scrum-guide.html. Accessed 18 July 2019.

Snowden, D., and M. Boone. 2007. A leader's framework for decision making. *Harvard Business Review* 85 (68–76): 149.

Stacey, R. 1996. *Complexity and creativity in organizations*. San Francisco: Berrett-Koehler.

Chapter 6
Test Early, Test Often

Box 6.1
Doug introduces the continuous acceptance testing strategy and explains why he insisted that Matt write this chapter.

I started writing books with Matt more than a decade ago when somebody sent me an article he had written called "The Case Against eXtreme Programming" and I realized that we had a common affinity for poking satirical fun at things that seemed to us to be bad ideas. Software engineering (and in particular, the Agile approaches to software development) is full of false gods, and over the years, Matt's abilities as a slayer of false gods have proven to be unparalleled.

One of the most insidious false gods in Agile software development is the notion that it's possible to unit test your way to a high-quality release. This is a false god because unit testing catches only coding errors that have been committed (errors of commission) and is completely useless at catching stuff that you never thought about when you were writing the code (errors of omission). The unfortunate reality of software projects is that it's the stuff you forgot about that tends to be the big troublemakers on your projects, commonly rainy-day scenarios that you didn't consider when coding the sunny-day scenario, as well as forgotten requirements (or, in Agile terms, missing user stories).

Matt wrote an article called "Green Bar of Shangri-La" (Stephens 2007) shown in the screenshot, which posited the (then daring) notion that running some unit tests and seeing a green bar appear might not necessarily mean that the code is free of bugs. (In fact, it's highly unlikely that the code will ever be free of bugs.) Bars that are 100% green and hit-and-miss acceptance testing lead to a false sense of security. This false sense of security causes problems in the world of continuous integration/continuous delivery (CI/CD), where software gets automatically deployed into production based on the unit tests lighting up green. In turn, all of this leads to a phenomenon that we call *hotfix-driven development*, where the development process is optimized around rapid response to bugs that are being reported by screaming customers.

© Springer Nature Switzerland AG 2020
D. Rosenberg et al., *Parallel Agile – faster delivery, fewer defects, lower cost*,
https://doi.org/10.1007/978-3-030-30701-1_6

By an interesting coincidence, the news headlines to the right of the article above have a common theme: buggy releases, all symptomatic of hotfix-driven development, where code is written to a strict timebox and released into production before it's ready.

To be clear, we're not suggesting that unit testing and automated regression testing are bad things; rather that an *overreliance on unit testing* is a dangerous thing. In Parallel Agile (PA), we focus a lot on acceptance testing and making our best effort to think about all of the rainy-day scenarios and corner-case requirements. In doing so, we draw on some of the work we did when we wrote *Design Driven Testing* (Rosenberg and Stephens 2010) together, including automation of acceptance test scripts from scenario descriptions.

On PA projects, we like to put a test team in place early, working side by side with the developers, but rather than directing these folks to start banging out JUnit tests, we have them start asking annoying questions about corner cases, edge cases, and potentially missing requirements. Then we start acceptance testing early (even while prototyping) and formalizing the acceptance tests during the MVP phase.

Testing is a fundamental part of any software project, and the quality assurance (QA) testing team is as vital as ever, particularly with the emphasis nowadays on hotfix-driven development. Gone are the days when the developers could simply write a bunch of code, throw it over the fence to the testers, and call the job done. Today, the developers are equally responsible for software quality (more about "quality" in a moment)—in other words, for testing their own work before they hand it over.

Software testing isn't something that developers do only once their code is complete; it's become an integral part of the development process. Similarly, on a well-run project the testers work closely with the developers[1] while writing automated acceptance test scripts. There's no fence (real or virtual) to throw anything over, or to stifle communication.

As we'll show in this chapter, having a clear, well-defined testing process is especially important on the kinds of rapidly developed, large-team projects that Parallel Agile (PA) is often used on. In the first part of the chapter, we'll cover some of the main reasons we recommend our particular approach to testing. After that, we'll illustrate how to incorporate automated software testing into a PA project. To do this, we draw heavily from Matt's own software testing process, domain-oriented testing (DOT), which just happens to be a perfect fit for PA.

6.1 A Note About Software Quality

Developers like to emphasize software quality (and that's a very good thing). But what does it mean to say that software has quality?

Quality in this sense really means fit for purpose—that is, the software meets the requirements. We could go further, and say "*provably* fit for purpose"—that is, the software provably meets the requirements. But provable how? With tests, naturally, or more to the point, with repeatable tests that are based on individual requirements.

A test can be in the form of a script that a human tester walks through ("Enter this amount, click this button, then check that a particular thing happens or doesn't happen"). But repeatable, formulaic tasks are what computers are meant to be good at, so we always try to automate tests wherever possible. Then rerunning the tests is simply a matter of clicking a button.

> **Note 6.1**
> As you've probably gathered by now, PA is very much about helping teams to work quickly in parallel by automating certain key parts of the process.

Say you have a use case that describes an ATM dispensing cash. You'll have a test (or group of tests) that assert that the money is dispensed and the user's account has been debited the correct amount. That's the sunny-day scenario. You'll also have tests covering all of the rainy-day scenarios—for example, the user's account has insufficient funds, the user's card is detected as lost or stolen, and so on.

---

[1] In Chap. 8, Barry identifies concurrent testing with development as a critical success factor for scalability.

"Base the tests on the requirements" might seem obvious, but there's a noticeable emphasis these days on driving tests from the code instead of from the requirements. The result is often a swath of unfocused tests that (when looked at objectively) just don't achieve much. It's the equivalent of pedaling a bicycle furiously in first gear.

When tests are driven from the requirements in a structured, formulaic way, you can use the result to prove that the software is fit for purpose. We cover some highly effective ways of doing that, in the context of a PA project, in this chapter.

6.2   Errors of Commission vs. Errors of Omission

It's always a good time for an overgeneralization, so here goes. There are two kinds of bugs that can get into code: bugs where somebody coded something wrong, and bugs where somebody forgot about a requirement (or a corner case, or a rainy-day scenario). We can call the first class of bugs *errors of commission* because they are the result of somebody having committed a coding error, while the second class of bugs are *errors of omission*.

Unit testing is helpful for the first kind of bug: you're coding this method, and the result should be as follows. Unit testing is completely valueless for errors of omission, where nobody thought of the case, it never got coded, and so of course it never got unit-tested.

Unfortunately for the legions of test driven developers who are busily making the JUnit bars turn red and then turn green, it's the errors of omission that are usually the biggest troublemakers on a software project. The much worshipped green bar is pretty much a false god.

We would go as far as to say that "free of bugs" is simply an unreasonable and virtually unprovable thing to declare; however, "meets the requirements without bugs" is completely achievable *and* provable. The way to do this is, quite simply, to make sure that each behavioral requirement (aka use case scenario) is covered by a series of tests. In this sense, requirements coverage is a far more important metric than code coverage, which unfortunately pervades the industry at this time.[2]

Hotfix-driven development can be prevented by (1) not developing to a strict timebox, and (2) driving your tests consistently and systematically from the requirements. You would be wise to follow the saying, "Test behavior, not your implementation."

In the sidebar, Doug channels the ghost of Edgser Dijkstra to talk about hotfix-driven development. See Appendix A for more insight and a real-world example of a hotfix-driven process, where timeboxes are absolute and overtime is always the answer. It's a real scream.

---

[2] Also check out Matt's article on the subject: http://bit.ly/never-bug-free.

Box 6.2: Hotfix-Driven Development Considered Self-Perpetuating
For a number of years, we have been familiar with the observation that the top priority of many software development organizations is to publish new software to their users on a daily basis, whether or not such software has been developed to a level of completion that might be suitable for the user community to experience.

More recently we discovered that many organizations have optimized their development processes to prioritize responding to "hotfixes" rather than doing sufficient planning to reduce the amount of dysfunctional software that is published, and we became convinced that this effect (as encouraged by the Agile Manifesto's explicit devaluing of planning as opposed to feedback) is sufficiently disastrous as to necessitate a more balanced approach to feedback-driven development.

At the time that Barry Boehm and Richard Turner wrote *Balancing Agility and Discipline* (Boehm and Turner 2003), and Doug Rosenberg, Matt Stephens, and Mark Collins-Cope wrote *Agile Development with ICONIX Process* (Rosenberg et al. 2005), we did not attach too much importance to the common viewpoint established in these independent works. However, during many discussions over the intervening years, as we have been experimenting with massively parallel software engineering and as we have watched (with some trepidation) the industry adopt feedback-driven processes in safety-critical systems, we now submit our considerations for publication.

Our first remark is that optimizing a development process to support rapid response to hotfixes inevitably requires "shortcuts" to be adopted, as the release process is tuned for quick response to high-priority interrupts. Prioritizing hotfix interrupts necessarily moves other tasks lower on the priority list, and these other tasks generally include independent quality assurance, testing against requirements, and sunny/rainy-day path coverage testing, in addition to all forms of pre-code analysis and design.

Our second remark is that the overall "temperature" of a software development practice in the field is increased with each hotfix interrupt that is received, and that the generation of new hotfixes is proportional to the temperature of the development process. Each hotfix that must be processed necessarily causes an interruption of other work that is in process. This continuous stream of interruptions places further constraints upon the work being undertaken during the current timeboxed sprint, and timeboxing already places development work under continuous time pressure. An absolute truth about software development is that the quality of software being developed is a decreasing function of the amount of time pressure applied to developers.

Our third remark is that the increase in temperature caused by processing a hotfix sets up a "greenhouse-effect" positive feedback loop, where optimizing the development process to respond to hotfixes creates an environment in which hotfixes are more frequently required, and that when this feedback loop gets out of control, it often results in a catastrophic event that may cause the company's stock price to plummet. Such stories are in the news on a regular basis.

Our fourth remark is that hotfix-driven development is the real-world name for a development process that more formally includes timeboxed sprints, test-driven development, and continuous delivery. Hotfix-driven development as it stands today is just too primitive an approach to software engineering; it is too much an invitation to make a mess of one's project. One can regard and appreciate the need to respond to customers in a timely manner and to drive the overall direction of a software project from customer feedback, but a more rational and sane development process needs to place quality of the released software as the top priority and avoid the positive-temperature feedback effects that cause buggy software to be continuously deployed to the field.

6.3   Acceptance Testing Fails When Edge Cases Are Missed

Given how important acceptance testing is the question becomes, How can we do a better job at it? Here are two common failure modes:

- Testing failed to exercise all sunny/rainy-day paths through the use case.
- Requirements were not stated completely and not comprehensively tested.

Let's walk through these one at a time.

Exercising all sunny/rainy-day paths through a use case requires that all of the alternate and exception paths through a scenario are detailed, and a test script is created for each one. Failure to completely understand all of the edge and corner cases when the code was written is as likely as anything else to be the culprit behind the hotfix, but in any event, it's QA's responsibility to make sure that all of these conditions get tested.

The most efficient way to proceed with documenting and testing all of the paths through a scenario is to use the Structured Specification feature in Enterprise Architect (EA) to describe the use case, and then generate both an activity diagram and a set of test scripts from Structured Specification.

Not stating the requirements completely (or, more precisely, not comprehensively testing against a complete set of requirements) is another likely hotfix culprit. The most efficient way to make sure you haven't forgotten to test all of the requirements is to do a requirements model in EA, review it carefully, and use the Agile/ICONIX design-driven testing (DDT) add-in to generate a test case for each requirement.

6.4 CarmaCam Example

So far in this chapter we've examined some of the problems that afflict projects where testing (and therefore software quality) is either considered secondary to the proceedings or approached suboptimally. For the rest of this chapter, we'll look at how to approach testing on a parallel/large-team project in an entirely optimal way.

The example we'll use is taken straight from some real-world development done with CarmaCam. The developer, Ankita, was tasked with allowing CarmaCam's bad drivers database to be queried. Here's Ankita's use case:

Box 6.3: Basic Course
System displays a list of reports from the database, based on the input license plate number.

Reports can be sorted based on the filter criteria such as severity, location, date, and time. System displays Bad Driver Report. Insurance company can review this report and check for severity claims and duplicate reports.

Alternate Courses
No report found for a license plate number:
    System displays a popup: NO records found.
    User enters another license plate number.
User reviews report by choosing severity, or location, or time, or incident ID:
    List of reports is sorted based on the selected criteria.
Bad Driver Report not found:
    User refreshes the system, as a report may have been reviewed earlier but not marked accordingly.

This use case was elaborated on the robustness diagram shown in Fig. 6.1.

Note 6.2
Robustness diagrams provide a standard notation for describing use cases in terms of models, views, and controllers—and the requirements/user stories that the use case satisfies. This standard notation makes it easy to express the intended conceptual design of a use case so that it can be reviewed before coding (Fig. 6.1 shows a sample robustness diagram).

Starting to think about the model, view, and controllers (and requirements) early in your design helps you to reach the correct design early, and saves on refactoring later, especially if you're already using a model-view-controller (MVC) UI framework such as Angular or Vue.

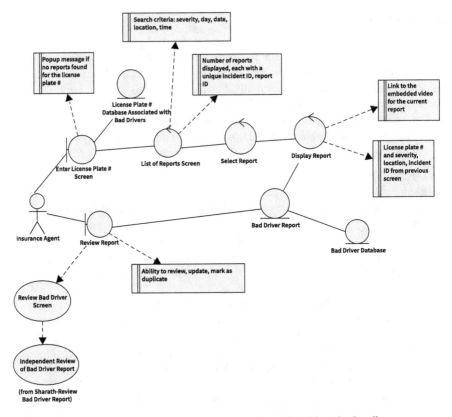

Fig. 6.1 MVC decomposition and user stories for the "Query bad driver database" use case

Stay tuned to see how we broke down this use case and its user stories into specific tests.

6.5   Testing at Different Levels

The testing process described in this chapter is formulated around two main tenets:

- *Broadly scoped tests* (where they each cover a relatively large amount of code) are useful for catching unexpected bugs. Always keep them around, even if finer-grained tests appear to cover the same code.
- *Fine-grained tests* (e.g., where one test covers just one class or function) aren't effective as regression tests; however, they're useful as a form of assurance that a unit of code works as intended.

You're either zoomed in at the microscopic unit test level (fine-grained tests), or zoomed out at the end-to-end acceptance test level (broadly scoped tests), with the majority of tests landing somewhere in between.

For the rest of this chapter we focus on three kinds of tests. All three happen to be functional tests—that is, they're concerned with proving that descriptions of system behavior have been implemented to specifications[3]: unit tests, component tests, and acceptance tests.

It can be useful to conceptualize the three levels of tests in this way:

- *Unit tests* verify the "how" of some code. They look inside a function and are closely tied to the implementation details.
- *Component tests* verify the "what" of the code. They check that if they pass a certain value to a component (group of closely related functions), they get back what they were expecting.
- *Acceptance tests* verify the "why" and the "who" of the code. They're a proxy for the business requirements, and they're defined in terms of the actors or users of the system.

There's some crossover, of course—unit tests also verify an element of "what," otherwise they wouldn't be much use at all. But the model outlined here is still useful to have in mind when discussing why the three levels of tests are needed.

6.6   A Capsule Summary of Domain Oriented Testing

DOT is "domain oriented" because everything within it is oriented towards the business domain model. The tests, in turn, are driven either from the code or from the requirements, depending on which tests.

A process needs a prescription—at least that's what my doctor told me. Here's DOT in an easily swallowed capsule form:

- Drive unit tests from the code.
- Drive component tests from the use case scenarios.
- Drive acceptance tests from the user stories[4] and use case scenarios.

Though component and acceptance tests are both driven from the use case scenarios, acceptance tests are far more end-to-end and will cover the complete scenario. In contrast, a use case scenario might be split out into several component test scenarios.

---

[3]Acceptance tests can also cover nonfunctional requirements—for example, "The system must handle up to 1000 transactions/second as a consistent load"—though DOT is chiefly concerned with identifying functional acceptance tests. That isn't to say that nonfunctional tests aren't important; they're just beyond the scope of this chapter.

[4]Remember from Chap. 5 that user stories are requirements from the user's perspective.

Note 6.3

In essence, DOT in its entirety is the preceding three bullet points, plus a lot of good advice on how to test well within the context of these guidelines. DDT, meanwhile, is essentially a way to accomplish the third bullet point by identifying the acceptance tests in a systematic way—plus some free automation in the form of an EA add-in.

Box 6.4: From DDT to DOT

Back in 2010 Matt and Doug collaborated on *design driven testing* (DDT), the process and a book by the same name. In essence, the process is about driving tests of various types from the use cases and an early stage design in the form of robustness diagrams. The process ties in neatly with the ICONIX Process, as robustness diagrams are at the core of both.

Since then, Matt has gone on to formulate *Domain Oriented Testing* (DOT), which is a holistic approach to testing and software quality, and is a complementary collection of structured good practices developed from decades of hard-won experience creating and delivering projects.

In fact, you can use DDT quite easily in conjunction with DOT, which is exactly what we're doing in this chapter.

DOT is an efficient, nonprescriptive (though rather opinionated) process that will allow your team to write *just enough* tests to get the job done. DOT also argues in favor of *requirements coverage* over *code coverage* as a useful metric. As with DDT, the idea is to drive the tests from requirements, so that you essentially know when you're done.

DOT is applicable to (and will benefit) most software processes, though it has a particular affinity with PA—probably not surprising given their common history.

Another difference is that component tests are much closer to the code and written by the developers, while acceptance tests are written by the testers as separate behavior-driven development (BDD)-style test scripts.

As these three core guidelines form the entirety of the testing effort in a DOT or PA project, we'll spend the remainder of the chapter walking through them. We'll spend the most time on acceptance testing (tests written and performed by testers), as this is at the heart of PA. We'll briefly cover unit testing and component testing (tests written and performed by developers).[5]

---

[5] If you're a developer and you want to know more, head over to https://www.domainorientedtesting.com/ or check out Matt's upcoming book (likely release early 2020), unsurprisingly called *Domain Oriented Testing*.

> **Note 6.4**
>
> Projects work best when the testers are working closely with the developers from the start. As the testers (writing acceptance tests) identify corner cases they let the developers know, and as the developers (writing component tests) identify corner cases they let the testers know. For each corner case identified by the testers, the developer creates a corresponding scenario within the use case. The level of requirements and test coverage that close collaboration between testers and developers inevitably creates (especially by the acceptance testing phase) puts the project in a good place.

6.7   Drive Unit Tests from the Code

Unit tests are zoomed-in white-box tests—their job is to test that an individual method does what it's intended to do. They are "white box" in the sense that they often have an uncanny amount of knowledge of the internals of the method and related code. If the implementation changes, the unit test might break. This isn't exactly an ideal to strive for; it's just how it is.

Truth be told, we're not great fans of unit tests (strictly in the definition just described). Or more accurately, we're not great fans of how unit tests tend to be used, and rampantly overused. If you cover the code with too many unit tests, the codebase turns into a rigid structure, unwieldy and expensive to refactor.

Unit tests do have a use—it's just important to recognize that their usefulness is limited to a certain set of scenarios, and their overuse (as foisted on us by certain code coverage tool vendors) will lead to the drawbacks previously mentioned.

You might wonder, then, why even write unit tests at all? There are definitely some good reasons, the main ones being to

- Catch bugs as early as possible, to prove that the individual function you're currently writing works as expected
- Better understand the zoomed-in design, and drive the design to an extent
- Question the code
- Provide additional test scenarios and permutations that might be difficult or unwieldy to add at a more zoomed-out level, e.g. in a component test

So, pretty essential then! However, you'll notice that the first three of these benefits occur right at the point when you're writing the code that the unit test is aimed at. Even if you've done a great deal of upfront design modeling, unit tests do still provide some feedback into the design at a low level—with the coding you're now doing the real work, discovering what's possible and what isn't. However, aside from the fourth benefit, the unit tests' window of utility soon passes and they can quickly turn from an asset to a liability.

It's tempting to keep unit tests around as a blanket form of regression test, but this isn't their area of strength. All they really test is that a function has been implemented in a particular way. They're far more effective as a temporary, *in situ* development tool than as regression tests.

With all of that said, it's still worth keeping them around. It's always possible that someone will accidentally break an individual function, so unit tests provide some level of assurance that a function continues to work. This assurance is also provided by the component tests, though, so if a unit test becomes more trouble than it's worth, have no qualms about deleting it, as long as the code and test scenarios are covered by a component test.

6.8   Drive Component Tests from the Use Case Scenarios

Compared with a unit test, a component test is slightly less zoomed-in. Its job is twofold:

- Validate a cluster of functionality, a closely related group of functions (in MVC terms, a controller) that together fulfill one particular item of system behavior
- Prove that a use case scenario (whether a happy path or an unhappy path) has been implemented to specifications

Component tests are black-box tests, in the sense that they know nothing of the internals of the method or methods under test. All they know is the interface that they're calling: the input and the expected output.

There are more good reasons to write component tests, namely to

- Catch bugs as early as possible, to show that the use case scenario you're implementing works as specified
- Capture the domain model as an executable specification that confirms *domain correctness* across your codebase
- Question the depth or shallowness of the requirements
- Validate the design
- Better understand the design, and drive the design to an extent
- Question the code
- Ensure error conditions are handled (e.g., a suitable error message is displayed, or a transaction rolls back correctly so data integrity is maintained)
- Provide a blanket of tests, a regression safety net, that can be rerun regularly

The topmost good reason is kind of interesting, as it reveals an important aspect of component testing DOT-style: the idea is to implement the component tests as early as possible, so that you can run the tests while you're coding. Then you can see exactly when the module has been completed to specification. Conversely, if all the tests are lighting up green but you feel that there's still code to be written, then you've identified some gaps in the use case scenarios, so you can flag this issue and revisit the use cases.

Notice that the "good reasons" overlap somewhat with unit tests, and not by coincidence. Unit tests and component tests operate within the same space. However, component tests are far more useful and long-lived than unit tests (long-lived in the sense that they continue to be useful for longer). If the code is written to accommodate testing in general, they are also easier to write than unit tests. You should find that you don't need to write mock objects, stubs, and so forth. Developers sometimes feel compelled to create mocks/fakes/stubs for unit tests, so that the test only ever runs the function under test. This tendency is because unit tests are oriented towards the code. Conversely, component tests are oriented towards the requirements – the business domain – so the same compulsion to spend extra time stubbing out code shouldn't be there. It simply doesn't matter if additional code gets run; in fact it's preferable, as you want a component test to cover as much of the "real" code (versus mocked functions) as possible.

6.8.1   When Should Component Tests Be Written?

The simple answer is, during the minimum viable product (MVP) phase.

During the earlier proof of concept phase, you'll mostly be focusing on prototyping the sunny-day scenarios. But at that stage you won't be writing accompanying test code anyway. You will, however, be identifying new use cases and rainy-day scenarios, in preparation for the MVP phase. Then, during MVP, you'll be writing the component tests directly from the use case scenarios.

Let's run through a quick example of writing a component test class from a use case scenario, returning to the CarmaCam example.

For this example, we'll use ScalaTest, as it provides a nice syntax for BDD-style test specs while still being close to the code (as these are developer-oriented component tests). We won't go "full BDD" with the syntax for this example, though.

For initial inspiration, turn to the use case. You'll want separate tests for the basic course and for each alternate course. Not all of the use cases will be relevant to this particular developer. He or she might be implementing only the API portion of the use case, while someone else is writing the web front-end. So "The system displays a list of reports···" won't be relevant here, but "list of reports from the database" definitely is.

Let's start with that:

```
"When queried, the API" should {
  "retrieve a list of reports from the database" in {
  }
}
```

Not a bad start. Before implementing the test itself, we should also add in all the alternate courses, like so:

```
"When queried with a license plate #, the API" should {
  "reject an empty license plate #" in {
  }
  "reject a badly formatted license plate #" in {
  }
  "if no reports were found, return an empty JSON array" in {
  }
  "retrieve a list of reports from the database" in {
  }
  "return the reports in a different order according to the sort-
  ing" in {
  }
}
```

We've also updated the outer When line to make it more focused on the API part of the implementation. A developer writes these component tests while in close collaboration with the UI developer, so that both developers know which parts of the use case are being handled by whom.

Whoa there—that's a few more scenarios than were in the original use case! It happens. As soon as you're at the keyboard thinking about how this is going to be developed, you'll think of caveats ("Oh, but what if this happens⋯"). These micro-revelations are gold dust. Rather than just coding safeguards in place, be sure to capture them all right away as test scenarios, and at some point feed them back into the use case.

A tester would, of course, also be closely involved, so that the additional discovered corner cases can be added to the use case as alternate courses, and added to the acceptance test scenarios. (This might seem like duplication, but remember the acceptance tests will be testing the system end-to-end and ensuring the corner case survives throughout, rather than just here in this relatively zoomed-in component test.)

But is this "test first" development? Yes and no. As the developers write the use cases, you identify individual test scenarios that can be code-generated into skeleton test classes, and you implement the tests themselves while writing the code itself.

6.9   Drive Acceptance Tests from the User Stories and Use Case Scenarios

Acceptance tests are about as zoomed-out as it gets. Their purpose is to validate that the code fulfills the requirements. Code coverage is definitely not your goal with acceptance tests.

There are a multitude of good reasons to use acceptance tests (actually, there are a *few* reasons, but they're such good reasons that they seem like a virtual army), specifically to

- Catch bugs as early as possible, to show that the module or use case you're implementing works exactly as specified
- Capture the domain model as an executable specification that confirms *domain correctness* across your codebase
- Question the depth or shallowness of the requirements
- Ensure error conditions are handled (e.g., a suitable error message is displayed, or a transaction rolls back correctly so data integrity is maintained)—*exceptions*
- Ensure additional corner cases are identified (e.g., atypical user access such as "I forgot my password")—*alternates*
- Provide a blanket of tests, a regression safety net, that can be rerun regularly
- Provide reliable cohesion between shared modules

Notice that there's some minor overlap there with component tests, and with good reason. Both levels of testing are driven from some form of requirement, and they are oriented heavily around the business domain model.

As previously mentioned, code coverage is not a goal of acceptance tests. If the testers have written the acceptance tests to cover each requirement, yet a swath of functionality is still untested, it would be the job of the component tests to fill these in rather than the acceptance tests. (But yes, you should also revisit the requirements in this case, as something might have been missed.)

6.9.1   Who Is Responsible for the Acceptance Tests?

You'll want all of the acceptance tests (whether automated or manual) to be written by the software testers, rather than by the developers. Where automated tests are concerned, it's tempting to just let the developers write them, but this is something to be avoided. The responsibilities and thought processes of the two groups are, of course, virtually opposite. Developers create, testers destroy. It's a totally different mindset. Also consider the following:

- A high bug count next to a developer's name looks bad. *Bad* developer!
- A high bug count next to a tester's name looks great. *Nice work*—now go find some more!

If required, the developers can still code struts, helper classes, and so on to pave the way, so the testers can focus on actual testing rather than writing more code. Of course, if you have test engineers available (testers with a bit more code-savvy), then so much the better.

The developers (or devops engineers) should also assist with architecting the test project so that it's fully containerized. It needs to be straightforward for a tester to quickly spin up a testing environment with the latest versions of everything, run whatever tests they want to, and tear it down again.

While PA has an acceptance testing phase, it's important that the testers become involved in the project before this stage. Ideally, they would have some level of involvement right from the start (even if they're still involved part-time in some other project at that point). This means that while the developers are creating the MVP, the testers are busy writing the acceptance tests in parallel. A big advantage of this approach is that if there's any area of the system that's difficult to test, it can be addressed or restructured early on, rather than a few weeks before the product is due to ship.

> **Tip 6.1**
> As team members write the user stories and use cases, they identify the acceptance tests in parallel. The acceptance tests closely follow the use case scenarios—they're virtually 1:1. As the use case is divided into sunny-day and rainy-day scenarios, create an acceptance test for each scenario.

6.9.2   Manual vs. Automated Acceptance Tests

You might be wondering at this point how you decide whether to turn each scenario into a manual or automated acceptance test. That's an easy one: you should turn every acceptance test that involves UI interaction into a manual acceptance test script that a "human" tester will use. However, in addition, the testers should—try to automate *all* of the acceptance tests (with assistance from the developers). UI testing frameworks have advanced a long way in recent times. Selenium, Browser Stack, Sauce Labs, and the like make it remarkably easy to write automated UI tests.

But if the same acceptance test exists in both manual and automated form, isn't that duplicated effort? The key is that manual and automated acceptance tests have different goals, and so are used differently:

- With manual tests, you're using human observation, intuition, and the brain's ability to process at an abstract level—to spot things that are missing or just look wrong. It's virtually impossible for an automated test to be as effective at this type of testing. This situation may change someday when we start to see AI-based testing tools with human-like reasoning power, though we're probably a long way off from that particular singularity just yet.[6]
- With automated acceptance tests, you're using a computer's robotic capability to retread the same ground at *(insert breathless superlative here)* speeds. This is mechanical testing, to ensure in a complete, consistent way that individual fields,

---

[6] Meanwhile, in a secret laboratory somewhere deep beneath the Swiss Alps the⋯is hovering

panels, grids, and so on contain the expected results. As these tests are so effective, they're perfect as regression tests that can be rerun every time some code is committed.

It really isn't a case of "Which do I use?" Manual and automated tests complement each other like your left and right hands clasped together.

- Manual testing catches the following:

  - "Oh, we missed something—that requirement must have been incomplete."
  - "That just doesn't seem right; the tests missed that bug."
  - "I accidentally clicked the Back button and it resubmitted the form."
  - "This panel is in the wrong place."
  - "This screen isn't particularly usable. See how it could be improved⋯"
  - "It feels like video uploading is too slow when we watermark the speed on each frame."
  - "My camera defocuses at night when the light level is too low."

- Automated testing catches the following:

  - "This field contains the wrong result."
  - "This grid contains the wrong number of rows."
  - "There are null values in the JSON response."
  - "This test that used to pass suddenly no longer passes." (meaning one of the requirements is no longer correctly implemented)

6.9.3   Acceptance Test Early and Often

You'll notice that the manual testing list from the previous section contains a lot of user experience–related items. On the CarmaCam project, for example, early user experience (UX) testing resulted in changes to triggering of video uploads from voice to touch due to ambient noise affecting reliability, responsive design on the web app, and other reasons.

Here are some actual examples of problems discovered during early acceptance testing of the various prototypes created during CarmaCam's proof of concept phase:

- Voice input didn't pass acceptance testing.
- License plate images needed to be brightened.
- The proper zoom level for the camera needed to be determined.
- A traffic map and speedometer were desired features.
- The initial video buffer design caused the camera to switch on/off, resulting in nighttime videos defocusing when the camera switched back on in low light.

These issues were all discovered during manual acceptance testing in the prototyping phase.

A fairly big moral to learn here is this: begin acceptance testing under real conditions as early as possible—as soon as there's something to test—and test often. Test the prototypes as if they're the finished product. This is a great way to reveal new rainy-day scenarios. As soon as you discover rainy-day scenarios, add them to the use case. Then, when you're developing the MVP, the component tests will be driven directly from all of these error conditions that might not otherwise have been discovered. This is fundamentally why PA has a distinct prototyping phase. When the production system is being developed, it will be far more robust, with the majority of error conditions discovered and scenario-driven tests at the ready.

One way to think about massively parallel prototyping and acceptance testing is that it's Darwinian evolution at work. The fittest prototypes survive and the others get thrown away.

6.9.4   Creating a Manual Acceptance Test Script

Creating a manual acceptance test script is pretty easy—it's simply the use case scenario. Here's a handy recipe for turning a complete use case into some acceptance test scripts:

1. Turn your sunny-day scenarios into positive test cases and your rainy-day scenarios into negative test cases.
2. Turn each step in the use case ("The user does something; the system does something in response") into a step that the tester should follow, and an expected response.
3. Carry over the preconditions ("The user should be logged in," "Product XYZ should be set up").
4. Turn the postconditions ("The BUY transaction should be complete," "The money should be transferred") combined with the use case title ("Buy a hamster") into the test success criteria.

You can also base the success criteria on the final system response (e.g., "The system displays a confirmation page").

In a moment we'll show how a little automation can help, courtesy of a free add-in available for EA. But first, you may be familiar with BDD, Cucumber, Gherkin, and the like, so here's a quick example using those.

6.9.5 Creating an Automated Acceptance Test with BDD and Cucumber

As mentioned earlier, you'll ideally want the acceptance tests to be automated as much as possible, so that you can rerun them at the drop of a hat or, more usefully, whenever some new code is committed.

Acceptance tests might be written in a different language than the main project, using Cucumber with Gherkin, Ruby, Python, and so on—whatever the testers are comfortable using. In fact, acceptance tests can (and really should) be written in the BDD style: given/when/then. This isn't a fast requirement by any means, but DOT and BDD fit very well together.

Returning to CarmaCam's Bad Driver Database Query example, previously we showed some component test scenarios as identified from the use case scenarios. Here's one way that the same use case scenarios could be turned into an automated BDD test script using the Gherkin syntax.

Recall that earlier, the scenarios were broken down into smaller pieces for the component tests, so that they match up more easily with the code modules being developed. Here, though, we're at a zoomed-out, end-to-end sort of level, which is reflected in the acceptance test. To illustrate, here's the basic course turned into a test scenario:

```
Feature: Query Bad Driver Database
Scenario: System displays a list of reports based on a license
plate number
  Given 3 reports exist for driver Bob's license plate in the
database
  Given the user is viewing the Bad Driver Reports page
  When the user enters Bob's license plate # and clicks Search
  Then the system finds the 3 reports and displays the results
```

You should then write similar scenarios for all the alternate courses.

We're skipping over the implementation details to keep the example brief, but of course you would also need to implement the test itself using Cucumber with your language of choice. We've found in practice, though, that implementing the first few tests are where the real effort goes. Once the test harness is all set up and can walk through webpages, make REST API requests, and so forth, then the whole exercise becomes quick and painless.

6.9.6   Creating an Automated Acceptance Test with DDT

If you were thinking that perhaps the "recipe" for driving tests from use case scenarios could be automated, you are correct. We thought the same thing, too, so we
collaborated with the folks at Sparx to create a free add-in for EA. It's the Agile/
ICONIX Design Driven Testing (DDT) add-in. We demonstrate how to use it in the
next few sections, while further exploring the idea of testing use case scenarios.

6.9.6.1   Scenario Testing

When you write a use case, you're writing it in the form of scenarios (sunny-day
scenario and rainy-day scenarios). It stands to reason that the tests you'll write for
these are called *scenario tests*. Scenario tests are end-to-end tests that verify that the
system behaves as expected when the user clicks the expected buttons, and also that
it copes when some unexpected buttons are clicked, too.

By "end-to-end," we mean that a scenario test verifies the complete scenario,
from the initial screen being displayed, through each user step and system response,
to the conclusion of the scenario. Sometimes scenario tests are automated, but they
don't have to be. There's plenty of mileage in simply creating scenario test scripts
that follow along the use case flow and handing these test scripts to your QA team.

Use cases generally have a sunny-day scenario (the typical sequence of user
actions and system responses) and several rainy-day scenarios (everything else that
can happen: errors, exceptions, and less typical usage paths). When you're modeling systems with use cases, you make an upfront investment in "writing the user
manual" one scenario at a time, with the expectation of recovering your investment
later on in the project. If you do it right, you virtually always recover your investment multiple times over.

One of the places you can leverage the investment you've made in writing use
cases is in scenario testing. If you have a use case with one sunny-day scenario and
two rainy-day scenarios (see Fig. 6.2), you can expand that use case into at least
three "threads" (see Fig. 6.3), each of which defines a potential scenario test for
some part of your system. There's one thread for the sunny-day scenario and others
for some portion of the sunny-day combined with each of the rainy-day scenarios,
in turn. When you've covered all of the permutations, you have a good start on
black-box acceptance testing your use case from the user perspective.

Fortunately, automation exists to make the generation of these test scripts less
tedious. The ICONIX Agile DDT add-in for EA, which we mentioned earlier, also
includes something called a use case thread expander that generates a complete set
of test scripts for each path. For a complete tutorial, refer to *Design Driven Testing*
(Rosenberg and Stephens 2010).

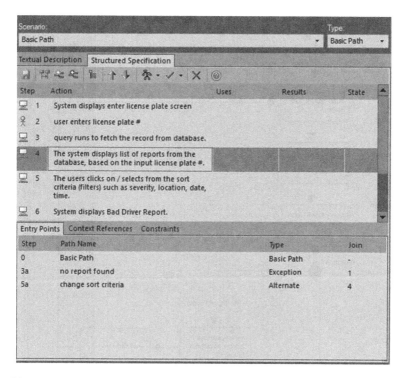

Fig. 6.2 Don't forget the corner cases (both exceptions and alternates)

6.9.6.2   Comprehensive Requirements Testing

Agile projects often have difficulty scaling beyond a small scrum team and a short two-week time horizon. Agile ceremonies like stand-up meetings, retrospectives, and backlog grooming don't carry you very far, and the JIRA tickets that represent the requirements (user stories) may not be written consistently nor to a detailed level. Most attempts at scaling Agile projects involve reintroducing requirements into the mix. Sometimes this is done with a Sprint Zero requirements pass.

6.9.7   Prototype to Discover Requirements, Review Them Carefully, and Test Each One

On PA projects, usually each developer is responsible for a use case. Generally, the use case is prototyped during the proof of concept cycle, with the intent of discovering what the requirements should be. At the start of the MVP cycle, the requirements are detailed on a UML diagram and reviewed for accuracy and completeness. Before we release the project, we generate a test case for each requirement and exercise the test case.

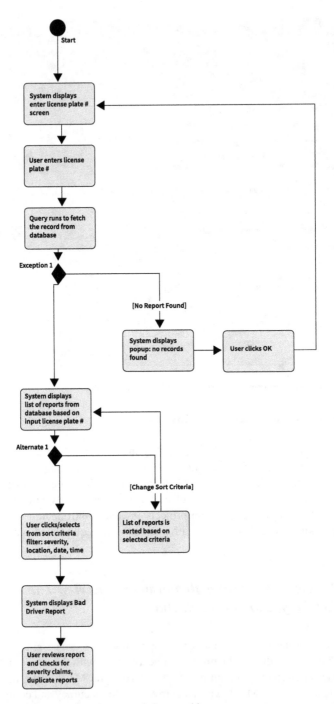

Fig. 6.3 At least three test threads are needed to test this use case

From a testing perspective, the main focus for each phase is as follows:

- **Proof of concept:** Test that the "normal" system usage works correctly by developing sunny-day scenario tests. Think of these as "story tests" that verify that the user can accomplish the desired goal.
- **MVP:** Identify corner cases while doing MVC analysis, often by identifying controllers to handle corner cases.
- **Optimization:** Focus on making sure all the corner cases are covered.

In other words, we prototype to discover the requirements, we review the requirements for completeness, and then we generate test cases for each and every requirement. The intent of this strategy is to try our best to catch errors of omission. Because the requirements work is done in parallel with a small scope of a single use case, it doesn't add significantly to the project schedule.

Once the requirements have been agreed on, the developer proceeds to implement the use case, and the test team can start filling in the test scenarios while the coding proceeds.

At the end of the MVP cycle, all of the requirements tests are collected and a test plan is generated. These tests, along with the scenario tests, form the starting place for getting the system ready for release.

6.10   Summary

Hotfix-driven development has become prevalent in the Agile universe. Hotfix-driven development is often caused by a misuse of timeboxing in conjunction with continuous delivery.

We feel that a dollar of acceptance testing is worth 10 dollars of unit testing, because errors of omission are the chief culprits of buggy software and because an overreliance on unit testing creates a false illusion of quality.

In this chapter, we introduced Domain Oriented Testing (DOT), which focuses on three types of tests: unit tests, component tests, and acceptance tests.

With PA, the most important kinds of acceptance testing are scenario testing and requirements testing. Scenario testing minimizes ignored corner and edge cases, while requirements testing minimizes forgotten requirements. Automation is available for scenario testing and requirements testing in the form of the Agile/ICONIX DDT add-in from Sparx Systems. We used Design Driven Testing (DDT) to illustrate acceptance testing.

PA does testing at each life-cycle phase, with testing becoming more rigorous as the project progresses toward release.

In the next chapter, we'll share some insights about how to manage large-scale parallelism to compress schedules and reduce cost. Testing in the manner described in this chapter is essential to ensuring that schedule compression does not come at the expense of quality.

References

Boehm, B., and R. Turner. 2003. *Balancing agility and discipline: A guide for the perplexed.* Boston: Addison-Wesley.

Rosenberg, D., and M. Stephens. 2010. *Design driven testing.* Berkeley: Apress.

Rosenberg, D., M. Stephens, and M. Collins-Cope. 2005. *Agile development with ICONIX process: People, process, and pragmatism.* Berkeley: Apress.

Stephens, M. 2007. Green bar of Shangri-La. The Register. http://www.theregister.co.uk/2007/04/25/unit_test_code_coverage. Accessed 18 July 2019.

Chapter 7
Managing Parallelism: Faster Delivery, Fewer Defects, Lower Cost

Box 7.1

This chapter is a free-ranging discussion on how to think about software engineering as a parallel processing activity, something that Doug has been doing for a few decades now. Here's the story of his first experience with managing parallelism on a NASA project more than 30 years ago.

Back around 1985–86, I was employed as a consultant at NASA Jet Propulsion Laboratories (JPL) on a project with the tongue-twisting acronym of ASAS/ENSCE[1] (ASAS for short).

ASAS was a "tactical data fusion" system that displayed icons for things like tanks and artillery on a map. To give you an idea of how long ago this was, the maps at the time were provided on 10-inch video disks.

One day, my boss Dave called me into his office with a worried look on his face and asked for my help. Our group was working on the Man Machine Interface subsystem (in simple terms, the UI) and there was a General coming to the lab to see our prototype, which was lagging at least 3 months behind schedule. The General's visit was scheduled in a little over a week and we had nothing at all to show. Could I help?

I suggested that I could try to help, but it would require Dave to temporarily deputize me with the authority to direct my co-workers (including my direct supervisor) for this particular task. Dave called a meeting and I was deputized. We had a cognitive psychologist named Gene assigned to our team, whose job was to evaluate the usability of our system under battlefield conditions (with people wearing gloves, HAZMAT suits, etc.). As it turned out, this crisis happened about a week before Super Bowl weekend and Gene was

---

[1] All Source Analysis System/ENemy System Correlation Element, a large tactical data fusion system.

© Springer Nature Switzerland AG 2020

D. Rosenberg et al., *Parallel Agile – faster delivery, fewer defects, lower cost*, https://doi.org/10.1007/978-3-030-30701-1_7

apologizing to our team about having to work through the Super Bowl, offering to host a party at his house near the lab, after which we could all go back to work.

Brimming with the overconfidence of youth, I informed Gene that I was going to split this problem into a bunch of small tasks, each of our dev team would be assigned one of these tasks, I would handle the integration, and we were going to be done by Friday afternoon with no need to work through the weekend. As it turned out, we pulled it off exactly as I planned: we caught up from being 3 months behind in about 5 days. I've been a believer in divide and conquer (aka parallel development) as an effective strategy ever since, and have never cared much for Brooks' Law.

Parallel Agile (PA) shortens development schedules similar to how multicore CPUs shorten computation time: by doing work in parallel. You first partition a development effort into small chunks of work that can be developed independently, then you develop them independently. The more developers you have available to attack a problem, the more you can get done in a similar time period. Staffing on PA projects is elastic, and you can add developers similar to how the Amazon Elastic Cloud brings new servers online.

This chapter's topic started out as cost estimation; however, estimating PA projects turns out to be a different sort of creature than either old-school waterfall cost estimation or new-age Agile/scrum estimation. With PA, most of your estimation effort is at the individual use case level, trying to make sure nobody has a task that's too big to complete in a month.

The chapter has now morphed into an overview of how to manage PA projects, driven largely by Doug's experience in managing our test projects. That experience was guided by several decades of software project management, along with an electrical engineering background and a couple of personal interests that helped shape the thought process.

From the electrical engineering background comes a firm belief that parallelism makes things run faster. From simple high school physics ("resistance in series versus resistance in parallel") all the way through to multicore CPUs and cloud computing, employing parallelism to go faster is a natural thought process—electrical engineers do this all the time.

This inherent belief in parallelism as an enabler of schedule compression tends to run afoul of Brooks' Law, which may not be so much of a law as a statement that back when it was written the strategies and tactics to enable parallel development weren't developed yet.

From the personal interest file comes a study of military history, notably World War II (Doug's father was in the U.S. Army in WWII) and General George Patton (Doug's father was in Belgium in December 1944 with the German army heading his way when Patton broke up the German attack during the Battle of the Bulge).

Patton was the master of adaptive planning and fast results, consistently slicing through less adaptable enemy armies like a hot knife through butter. Redeploying his army during the Battle of the Bulge is one of the greatest examples of rapid, flexible, yet careful planning in history, with monumental consequence.

Patton's book *War as I Knew It* (1975) gives great insight into his thought process. In particular, how he deployed his staff is relevant to any sort of parallel project management activity. He continually adapted his plans to conditions on the ground. One of his many pearls of wisdom is, "One does not plan and then try to make circumstances fit those plans. One tries to make plans fit the circumstances."

Among Doug's other personal interests is chess, with a strong appreciation for the Russian two-time world champion chess player Alexander Alekhine, who wrote up detailed analysis of hundreds of his chess games (2013) in a fascinating narrative style that gives enormous insight into his thought process.

Alekhine held the world championship for 17 years and was famous for simultaneous chess exhibitions, including a mind-boggling ability to play simultaneous chess blindfolded. On July 16, 1934, in Chicago, Alekhine set the new world record by playing 32 blindfolded games with 19 wins, 4 losses, and 9 draws (LearningChess 2015). It seems clear that if you can play 32 chess games in parallel while wearing a blindfold, your thought process is relevant to managing any sort of parallel activity.

What do General Patton's and Alexander Alekhine's thought processes have in common that relates to how to manage a parallel software project? We can boil it down to a few things:

- Instant tactical assessment
- Rapid and adaptive planning
- Seizing the initiative
- Redeploying resources as the situation evolves

This turns out to be a very helpful checklist for software project management as well.

In this chapter, we'll focus on how to plan rapidly, adaptively, and flexibly, and cover some general strategies for keeping track of large numbers of parallel threads, with a focus on enabling parallelism in development because that's what lets you get done faster. We'll also discuss some strategies for improving quality at the same time you're going faster.

7.1   Believe in Parallelism: Resistance Is Futile

If you have some familiarity with electrical engineering, you might recognize the inherent belief in parallelism as an accelerator of processes and computations, via the idea of series versus parallel circuitry. Basically, an electrical circuit is a path by which electrons can find their way from some electrical potential to ground. Resistors impede the path of the electrons. When you connect resistors in a series (one after the other, exactly like a series of 2-week sprints), the overall resistance is

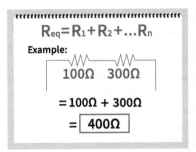
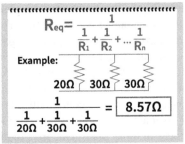

Fig. 7.1 In theory, you should be able to shorten schedules by working in parallel

the sum of the resistors you connect (similar to how the calendar time is consumed in some multiple of 2-week sprints on a scrum project). But when you configure the resistors in parallel instead of putting them in a series, the equivalent resistance goes down (much like how deploying your developers in parallel shortens the time to project completion). Theoretically, we should be able to compress project schedules in a similar manner to reducing the resistance of an electrical circuit laid out in series rather than in parallel, as shown in Fig. 7.1.

As anyone who has taken Physics 101 has probably forgotten, in parallel resistor networks, the more parallel branches there are, the lower the overall resistance becomes. In theory, it seems like we might be able to do this with software project schedules, but in practice, as Brooks' Law suggests, it usually doesn't work that way.

It's interesting to consider the reasons it doesn't normally work. Two of the reasons it doesn't work in practice are as follows:

- Adding more developers to a software project increases communication overhead and presents a lot of practical difficulties. For example, the scrum room might hold only a dozen programmers, and the standup meetings might take a long time if there are 50 or 60 developers. Brooks cites time spent by experienced developers in training new developers.
- Integrating the work of a large number of developers working independently presents difficulties, particularly from a database standpoint. Prototype code developed independently often is limited to user interface (UI) prototyping, with no database connection even attempted.

PA mitigates these two problems by using standard UML design notation to improve communication and by code-generating an executable architecture at project inception to facilitate integration.

7.1.1 Multicore CPUs

In hardware, performance is accelerated using parallel processing *all the time* (see Fig. 7.2). It's somewhat bewildering that we don't do something similar in software engineering.

Multicore CPUs aren't really big news anymore. But a multiprocessing thought process isn't typically applied to Agile software development, which usually proceeds with a small team involved in a never-ending continuum of two-week sprints.

Everything is sequential—no wonder it's slow.

7.1.2 Elastic Cloud of Developers

Adding developers to a PA project makes it go faster, just like Amazon Web Services (AWS) autoscaling brings more servers online to improve performance. Adding a lot more developers to a PA project makes it go a lot faster. More precisely, you can get much more accomplished in the same amount of time, because your developers are deployed in parallel, working on tasks that all interface to a common API that gets generated at project inception.

An interesting analogy to elastic staffing is the Amazon Elastic Cloud, which dynamically scales server capacity as loading increases. The AWS website describes autoscaling as follows (Amazon n.d.):

> Amazon EC2 Auto Scaling helps you ensure that you have the correct number of Amazon EC2 instances available to handle the load for your application. You create collections of EC2 instances, called Auto Scaling groups. You can specify the minimum number of instances in each Auto Scaling group, and Amazon EC2 Auto Scaling ensures that your group never goes below this size. You can specify the maximum number of instances in each Auto Scaling group, and Amazon EC2 Auto Scaling ensures that your group never goes above this size. If you specify the desired capacity, either when you create the group or at any time thereafter, Amazon EC2 Auto Scaling ensures that your group has this many instances. If you specify scaling policies, then Amazon EC2 Auto Scaling can launch or terminate instances as demand on your application increases or decreases.

We'd like to do something analogous to EC2 autoscaling with developer staffing. It's a hard premise to prove unless you have a couple hundred graduate students that sign up for Barry's Directed Research class every semester, which has allowed us to experiment with the elastic staffing model for 4 years prior to writing this book.

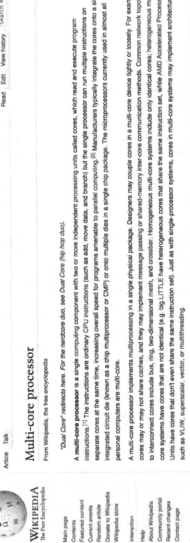

Fig. 7.2 Parallel processing is routinely used to accelerate computation. (Wikipedia 2019)

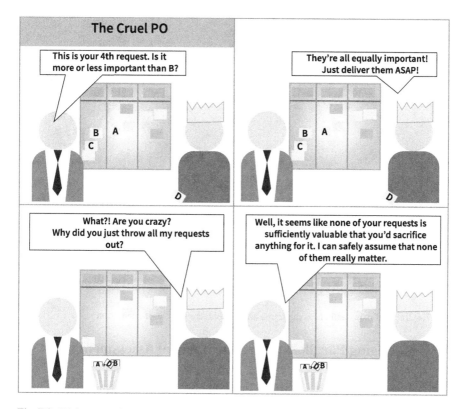

Fig. 7.3 PA lets you add more developers when management wants everything right away

7.1.3   You Want It WHEN?

With PA projects, you can scale the number of developers based on how many tasks you need to get completed. This lets your development team respond better to management's request to deliver all of the features they want, right now. The classic Agile response to these unreasonable management demands is shown in Fig. 7.3.

When management absolutely, positively needs it overnight (figuratively speaking), you can deploy more developers working in parallel. In other words, if you're running a PA project and management comes to you with "I need everything right now," you can push back and say, "I can have that for you by X date, but you're going to have to give me Y more developers."

But how do you, as a development manager, know how many developers you need? You can estimate from use cases, sprint plans, and model-view-controller (MVC) decompositions. Estimation of PA projects works a little differently, as you are mainly aiming to ensure that no developer task is so large that it might take more than a month to complete. We'll discuss both task estimation and use case estimation a little later in the chapter.

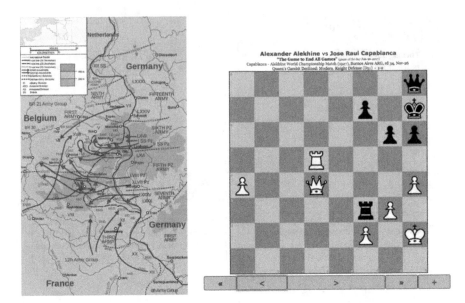

Fig. 7.4 Tactical maps and chess diagrams allow rapid assessment of a situation

7.2   Managing Parallelism: Instant Tactical Assessment

If you're going to manage a project that employs large-scale parallelism, you'll need to keep track of a large number of parallel development threads. Presuming your name isn't Alexander Alekhine or Garry Kasparov, it's probably going to be more data than you can keep in your brain at one time (for normal humans, cognitive science tells us that 7 +/− 2 is about what you can keep in your head). Using a visual aid from which you can quickly recover the context of the conversation with any particular developer is going to be a great help.

Standard notations are essential for your visual aids to work effectively because they use abstraction to clearly communicate a situation with unambiguous meaning to both the producer of the diagram and the consumer of the diagram.

General Patton, for example, had a staff of intelligence officers producing tactical maps on a daily basis. When he needed to know how far the German army had advanced during the Battle of the Bulge, he simply consulted a tactical map (Matthewedwards 2012).[2] Similarly, when Alexander Alekhine prepared to play Jose Raul Capablanca for the world chess championship (Chessgames.com 2017),[3] he could review all of Capablanca's past games visually. See Fig. 7.4.

---

[2] Personal footnote: if you find Liege Belgium on the map in Fig. 7.4 (just below the legend), you'll know why Doug is a big fan of General Patton, whose attack from the south broke up the German offensive just before it got there.

[3] In the position shown, with material otherwise even white's passed pawn wins.

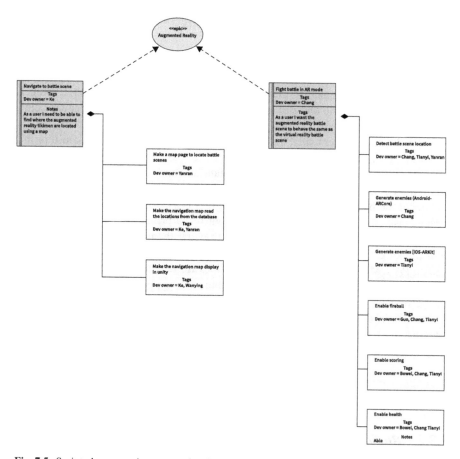

Fig. 7.5   Sprint plans organize your sprints into user stories, tasks, and epics

On PA projects we use standard diagrammatic notations for both management plans and technical plans. The management plans give context to the developers, who individually (in parallel) produce the technical plans so they can be reviewed with management.

PA follows a feedback-driven, agile project management approach, so the standard management diagram for PA is the *sprint plan*. Sprint plan diagrams like the one in Fig. 7.5 enable you to organize user stories into epics, and decompose each user story into its constituent tasks. We've built a UML profile for sprint plans into the PA add-in for Enterprise Architect (EA), which you can find at http://www.parallelagile.com/Parallel-Agile-Sparx-Add-in.pdf.

One important use of the sprint plan is to help visualize dependencies between various tasks. Just drawing the sprint plan diagram tends to make these dependencies visible, but if interdependencies are a problem, it's a simple matter to show these dependencies by drawing <dependency> arrows on the diagram.

7.2.1 Task Estimation from Sprint Plans

If you're going to try to follow the PA three-phase approach of proof of concept, minimum viable product (MVP), and optimization, and allocate about one calendar month to each of these phases, then it's important to make sure that each developer is tasked with something that's of a size and scope such that the developer can complete it within a month.

From the management side, the visual model sprint plan is the tool you'll probably use. From the technical side, if you've written use cases and elaborated them with something like an activity diagram, state machine, or MVC/robustness diagram, there's some additional help available—more on that shortly.

One of the best uses for a sprint plan diagram is as a basis for estimation of the various tasks that need to be done. You might be surprised at how the exercise of breaking each user story into its tasks and drawing them on a diagram organizes your thinking.

The PA UML profile supports tagged values for developer estimates and manager estimates. We recommend using a weighted average of the developer and manager estimates. You can invent your own weighted average formula, but on the theory that the developer has the best idea of the details about what needs to be done (and managers often estimate with when they would like it to be done), we suggest something like the following as a reasonable place to start:

```
weightedEstimate = (2 * developerEstimate + managerEstimate)/3
```

7.2.2 Rapid and Adaptive Planning

To effectively apply parallelism, you need to plan a little more than you do on most Agile projects. (Many Agile teams aren't doing much planning because planning is explicitly devalued in the Agile Manifesto.) Specifically, you need to be able to partition a system into "parallelizable" tasks, and you need to be able to integrate the work that's done in parallel back into a cohesive whole. In other words, you need to be able to take the system apart (into its use cases) and then make all the pieces fit back together when they're done (integrating all of the use cases through a common executable architecture).

The fundamental unit of work partitioning in PA is the (ICONIX-style) use case, so planning generally focuses on describing use cases. These small (roughly two paragraphs of narrative) scenario descriptions detail the behavior requirements for a scenario. With ICONIX-style use cases, there's a single sunny-day scenario and usually several rainy-day scenarios that are kept together as a unit.

Having each developer write a two-paragraph narrative description, all working in parallel, means that you can get all of your use case narratives done in the time it takes to write two paragraphs of narrative. If your developers think better in code, they can code a prototype of their use case and then write the use case narrative as a user guide for their prototype. Whichever angle you attack from, it doesn't take much time—there's no big design up front (BDUF) delay built into your schedule.

It's important not to skip the use case writing step, though (as often happens on Agile projects). The activities that enable parallelism in software development are greatly assisted by having a UML model. Without the UML model, you can't use code generation to make that model executable. And to state the obvious, you also use UML for planning—the use cases (and the executable domain model) are the core of the development plan.

7.2.3 Seizing the Initiative

General Patton always preferred retaining the initiative by attacking quickly before the enemy had prepared to defend against his army, and he used this technique to minimize casualties among his troops. Similarly in chess, Alexander Alekhine was the master of seizing the initiative with the first 10 moves of a game and then exploiting his advantage throughout the match.

Seizing the initiative works effectively with software projects as well, and it is enabled by code-generating your domain model into an executable architecture. Getting something up and running quickly has an enormous motivating effect on your team and kicks the feedback-driven part of the equation into gear.

With PA, you don't dawdle around through months of extended upfront design before building anything. Instead, you get right down to it and attack many use cases in parallel following the three-phase pattern of

1. Proof of concept (prototyping)
2. Minimum viable product (modeling)
3. Optimization (acceptance testing)

Depending on the technical risk involved with the use case, you can incorporate some use case and MVC modeling into the prototyping phase or just jump directly into experimental code for things like voice recognition and augmented reality. Given half a day or so for drawing the initial domain model and code-generating an API, your coding attack can jump off almost immediately—no need for a two-week planning sprint.

Doing a little bit of upfront planning actually tends to make development of each use case go a lot faster. PA does not use strict timeboxing, but our experience to date has been that allowing a month for each of the three phases has generally worked well, and in many cases some developers complete early. Which means that you can get from project inception to a set of well-designed and rigorously tested use cases in around 3 months. How big that set is depends on how many developers you have available, so you can consider elastic staffing approaches.

PA's three-phase approach follows the project management pattern of prototype–design–code–acceptance test. If you've partitioned your project properly into small

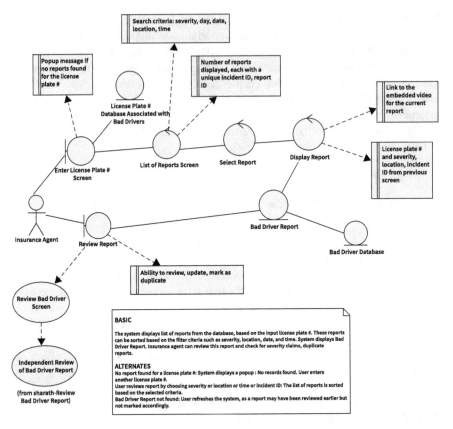

Fig. 7.6 MVC diagrams explain use cases in terms of models, views, controllers, and requirements

use cases, and you have enough developers to assign to all your use cases, each of these phases generally takes around a month. That means you can get from zero to a fairly complete project in a short period of time, and the size of the projects you can take on scales up with the number of developers you have, rather than proceeding with a never-ending series of short sprints.

Technical planning on PA projects happens rapidly, because the planning is done by each developer for his or her individual tasks so that all the planning happens in parallel. One particularly useful diagram for bottom-up technical planning is the MVC decomposition (aka robustness diagram), which explains a use case in terms of its models, views, and controllers. As shown in Fig. 7.6 (CarmaCam's "Query database by license plate number"), it's good practice to include requirements on this diagram as well. Note that in UML, a User Story is simply a Requirement with a stereotype of <User Story>.

After you write the behavior description in narrative form, you refine (disambiguate) it by doing an MVC decomposition that describes the use case in terms of its data (the model), its UI (the view), and the logic that glues the UI to the data (the controllers). Because the scope of each use case is small, it's possible for a developer to complete various tasks (prototyping, describing, analyzing, coding, and testing) in a short period of time.

A PA technical manager needs to be able to read these diagrams, and developers need to learn how to create them. It shouldn't take more than an hour or two for developers to explain their intention on an MVC diagram, and it shouldn't take more than a few minutes for a manager to determine whether the developer is on the right track or veering off on some tangent.

Doing planning in parallel from the bottom up addresses a key objection that many Agilists have about UML-based processes in general: the fear that BDUF takes too long before people start coding. Since each developer is working on a single use case that's small in scope, it doesn't take long for the developer to produce a fairly detailed plan of how to implement a use case.

7.2.4 Analyzing Use Case Complexity

Rapid use case complexity analysis is a particularly valuable capability to have when you're partitioning a project for parallel development. The trick to keeping the three PA development phases at a month apiece is to make sure that *no developer gets assigned a task that will take more than a month to complete*. If you can arrange this, then all of your parallel tasks should complete in a month.

Following the three-phase paradigm, your team would write first-draft use cases and do some MVC analysis at the beginning of the prototyping phase, perhaps do a few sequence diagrams or state machines during the MVP phase, and then generate acceptance test activity diagrams during the optimization phase. Developers have flexibility in how they choose to elaborate their use case, and the modeling doesn't take a long time because everybody's working in parallel on a small-scope single use case.

To help you estimate, we've built a use case complexity analyzer (see Fig. 7.7) that looks at any nested diagrams within the use cases (e.g., activity diagrams, sequence diagrams, robustness/MVC diagrams); scores the complexity of your use cases as easy, medium, or difficult; and then color-codes the use cases on the diagram. You can run the complexity analyzer at any time as your design evolves.

In general terms, the idea behind the use case analyzer is to read any nested diagrams that are "contained" within a use case in the UML model, and count things (elements on child diagrams). Then our algorithm takes a weighted average of the complexity score across all nested diagrams. What sorts of things can we count?

On an MVC diagram you're generally looking at how many controllers are in the use case, and how many screens (boundary objects) are in the use case. If your use case has 23 controllers in it (or more than 10), that's a clue that it needs to be broken up, and it will light up in red in the analyzer. On a sequence diagram, the analyzer counts the number of objects and the number of messages. On an activity diagram (including an automatically generated acceptance test diagram), the analyzer counts

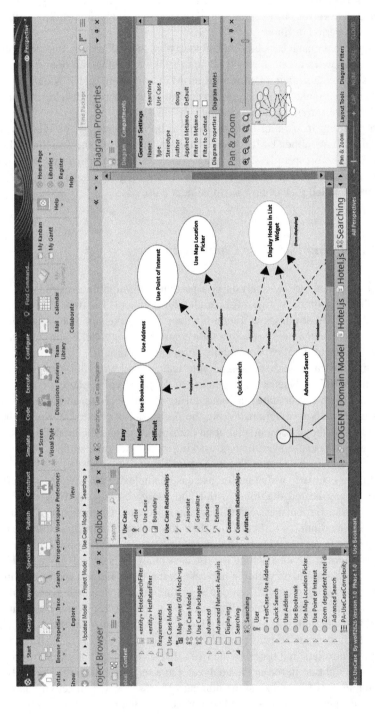

Fig. 7.7 Estimate use case complexity by looking at nested diagrams

the number of branches. On a state machine, the analyzer looks at states and transitions.

The benefit of the complexity analyzer is that you can get an instant tactical assessment of where your use cases are at any moment as the project evolves. If your team analyzes use cases rapidly and in parallel at the beginning of each sprint, you can predict where your hotspots are going to occur and plan adaptively to provide help in those areas.

7.2.5 Redeploying Resources as the Situation Evolves

To repeat the quote from General Patton, "One does not plan and then try to make circumstances fit those plans. One tries to make plans fit the circumstances."[4]

In software development, as in war, circumstances are subject to change from outside forces (new or changing requirements). And sometimes even without disturbance from outside, projects don't always go exactly as planned. People get stuck, people get sick, somebody has a family emergency—delays happen. Management is largely a process of finding out who is stuck and getting them unstuck.

Full-scale PA presumes a developer pool from which you can elastically staff your project, which is organized into user stories that each have tasks. At the beginning of your sprint, you do an initial mapping of developers to tasks. But you're not done after your initial assessment. PA managers need to continuously monitor for "stuck tasks" and reassign resources to help them. Managing a PA project involves an ongoing effort of assessing the circumstances and adapting to them—in other words, your planning needs to be fluid.

A lot of the ongoing assessment relates to schedule. In contrast to scrum, PA embraces "project thinking" and the idea of "getting done" (meeting delivery schedules). When we talk about developers completing a task on schedule, there are three possible outcomes: they complete the task on time, they complete the task early, or they run late. You should continuously redeploy those developers who finish early to help those who are running behind. Figure 7.8 shows this process of continuous redeployment.

7.2.6 Accelerating a Late Project by Adding Developers

The sprint plan in Fig. 7.5 is an example from one of the PA test projects—a virtual reality/augmented reality (VR/AR) mobile game project called TikiMan Go. At the time of this writing, we're in the middle of trying to accelerate the development of our augmented reality "battle scene" by adding more programmers. Despite Brooks'

---

[4]This philosophy paid off in December 1944 when the German army staged a huge attack from the Ardennes and surrounded Bastogne. Patton's Third Army was the only one agile enough to react as he famously "attacked with three divisions in 48 hours."

Accelerate Late Project

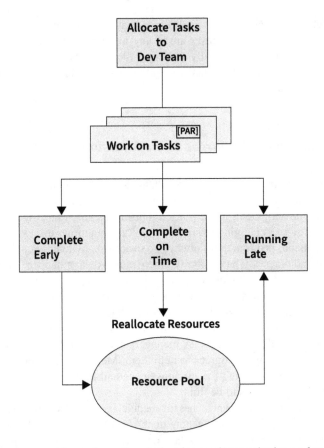

Fig. 7.8 Resources must be continuously redeployed to accelerate tasks that run late

Law claiming this is an impossibility, our experimental evidence is that it happens on a regular basis.

One way to explain this ability to accelerate schedule by adding developers is that projects are not monolithic. PA decomposes projects into use cases and allocates development staff on a per-use-case basis, splitting up complex use cases into their tasks as needed and attacking various tasks in parallel. Some use cases get done early and some run late. You can deploy additional resources to speed up the ones that are running late.

Thanks to Neil Siegel for pointing out that there are a couple of important and nontrivial preconditions that have to occur in order for this approach to be successful. One is that tasks have to be isolated from design dependencies as much as possible (i.e., you need a good architecture and a careful design), and the other is that the developers assigned to help the late developers need to have enough knowledge to be useful (i.e., assigning a Python programmer to a JavaScript task may not work out well).

When these preconditions are met, our experience has been that acceleration by adding developers can certainly be successful. In fact, as noted in the chapter introduction, Doug's first experience with managing parallelism (more than 30 years ago) happened because of the need to accelerate a late project.

7.3 Improving Quality While Going Faster

By now we hope you're thinking, "OK, I can see how leveraging parallelism and doing a little bit more planning helps to get the coding done faster." But you might be wondering if the speed improvement comes at the cost of decreased quality.

In a word: *no*. PA includes a number of techniques for improving the quality of the software that you're developing. The big three wins from a quality standpoint are achieved by

* Generating code for the database and API (aka executable architecture)
* Generating acceptance test scripts for each use case
* Removing the continual time pressure brought by timeboxed sprints, giving your team enough time to do a quality job

7.3.1 Generating Database Access Code

Slice it any way you like, at the end of the day, writing code by hand is an error-prone activity compared to what a good code generator can produce. Not all code is amenable to generation, but the code that handles basic database access is, and so is the code to wrap those database access functions in a REST API. These parts of the code tend to be boring, repetitive, and tedious, so it makes sense to automate them. From a quality standpoint, generating the data access layer of your code removes a lot of opportunity for bugs to creep into the system.

Of course, if you skip the UML model, you have nothing from which to generate code. Presuming you don't skip the UML model, you can use your use case narratives and your requirement definitions to help generate acceptance tests.

7.3.2 Generating Acceptance Tests from Use Cases

There are many aspects to testing software, but two of the most important are comprehensive test coverage of all sunny/rainy-day paths through a use case and comprehensive testing against all requirements. These two important forms of testing

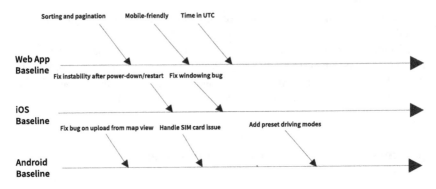

Fig. 7.9   Each baseline must be acceptance tested after every merge of a new capability

are often not even attempted on many Agile projects because nobody writes comprehensive lists of requirements and nobody writes behavior (use case) specifications that list all of the corner cases. You'll find that adding these layers of testing to your QA strategy will decrease your defect rate significantly, because it's always the "Whoops, I forgot that requirement or corner case" bugs that bite the hardest on software projects.

As you saw in Chap. 6, PA adds the missing use case and requirements models back into an Agile project management framework, and then uses automation to leverage both of these models by generating a set of requirement tests and a set of use case path coverage test scripts from the models.

7.3.3   Testing in Parallel with Developing

Another tactic that PA shares with its relative, the Incremental Commitment Spiral Model (ICSM), is to have a test team working concurrently with the developers. It's never too soon to start removing bugs from your software and developers love getting quick feedback on their code. PA's approach is to have the test team start testing against corner cases and rainy-day scenarios as soon as the code is written, and get this feedback to the developers immediately so that each use case can be bullet-proofed as development proceeds.

When you have many parallel threads being developed, it's important to maintain working baselines and to do some integration testing after each new capability is merged into the baseline. Figure 7.9 shows eight new capabilities being merged into three CarmaCam baselines. We did these merges (and a bunch of others) successfully over a period of 2–3 weeks while we wrote this chapter.

Note that the acceptance testing doesn't wait until the end of the sprint; it should happen after each merge into the baseline. It's a good idea to have your most experienced developers (who are usually the most thorough testers) managing the baselines, as a lot of bugs can be intercepted at this stage when the merge is being accomplished. After this first level of testing, it's a great idea to have your test team jump on the testing of each baseline right after the merge occurs.

7.3.4 Hurry, but Don't Rush

Short, timeboxed sprints are a key Agile tactic to achieve high project velocity. But timeboxing comes at a cost. Quality suffers when developers feel rushed. It's a pretty simple equation: relax the time pressure, improve quality.

Doug recently talked to Barry's Computer Science 510 students about timeboxing, and the conversation went something like this:

Doug: So let's talk about timeboxing. Have any of you ever stayed up until 3:00 am working on a programming assignment? Of course you have, you're grad students.

Class: *Smiles and nods*

Doug: In general, do you think those assignments where you're under massive time pressure result in your highest quality work?

Class: *Heads shake "no" and more smiles*

Doug: Well, when you graduate and get into industry, you're going to find that you're working in an Agile shop with timeboxed sprints and you're going to be under time pressure all the time, by design. Now let me ask you another question. When you're up at 3:00 am trying to finish by the deadline, what's the first thing you skip? Is it unit tests?

Class: *Bigger smiles and nods*

Doug: How about corner cases and edge cases? Do you skip those, too?

Class: *Smiles turn to grins, more nods*

Doug: So you're going to graduate, go out into industry, and work on projects where the primary mechanism for software quality is comprehensive unit testing and where your success is defined by your project velocity, and timeboxes are going to be used to make sure your velocity is high. As a result, you're going to skip a lot of unit testing, and you won't have time to design for all the rainy-day scenarios.

Class: *Some head scratching along with the nods*

To sum up PA's "fewer defects" strategy: generate code instead of writing it manually where you can, test against rainy-day scenarios, and give your team enough time to do a quality job.

7.4   Lowering Development Cost

Can PA's project management tactics lower your development cost? We think so, and we'll outline our reasoning in this section.

7.4.1   Doing "Just Enough" Design Reduces Costs

You're going to save money by spending less of your development budget building repetitive, tedious code, by having the database and API be generally bug-free, by getting feedback from working software early in the process, by reducing the need to refactor code, by more cost effective acceptance testing, and by getting your project to market faster.

- *Code generation saves money.* Generating code is not only faster than writing code, it's also cheaper. A lot cheaper. Consider a use case that we've decomposed into models, views, and controllers, and let's make an oversimplified assumption that the work is divided one-third each across M, V, and C. If you generate the database and API from the domain model, you've just reduced your cost by about one-third. Given that the automatically generated code is pretty reliable, there's no need to unit test the generated code, nor will you spend much time chasing bugs in the persistence layer of your software.
- *Prototyping gets you early feedback.* Prototyping during the proof of concept phase gets you all of the feedback-driven advantages of learning from working code, but since you're not going to put the prototype into production, you don't need to unit test your prototype code either.
- *Design reduces refactoring.* Since all of your use cases are carefully designed, you're going to need a lot less refactoring than you might if you had skipped the design part trying to fit into your short timebox. Design by refactoring is actually an insanely expensive way to develop software.
- *Acceptance testing reduces hotfixes.* Since all of your code will be acceptance tested against a fairly complete set of corner cases and exceptions, you're going to ship cleaner, less buggy software to your customers, so you'll have fewer hot-fixes disrupting your progress. Hotfixes are incredibly expensive because your most experienced people are inevitably going to be pulled off their current tasks to deal with screaming customers.
- *Shortening schedules increases profits.* The quicker you get your project done, the more cost effective it is. Presuming that the software you're building is some-how related to your business making money, you'll start making that money sooner if you get done faster. How does this fit with the Agile approach of deliv-ering "product value" rather than thinking about projects and schedules? Simple - we deliver product value one project at a time, on very short schedules.

7.4.2 Combining Planning with Feedback

Many Agile practitioners are likely rolling their eyes at this discussion of planning, and especially UML-based planning. That's because they (and their fellow adherents of the Agile Manifesto) deeply believe that software development should be a feedback-driven process, with real code put into the hands of real users at the earliest possible moment.

PA recognizes the value of feedback in software engineering, and that's why our first activity after generating the database and API is a prototyping phase where we attack the problem to be solved by actually starting to build the system (with each developer prototyping his or her own use case, working in parallel). Only after we've gained feedback from prototyping do we step back and carefully model the system. So, in an Alice In Wonderland like twist, it's "code first, design afterwards".

Generally speaking, the prototyping goes quickly because you can focus on building only the sunny-day part of each use case, and because you're free to skip unit testing of prototype code. When you do start modeling the use cases, it's generally with an eye toward anticipating the rainy-day scenarios, edge cases, corner cases, and exceptions. Since each developer is modeling only a single use case (and all the developers are working in parallel), the modeling goes rapidly, too.

After the modeling is done and the code is written (which generally goes quickly because each developer is starting from a working prototype and an MVC decomposition of his or her use case that comprehensively covers both sunny- and rainy-day scenarios), you leverage automation in the form of acceptance test script generation. Testing goes pretty quickly, too.

7.5 Summary

Since massively parallel software development is a bit different from "normal" Agile software development, we covered a lot of unexplored territory in a chapter on managing parallel projects:

- Lessons about parallelism from electrical and systems engineering
- Lessons learned from successful parallel thinkers, including instant tactical assessment, rapid and adaptive planning, seizing the initiative, and redeploying resources as the situation evolves
- Sprint planning
- Estimation from tasks and use cases
- Accelerating late projects by adding developers
- Improving quality while going faster
- Relaxing time pressure to improve quality
- Improving quality via code generation and test case generation
- Acceptance testing in parallel with development
- Balancing feedback and planning

In the next chapter, Barry shares some wisdom gained from managing many successful very large (on the order of a million lines of code) software projects using parallel development. Barry's ICSM process was derived from this experience.

References

Alekhine, A. 2013. *My best games of chess, 1908–1937, 21st century edition*. Milford: Russell Enterprises, Inc.

Amazon. n.d.. What is Amazon EC2 auto scaling? https://docs.aws.amazon.com/autoscaling/ec2/userguide/what-is-amazon-ec2-auto-scaling.html. Accessed 18 July 2019.

Chessgames.com. 2017. Alexander Alekhine vs Jose Raul Capablanca. http://www.chessgames.com/perl/chessgame?gid=1012518. Accessed 18 July 2019.

LearningChess. 2015. Chess curiosities – Blindfold simultaneous game records by Alekhine. https://learningchess.net/blog/?p=783. Accessed 18 July 2019.

Matthewedwards. 2012. Battle of the Bulge map. https://commons.wikimedia.org/wiki/File:Wacht_am_Rhein_map_(Opaque).svg. Used under CC BY-SA 3.0 license. Accessed 18 July 2019.

Patton, G. 1975. *War as I knew it: The battle memoirs of "blood 'N guts"*. New York: Bantam.

Wikipedia. 2019. Multi-core processor. https://en.wikipedia.org/wiki/Multi-core_processor. Accessed 18 July 2019.

Chapter 8
Large-Scale Parallel Development

Box 8.1

Doug introduces the topic and explains why Barry is uniquely qualified to write this chapter.

Scalability is an interesting and important topic with multiple dimensions. You can consider the number of transactions, size of the database, number of developers employed, number of lines of code written, and multiple other factors.

During 2015 when we were developing our second Parallel Agile test project and Bo Wang was just beginning his PhD research on executable domain models, I was working on a big satellite TV project. One of my responsibilities was as requirements lead for a service that handled all communication between the set-top box and "head end" (broadcast center). This service had to handle over 100 million transactions per day. Another project I was involved in was a complete rework of the set-top box user interface; this project was being staffed by several dozen developers. Both projects were implemented with NoSQL databases and REST APIs, which made me believe that we were targeting a very scalable set of technologies for code generation.

On the user interface project, I was invited by the scrum master to help disambiguate some whiteboard sketches drawn during planning meetings that seemed to have no semantic integrity whatsoever. After a bit of head scratching, I asked him if he was actually trying to diagram out the sprint plans for the project using user stories, epics, and tasks. When it turned out that was exactly what he was trying to do, I found a UML profile that allowed us to diagram these out clearly and provided a basis for project estimation, as they needed to hire a significant number of new developers to complete the work.

The inspiration to start the CarmaCam project happened during my commute to this consulting assignment, and when we got that project started, I used the visual model sprint plans to organize our student work for 75 developers with great success. We used the code generator for the first time, with even greater success.

© Springer Nature Switzerland AG 2020
D. Rosenberg et al., *Parallel Agile – faster delivery, fewer defects, lower cost*,
https://doi.org/10.1007/978-3-030-30701-1_8

Hitting the rewind button on my career almost 40 years, I graduated college around 1980 and went to work at a company called TRW (now part of Northrup Grumman) as a programmer. My work involved computer-aided design for integrated circuits (VLSI CAD) at a time when the semiconductor industry was moving from around 100,000 transistors on a chip to millions. I was exposed to issues of scaling software very early in my career.

While I was working as a junior programmer at TRW I was vaguely aware that the company, which was doing some enormous software systems including satellite communications and many defense projects that nobody could talk about had a chief scientist named Barry Boehm who had pioneered the science of software cost estimation.

What I was completely unaware of until we started work on this book was that Barry's team, led by people including Walker Royce and Neil Seigel, had done some pioneering work on large scale (large scale as in multimillion lines of code) parallel software development. Over the intervening decades, this work has largely gone unnoticed, but the lessons learned went into Barry's work on the Incremental Commitment Spiral Model (ICSM). And we're all fortunate that Barry's going to tell you about those lessons learned in this chapter.

Some forms of Agile development have scaled well, some have not. Early failures include the Chrysler Comprehensive Compensation (C3) project, which started out well, but failed later when the initial Agile gurus left the project, along with the on-site customer representative, who had a strong understanding of the customer organization and of the software, and over full-time dedication to the project. The customer rep turned out to be a single point of project failure when she wore out from overwork and was replaced by a Chrysler employee who was competent but far less knowledgeable and energetic (Stephens and Rosenberg 2003).

Another Agile scalability failure was the Thought Works ATLAS lease management project, which started out well using eXtreme Programming (XP) but found that when the project reached 50 people and 500,000 lines of code, XP practices such as daily standup meetings, shared tacit knowledge of the code, two-week system sprints, and lack of a project architecture, or Big Design Up Front (BDUF), were leading to project failure (Elssamadisy and Schalliol 2002).

You might think that the four diverse software projects we piloted PA on would have had similar problems with a part-time project-set manager and up to 47 part-time University of Southern California (USC) students working in parallel. However, the projects satisfied a set of critical success factors (CSFs), mainly due to Doug

Rosenberg's CSF skills and experience in interactive system development and project management, and partly due to the similarities between the Parallel Agile (PA) CSFs and the CSFs in the Incremental Commitment Spiral Model (ICSM), which many of the student developers were familiar with, as the ICSM book (Boehm et al. 2014) was the textbook for USC's two primary software engineering courses.

In this chapter, you'll first learn how the ICSM CSFs were primarily derived from a set of successful large interactive TRW command and control software projects, which also satisfied and extended the CSFs to address forms of PA for very large systems. You'll then look at couple of examples. The first example is the three-version, million-line Command Center Processing and Display System–Replacement (CCPDS-R) project. The second example is a series of even larger TRW command and control–type projects that extended the set of CSFs and delivered highly successful results.

Later in the chapter, we compare the PA approach and CSFs with other successful scalable Agile approaches, such as the speed, data, and ecosystems (SDE) approach (Bosch 2017) and the Scaled Agile Framework (SAFe; Leffingwell 2017).

8.1 Parallel Agile and the Incremental Commitment Spiral Model

The Incremental Commitment Spiral Model (ICSM) is a principles-based process framework or meta-model that supports the definition of life-cycle processes based on the characteristics, constraints, and risks associated with a given project or program. PA is one of those life-cycle processes—in other words, you can think of PA as an ICSM process instance.

ICSM is both technology- and stakeholder-aware, and you can use it to handle projects of all sizes. ICSM is incremental and concurrent in nature, has specific approaches for establishing stakeholders' commitment for those increments before moving forward, and is dependent on evidence- and risk-based decisions.

ICSM is based on four underlying principles:

- Stakeholder value-based guidance
- Incremental commitment and accountability
- Concurrent multidisciplinary engineering
- Evidence- and risk-based decisions

PA is fully compliant with these principles. In particular, PA's proof of concept phase employs extensive prototyping that enables stakeholder guidance and evidence-based decision-making while minimizing risk. In PA, you make every effort to maximize the use of concurrency, in particular with respect to coding, testing, and design of use cases.

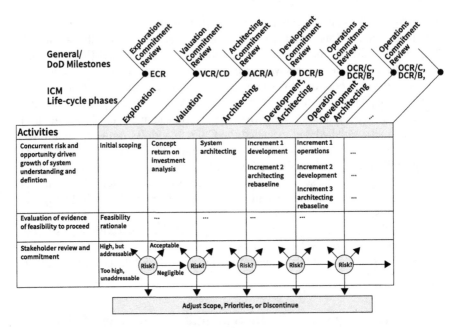

Fig. 8.1 ICSM life-cycle phases

8.1.1   ICSM Phases Map to Proof of Concept, Minimum Viable Product, and Optimization

Figure 8.1 shows the ICSM life-cycle phases of exploration, valuation, architecting, development, and operation in linear format, with risk assessment "gateways" after each phase.

PA projects follow this sequence with a somewhat simplified terminology of proof of concept (essentially ICSM exploration and valuation), minimum viable product or MVP (ICSM development), and optimization (ICSM operation).

8.1.2   ICSM Spiral Includes Prototyping, Design, and Acceptance Testing

Figure 8.2 shows the ICSM phases wrapped into a spiral, with activities during each trip around the spiral (starting from the inside) including prototyping, design, and acceptance testing. PA focuses on these activities.

PA simplifies the ICSM spiral, as shown in Fig. 8.3. Larger projects will benefit from the detailed breakdown described in ICSM.

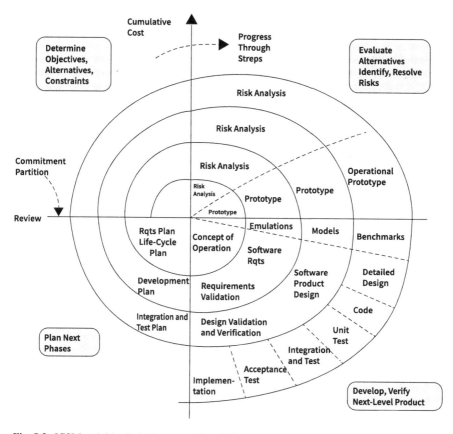

Fig. 8.2 ICSM activities include prototyping, design, and acceptance testing

Fig. 8.3 Parallel Agile follows ICSM principles with simplified terminology

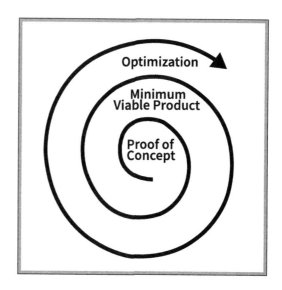

8.1.3 ICSM Principles Were Developed on Very Large Projects

A well-documented, successful government-acquisition project using the ICSM principles was the CCPDS-R project (Royce 1998). Its U.S. Air Force customer and contractor reinterpreted the traditional defense regulations, specifications, and standards. It held a preliminary design review, but it was not a PowerPoint show at month 4. Instead, it had a fully validated architecture and demonstration of the working high-risk user interface and networking capabilities at month 14. The resulting system delivery, including more than 1 million lines of software source code, exceeded customer expectations and was delivered within budget and schedule.

8.2 Parallel Agile Critical Success Factors

The critical success factors for PA modify and extend the ICSM three-team approach shown in Fig. 8.4, resulting in Fig. 8.5.

The main difference in the two approaches is that the 2014 ICSM three-team approach is organized around incremental development, while PA is organized to support either incremental or continuous development and deployment.

The upper Architecture and Capabilities Evolution team determines the following:

- Win conditions of a system's primary success-critical stakeholders (clients, end users, safety/security regulators, maintainers, investors, etc.)
- The choices of system infrastructure, commercial services, and technology options, likely directions of future growth, and needed developer skills

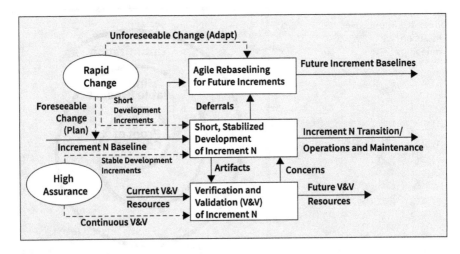

Fig. 8.4 ICSM 2014 three-team approach

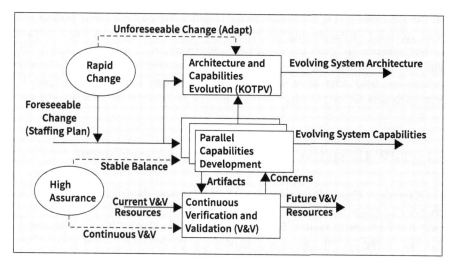

Fig. 8.5 Parallel Agile three-team approach

- The development of prototypes such as with geofencing alternatives for the Location-Based Advertising project or voice vs. button-pressing for CarmaCam (evaluated by the Continuous Verification and Validation [V&V] team)
- Overall responsibilities of the Keeper of the Project Vision (KOTPV) success-critical function identified in the study of 19 large project practices and outcomes (Curtis et al. 1988)

Across the system life cycle, the Architecture and Capabilities Evolution team provides the continuing KOTPV activity.

Many KOTPV functions require more than one person, often a combination of a domain expert and a technology expert. In some domains, a single person can provide such a combination, but it is rare to find an individual who can perform the KOTPV function across several domains, as Doug Rosenberg does in the earlier chapters. For the large-scale TRW projects described in the next two sections, the KOTPV function is provided by a team of experts, although there will generally be a team leader, such as Walker Royce for CCPDS-R and Neil Siegel for the series of large command-control systems.

The central Parallel Capabilities Development team generally develops the desired capabilities in a series of increments determined by the stakeholders, while providing updates to earlier increments as needed. The team's CSFs include the skills and facilities needed to accomplish the work, plus negotiation with the Architecture and Capabilities Evolution team on the priorities of evolving desired system capabilities vs. availability of developers with the required skills.

The Continuous Verification and Validation (V&V) team does not wait for some code to be tested. It starts at the beginning of the project getting ready to support the ICSM principle and PA CSF "evidence and risk-based decisions" by evaluating the feasibility of the initial decisions of the first two teams, such as the prototypes to use off-the-shelf geofencing algorithms in the Location-Based Advertising project and voice reporting of bad driving in CarmaCam. As shortfalls in feasibility evidence are uncertainties and probabilities of loss, and risk exposure is calculated as (probability of loss) × (impact of loss), such evaluations enable the first two teams to explore less risky alternative solutions. The Continuous V&V team continues to prepare for and perform testing and evaluation of the first two teams' later artifacts.

8.3   TRW-USAF/ESC CCPDS-R Parallel Development

The Command Center Processing and Display System Replacement (CCPDS-R) project's goal was to reengineer the command center aspects of the United States early missile warning system. It covered not only the software but also the associated system engineering and computing hardware procurement. The software effort involved over 1 million lines of Ada code, across a family of three related user capabilities. The developer was TRW; the customer was the U.S. Air Force Electronic Systems Center (ESC); and the users were the U.S. Space Command, the U.S. Strategic Command, the U.S. National Command Authority, and all nuclear-capable Commanders in Chief. The core capability of 355,000 lines of Ada code was developed on a 48-month fixed-price contract between 1987 and 1991. While this was admittedly a long while ago in software time, the project closely mirrors current systems being developed in government and the private sector, and so is relevant as an example.

> **Note 8.1**
> You can find a more detailed description of the CCPDS-R project in Appendix D of the book *Software Project Management* (Royce 1998).

The project had numerous high-risk elements. One was the extremely high dependability requirements for a system of this nature. Others were the ability to reengineer the sensor interfaces, the commander situation assessment and decision-aid displays, and the critical algorithms in the application. Software infrastructure challenges included distributed processing using Ada tasking (a major problem with previous Ada projects was the proliferation of software control threads caused by unrestricted use of Ada tasking) and the ability to satisfy critical-decision-window performance requirements. Many of these aspects underwent considerable change during the development process. The project involved 5 administration and 77 software personnel, most of whom had training in Ada programming but had not applied it to real projects.

CCPDS-R used standard Department of Defense (DoD) acquisition procedures, including a fixed-price contract and the documentation-intensive DoD-STD-2167A software development standards. However, by creatively reinterpreting the DoD standards, processes, and contracting mechanisms, USAF/ESC and TRW were able to perform with agility, deliver on budget and on schedule, fully satisfy their users, and receive Air Force awards for outstanding performance.

8.3.1 CCPDS-R Evidence-Based Decision Milestones

The DoD acquisition standards were acknowledged, but their milestone content was redefined to reflect the stakeholders' success conditions. The usual DoD-STD-2167A Preliminary Design Review (PDR) to review paper documents and briefing charts around month 6 was replaced by a PDR at month 14 that demonstrated working software for all the high-risk areas, particularly the network operating system, the message-passing middleware for handling concurrency, and the graphical user interface (GUI) software. The PDR also reviewed the completeness, consistency, and traceability of all of the Ada applications software interface specifications, as verified by the Rational Ada compiler and R-1000 toolset. The team completed a great deal of system integration before the software was developed, and verified that the individual Ada application functions could be developed by sequential-Ada programmers.

TRW invested significant resources into a package of message-passing middleware that handled the Ada tasking and concurrency management, and provided message ports to accommodate the insertion of sequential Ada packages for the various CCPDS-R application capabilities. For pre-PDR performance validation, simulators of these functions could be inserted and executed to determine system performance and real-time characteristics. Thus, not only software interfaces, but also system performance could be validated prior to code development, and stubs could be written to provide representative module inputs and outputs for unit and integration testing. Simulators of external sensors and communications inputs and outputs were developed in advance to support continuous testing. This created an executable architecture skeleton, within which hardware and software component simulators could be replaced by completed components for performance and interoperability assurance (more recently called a Digital Twin). Also, automated document generators were developed to satisfy the contractual needs for documentation.

Evidence of achievable software productivity was provided via a well-calibrated cost and schedule estimation model, in this case an Ada version of the Constructive Cost Model (Ada COCOMO), which was available for CCPDS-R. Developers, customers, and users could use Ada COCOMO to better understand how much functional capability could be developed within an available budget and schedule, given the personnel, tools, processes, and infrastructure available to the project. Another major advantage of the Ada COCOMO cost/performance tradeoff analyses was to determine and enable the savings achieved via reuse across the three different installations and user communities.

Since the CCPDS-R plans and specifications were machine processable, the project was able to track progress and change at a very detailed level. This enabled

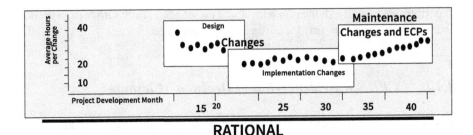

Fig. 8.6 Cost of changes vs. time: CCPDS-R

the developers to anticipate potential downstream problems and largely handle them via customer collaboration and early fixes, rather than delayed problem discovery and expensive technical contract-negotiation fixes. Figure 8.6 shows one such metrics-tracking result: the cost of making CCPDS-R changes as a function of time.

For CCPDS-R, the message-passing middleware and modular applications design enabled the project to be highly agile in responding to change, as reflected in the low growth in cost of change shown in Fig. 8.6. Further, the project's advance work in determining and planning to accommodate the commonalities and variabilities across the three user communities and installations enabled significant savings in software reuse across the three related CCPDS-R system versions.

8.3.2 CCPDS-R Parallel Development

The 48-month CCPDS-R core capability schedule included 20 technical personnel and 14 months of system definition and user prototyping (13 people), infrastructure definition and initial development (4 people), and initial testing and full-scale test planning (3 people). After a successful PDR, the full-scale core capability development included 77 technical personnel and 34 months of extending and evolving the infrastructure (11 people), with parallel sequential-Ada programmers developing and evolving the system capabilities (47 people), and continuous V&V, test preparation and testing (23 people). It also included the full team adapting to organizational and mission changes during development.

8.4 Parallel Development of Even Larger TRW Defense Software Systems

Dr. Neil Siegel spent several years as the designated "project fix-it person" at TRW, during which time he actually did "fix" several big DoD software programs. During this hands-on experience, he developed a theory of the root cause of the problems that affected these particular programs, and worked with some smart people to develop a reusable design pattern and methodology based on that theory. Over the next 20 years, as an executive at TRW (and at Northrop Grumman, after Northrop acquired TRW in 2002), he had the opportunity to implement this approach on a dozen or so major software-intensive development programs. All finished on time and on budget, and all are liked by their users. Many are still in operational use 25 years later, and have proven to be not only good products, but also highly maintainable and adaptable.

Siegel's theory postulated that large software system overages in time and money, low-achieved system reliability, and expensive yet ineffectual attempts at implementing fixes are due to the degree of entanglement between the product's software control structure and its functional mission capabilities. (Note that the CCPDS-R project team in the previous section was aware of previous projects' difficulties with mixing functional software and control software, particularly Ada tasking, and created an architecture and control software that kept them separate.) Siegel extended this idea by creating a general architecture (design pattern) for separating these concerns, creating an accompanying methodology for partitioning work based on this design pattern, and also had a team create a more generalized version of the system architecture skeleton, which could be applied to a wider variety of applications, including weapon systems, sensors, and information systems, as well as command and control systems. He also developed a set of quantifiable design criteria, such as the need to specify every independently schedulable software entity within the system.

In his PhD research, Siegel used data from several real DoD software-development programs retrospectively to establish a controlled observational case study, comparing programs that were implemented using his design pattern and methodology with those that did not. He also had data from programs that started without his design-based technique and then switched to it mid-course, and even data from one program that started with the technique (and used it to successfully deliver an initial capability), then did a next capability without the technique (and had problems), and then re-adopted the technique for third and subsequent deliveries.

Figure 8.7 shows the result of the analysis of the monthly defect report density for three projects each that did or did not use the technique. It is clear that the design-based technique resulted in far fewer defects, which in turn allowed the projects to stay on schedule (and therefore, on budget), while projects not using the technique did not. The Force XXI Battle Command, Brigade and Below (FBCB2) project used the technique in period I, did not use it in period II, and returned to its use in period III. As with CCPDS-R, the design-based technique had an infrastructure team and a functional capabilities team operating in parallel.

Figures 8.8 and 8.9 provide additional detailed perspectives of FBCB2's monthly mean time between failures and cost performance (e.g., overruns and underruns) for the periods using and not using the design-based technique.

Clearly, the FBCB2 results were markedly better when the infrastructure team and the functional capabilities team were operating in parallel.

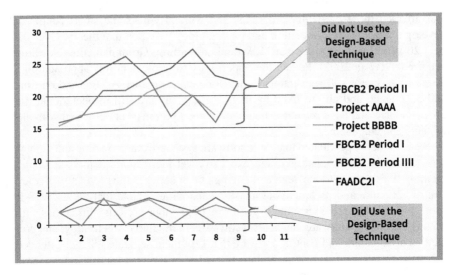

Fig. 8.7 Monthly defect report density of projects using and not using the design-based technique

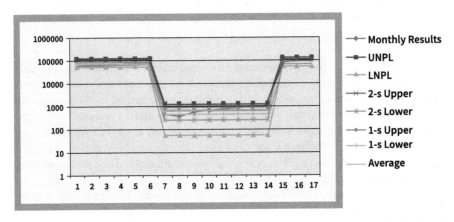

Fig. 8.8 Monthly FBCB2 mean time between failures in hours with and without the design-based technique

8.5 Comparing the Parallel Agile Approach and CSFs and Other Successful Scalable Agile Approaches

PA isn't the first attempt to make Agile development scale better. In this section, we'll compare it to some other approaches.

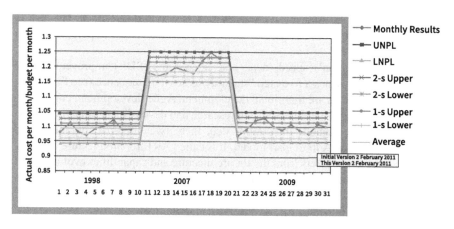

Fig. 8.9 Monthly FBCB2 actual vs. budgeted cost with and without the design-based technique

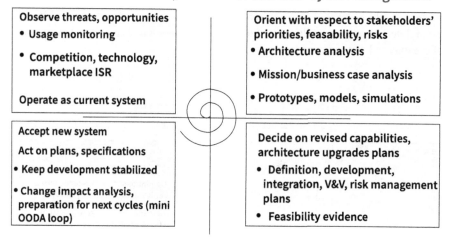

Fig. 8.10 Observe–orient–decide–act loop

8.5.1   The Speed, Data, and Ecosystems Approach

In today's and tomorrow's fast-moving and competitive world, a key concept is John Boyd's OODA loop (Bosch 2017), for observe–orient–decide–act, shown in Fig. 8.10.

If your OODA loop is slower than your competitor's, you are going to lose business. Over 50 percent of the Fortune 500 companies from the year 2000 are now gone. Software is increasingly critical to this need for speed, not only in information-based companies like Amazon with a new release every 11 seconds, but also in industries like automobiles, where software provides over 80 percent of the functionality.

For an organization's speed, data, and ecosystems (SDE) improvement, the Bosch approach provides a five-step "stairway to heaven" sequence (see Fig. 8.11).

For speed, the steps are traditional development, Agile development, continuous integration, continuous deployment, and research and development as an innovation system. For the continuous integration step, there is a three-part organizational model similar to the PA three-part model. It is called ART, for architecture, requirements, and testing. It differs from the PA architecture and capabilities evolution part by preceding requirements by architecture. Testing is about the same for both, although PA includes V&V of the architecture and capabilities.

For data, which is critical for the observe and orient parts of the OODA loop, the five steps are ad-hoc, collection, automation, data innovation, and evidence-based organization. Evidence-based organization is similar to the PA and ICSM principle of evidence and risk-based decisions, while the stairway is stronger in data collection for improvement experiments.

For ecosystems, the five steps are internally focused, ad-hoc ecosystem engagement, tactical ecosystem engagement, strategic single ecosystem engagement, and strategic multi-ecosystem engagement. PA does not have a counterpart, although the architecture and capabilities evolution part includes active search and evaluation of commercial services and products.

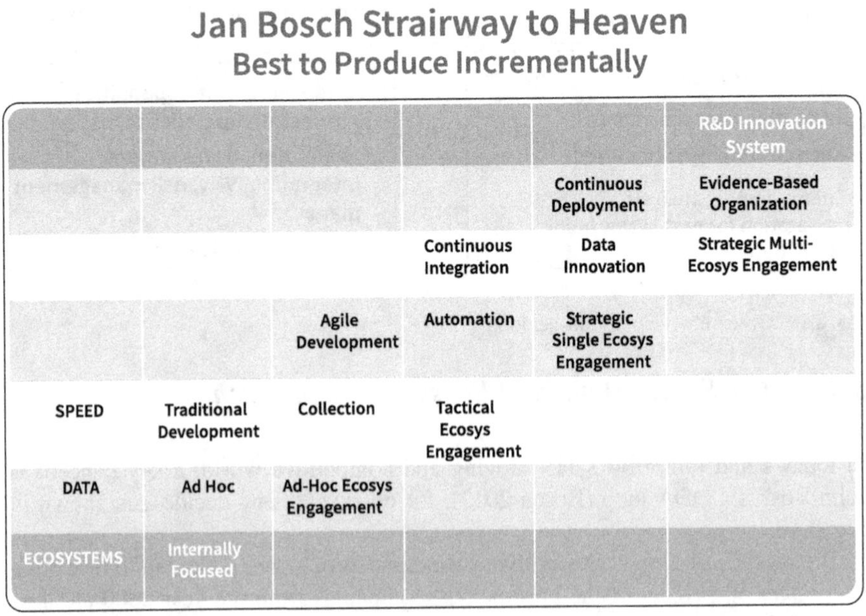

Jan Bosch Strairway to Heaven
Best to Produce Incrementally

					R&D Innovation System
				Continuous Deployment	Evidence-Based Organization
			Continuous Integration	Data Innovation	Strategic Multi-Ecosys Engagement
		Agile Development	Automation	Strategic Single Ecosys Engagement	
SPEED	Traditional Development	Collection	Tactical Ecosys Engagement		
DATA	Ad Hoc	Ad-Hoc Ecosys Engagement			
ECOSYSTEMS	Internally Focused				

Fig. 8.11 Step-by-step improvement

8.5.2 The Scaled Agile Framework (SAFe) Approach

For sizable products and services, the SAFe approach (Leffingwell 2017) has another ART construct, the Agile Release Train (ART). ARTs are long-lived, cross-functional teams of Agile teams. Typically, they are virtual organizations (50–125 people) that create a solution or capability. Types of Agile teams participating in an ART could include business, product management, hardware, software, quality, testing, compliance, security, or other domain-specific specialties. For scalability to very large systems, SAFe also has solution trains, which coordinate the work of several ARTs, and super trains, which coordinate the work of several system trains.

SAFe has nine fundamental principles:

1. Take an economic view
2. Apply systems thinking
3. Assume variability, preserve options
4. Build incrementally with fast, integrated learning cycles
5. Base milestones on objective evaluation of working systems
6. Visualize and limit work-in-progress, reduce batch sizes, and manage queue lengths
7. Apply cadence, synchronize with cross-domain planning
8. Unlock the intrinsic motivation of knowledge workers
9. Decentralize decision making

The SAFe principles are similar to the four ICSM principles. Stakeholder value-based guidance is partially addressed by "Take an economic view" and "Apply systems thinking." Incremental commitment and accountability are addressed by "Build incrementally." Concurrent multi-discipline engineering is addressed by the ART construct. Evidence and risk-based decisions are addressed by "Base milestones on objective evaluation." SAFe and PA also both use the Unified Modeling Language (UML) and the Systems Modeling Language (SysML) for software and systems modeling.

In addition, SAFe incorporates other lean/Agile methods. For example, the SAFe principle "Visualize and limit work-in-progress, reduce batch sizes, and manage queue lengths" basically adopts the Kanban approach (Anderson 2010).

8.6 Conclusions and Latest Parallel Agile Scalability Experience

One way to look at scaling up PA might be to view it as "speeding up the Incremental Commitment Model (ICSM)." Both address three-team approaches for developing and evolving a software product's architecting, developing, and V&Ving in parallel. ICSM has provided PA with a method for large-scale software development, while

PA has provided the 2014 version of ICSM with capabilities to support increasing demands for rapid, continuous system development and deployment.

Both PA and ICSM include a set of critical success factors (CSFs) in terms of three-team responsibilities: Architecture and Capabilities Evolution using a Keeper of the Project Vision (KOTPV); Parallel Capabilities Development; and Continuous Verification and Validation (V&V). We showed evidence of the scalability of PA and continuous ICSM through a set of very large TRW projects that used the CSFs to succeed in rapid and reliable development, including one project where once the CSFs were cut off, speed and reliability seriously fell and were only restored when the CSFs were restored.

Based on the CSFs, PA and ICSM are comparably scalable to the two main scalable Agile approaches: speed, data, and ecosystems (SDE) and the Scaled Agile Framework (SAFe).

8.7 Summary

Parallel Agile is descended from two highly scalable approaches to developing software: ICONIX Process and the Incremental Commitment Spiral Model (ICSM). PA is fully compatible with the four underlying ICSM principles.

In this chapter, we provided an introduction to ICSM and its roots in million-line-of-code systems developed using parallel development at TRW while Barry was Chief Scientist. We explained common critical success factors between PA and the TRW process (including the use of a test team working concurrently with the development team). Significantly, both PA and the TRW process leverage "executable architecture" to help enable parallelism.

Finally, we compared PA to other approaches to scaling Agile, including the Scaled Agile Framework (SAFe).

References

Anderson, D. 2010. *Kanban: Successful evolutionary change for your technology business.* Seattle: Blue Hole Press.

Boehm, B., J. Lane, S. Koolmanojwong, and R. Turner. 2014. *The incremental commitment spiral model: Principles and practices for successful systems and software.* Upper Saddle River: Pearson.

Bosch, J. 2017. *Speed, data, and ecosystems.* Boca Raton: CRC Press.

Curtis, B., H. Krasner, and N. Iscoe. 1988. A field study of the software design process for large systems. *Communications of the ACM* 31 (11): 1268–1287.

Elssamadisy, A., and Schalliol, G. 2002. Recognizing and responding to 'bad smells' in extreme programming. *ICSE*: 617–622.

Leffingwell, D. 2017. *SAFe reference guide.* Boston: Addison Wesley.

Royce, W. 1998. *Software project management.* Boston: Addison Wesley.

Stephens, M., and D. Rosenberg. 2003. *Extreme programming refactored: The case against XP.* Berkeley: Apress.

Chapter 9
Parallel Agile for Machine Learning

Box 9.1

Doug explains how the CarmaCam project evolved to incorporate machine learning.

On the CarmaCam project, we didn't go looking for machine learning, but (as with so many other applications) the need for it found us.

First, when we developed our emergency alert system, which directly transmits potential driving under the influence (DUI) and other emergency videos to nearby first responders in the field without an accompanying incident report, it became obvious that some form of real-time prescreening of videos was essential to prevent "spamming" of already overloaded law enforcement personnel. Machine learning could come to the rescue if we could develop the ability to detect potential DUIs from video based on characteristics such as a vehicle making multiple lane changes (weaving) and speeding.

Second, CarmaCam was conceived as a system including both crowd-sourced data capture and reviews, with unanimous approval by three independent (human) reviewers for each incident report being the quality assurance guarantee that we intended to offer. As we built the system and our release grew closer, the issue of where we would find enough human reviewers began to loom large. Once again, machine learning could come to the rescue, if we could figure out a way to check the characteristics of the video against the categorization provided when the report was filed. For example, if a report was filed as "red light violation" and the video did not include a traffic light, we could score that report as having a low probability of being correct. Our crowdsourced review process would then work against a prioritized database so that the human reviewers would waste less time watching videos that would ultimately be rejected.

© Springer Nature Switzerland AG 2020

D. Rosenberg et al., *Parallel Agile – faster delivery, fewer defects, lower cost,*

https://doi.org/10.1007/978-3-030-30701-1_9

In this chapter, we'll explore how we used Parallel Agile (PA) to do a machine learning proof of concept with 15 grad students over one semester and then began work on the minimum viable product (MVP) the following semester. This work remains ongoing (with a couple of patents pending) as we're writing the book.

9.1 Phase 1: Proof of Concept and Initial Sprint Plan

The need for Machine Learning on CarmaCam manifested itself in two major areas (screening Emergency Alerts and verifying Incident Reports) as shown in Fig. 9.1. In order for all of this to work, we needed to design a video-processing pipeline that gets activated any time a video is uploaded from the CarmaCam mobile app.

It turns out that machine learning was an appealing career path for computer science graduate students in 2018, so it was easy to find 15 master's degree students who had taken some courses in machine learning and wanted to gain some real-world experience. Without a clear advance picture of where the proof of concept would take us, we guessed at our initial allocations of developers to user stories, and those guesses turned out to hold up well.

Figure 9.2 shows the initial sprint plan for the proof of concept phase.

Following the standard Parallel Agile pattern, we spent the first phase of our project exploring technical alternatives, and then developing prototypes to assess risks. We quickly settled on OpenCV and TensorFlow as a promising set of tools and decided to prototype various video classifiers. This was a stroke of luck, because while we were researching the available tools, we found a small gold mine: the makers of self-driving cars had visited these problems before we arrived on the scene, and many of the TensorFlow models and training datasets were readily available. The CarmaCam machine learning team quickly began to collect these models, train them, and run them against CarmaCam videos.

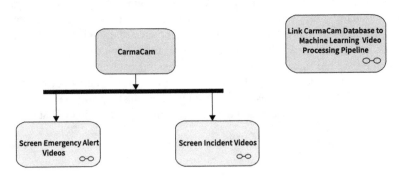

Fig. 9.1 CarmaCam uses machine learning for emergency videos and incident reports

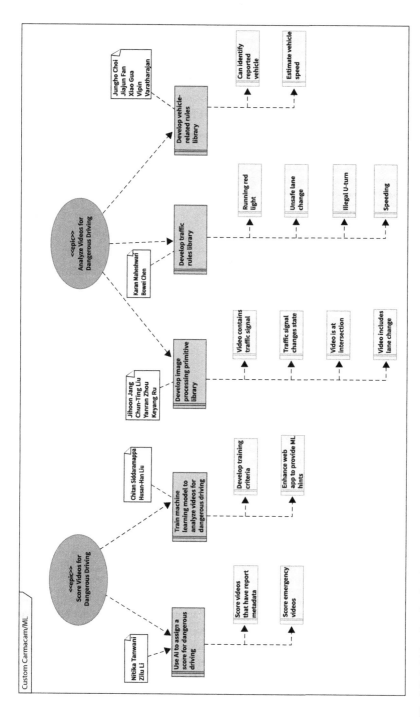

Fig. 9.2 Initial sprint plan for the machine learning proof of concept phase

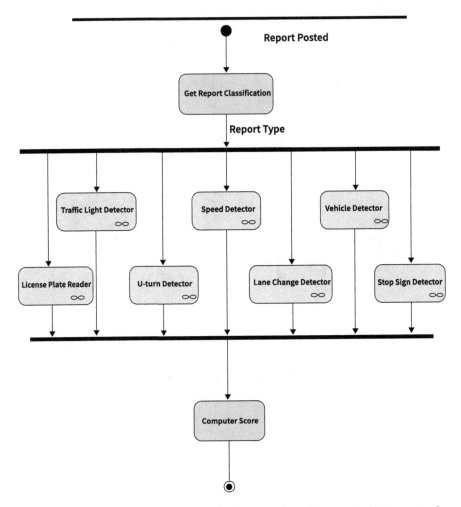

Fig. 9.3 CarmaCam's video processing pipeline compares videos to incident reports for accuracy

9.1.1 CarmaCam Incident Reports

Figure 9.3 shows the overall flow of evaluating an incident report to score videos with a probability that the report has been filed accurately. Based on the report classification, the video is routed through various pipeline stages that evaluate the video to see if it possesses the requisite characteristics. Each classifier attaches metadata to the report, and then a score is computed after all classifiers have been run against the video.

<table>
<tr><td>Vehicle Detection 1</td><td>Vehicle Detection 2</td></tr>
</table>

Vehicle Detection 1   **Vehicle Detection 2**

Fig. 9.4 Pretrained models for vehicle detection

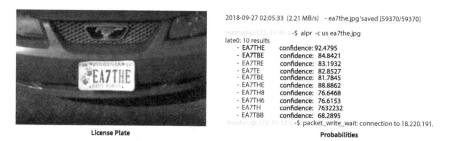

License Plate   **Probabilities**

Fig. 9.5 License plate readers help verify incident reports and eliminate errors when reports are filed

We prototyped multiple classifiers in parallel. Figures 9.4 and 9.5 show examples of classifiers under development for vehicle detection, as well as a license plate reader.

From a project management standpoint, we assigned one machine learning classifier per developer rather than assigning a traditional use case. Because classifiers are developed in parallel, like use cases, the whole process doesn't take much time.

Figures 9.6, 9.7, and 9.8 show classifiers under development for stop sign detection, traffic light detection, and U-turn detection.

We developed the entire set of incident classifiers in parallel with classifiers focused on identifying potential DUIs from emergency videos.

9.1.2   CarmaCam Emergency Alert Videos

Users upload emergency alerts in the CarmaCam app by tapping the Alert icon, and these videos are sent to a special alert connection in the CarmaCam database. We developed a separate Alert Receiver app (now officially named CarmaCam/LE) that

Fig. 9.6 Stop sign detector

Fig. 9.7 Traffic light detector

Fig. 9.8 U-turn detector

monitors the alert connection on a timer, performing a geospatial query that allows immediate viewing of emergency videos by nearby first responders in the field.

While users may capture many kinds of emergency videos, including hit-and-runs and fender-bender accidents, our initial focus on using machine learning for emergency videos has been to identify likely DUIs, with a goal of getting drunk and impaired drivers off the road in the shortest possible timeframe. Identifying potential drunk and impaired drivers generally involves looking for vehicles making multiple lane changes (i.e., the car is weaving, or wandering all over the road), with lane changes occurring at high speed being an even stronger indicator. Figure 9.9 shows the classification process.

9.1.3 Identifying Multiple Lane Changes at High Speed

Identifying a potential DUI from video proved to be a problem. We were starting to push the envelope with respect to off-the-shelf TensorFlow models that we could find, and we began researching techniques for classifying videos showing multiple lane changes (see Fig. 9.10).

In parallel with detecting lane boundaries, a small team of developers tried a few different approaches to using optical techniques to estimate the speed of another vehicle from a moving camera. Figure 9.11 shows one of those attempts.

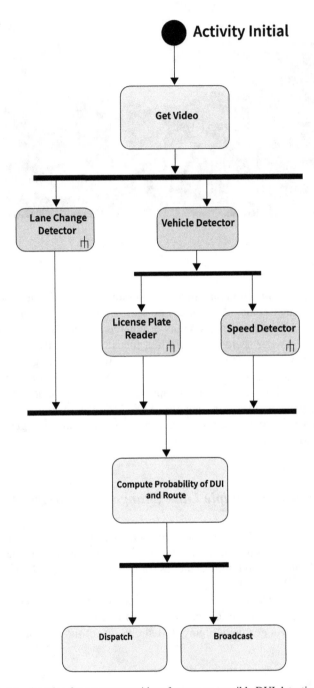

Fig. 9.9 Machine learning for emergency videos focuses on possible DUI detection

Lane Boundaries 1

Lane Boundaries 2

Fig. 9.10 Machine learning classifier to detect lane boundaries

9.1.4   Training Machine Learning Models from CarmaCam Videos

Early in the proof of concept phase, it became clear that because pretrained models that met our requirements were not always available, we would eventually need to develop some infrastructure to use the CarmaCam crowdsourced database to train TensorFlow models. We decided to start developing this capability in parallel with developing the classifiers and the video pipeline.

CarmaCam videos are typically between 10 and 20 seconds long, and a typical traffic incident lasts only a few seconds. Because machine learning video classifiers need to analyze each frame of video, we decided to start trimming the videos in the CarmaCam web app since using shorter videos would cut our compute time by about 90%.

Speed Detection 1

Speed Detection 2

Fig. 9.11 Estimating the speed of another vehicle from a moving camera is technically challenging

The process of training TensorFlow models involves annotating images by a human drawing a box around something (like a traffic light) and labelling it something like "traffic light." These annotations are then exported to an XML file and converted to a spreadsheet that is fed to the statistical analysis model. When you run 20,000 or 30,000 annotated images through the statistical model, it "learns" what to look for when you give it an image that's not annotated.

As discussed in Chap. 3, we generated the code for the database extensions from a whiteboard domain model sketch. We then assigned a developer to build the video trimming and annotation pages (see Fig. 9.12).

The CarmaCam crowdsourced database is potentially a rich source of training videos, so we decided to build an image annotation tool into the web app as well (see Fig. 9.13). This work remains ongoing.

With the database extensions and API code generated by CodeBot and deployed quickly (within a couple of hours), we were able to make significant headway on the front end of these use cases.

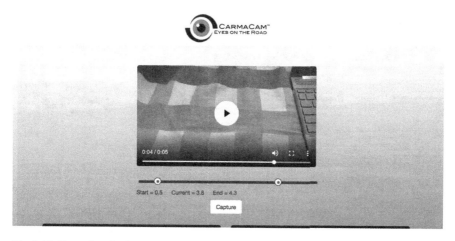

Fig. 9.12 Extending the CarmaCam web app to capture incident start and stop

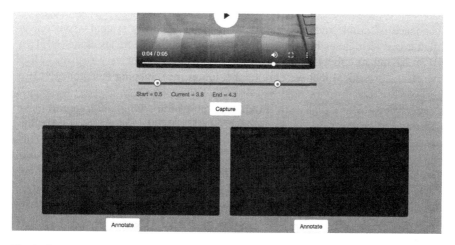

Fig. 9.13 Keyframes of videos will be annotated for training

9.1.5   Training Machine Learning Models Using Video Games

Machine learning models require extensive training—on the order of 20,000 training videos are required to get high-accuracy output from neural net models. Even with an automated video processing pipeline, it's a daunting amount of work to do this training using only CarmaCam videos.

For some cases, notably detection of a possible DUI from a video, this problem approaches showstopper status. While it's an unfortunate reality that there is an

Fig. 9.14 Exporting training videos from video games

abundance of drunk and impaired drivers on the highway system—someone is killed every 48 minutes by an impaired driver in the United States alone (NHTSA 2017), having to collect 20,000 possible DUI videos is not very realistic. More important, it's critical that we develop a solution for screening emergency videos more rapidly than this would allow.

This brings us to a real-world example of how prototyping and trying to make something work can help you to discover what's possible and what your requirements should be. Midway through the proof of concept phase, a student named Zilu, who had been working on the license plate reader, suggested that he thought it was possible to export training videos from a video game. The great thing about prototyping is there are no rules or restrictions holding you back—you're just building experimental code and you have total freedom to try new approaches. A few weeks after suggesting his idea, Zilu made it work, as shown in Fig. 9.14.

Parallel Agile as a development process includes a proof of concept/prototyping phase specifically to allow for flexibility in discovering what is possible and figuring out a good set of requirements.

9.1.6 Phase 1 Results and Summary

The machine learning team consisted of 15 students working in parallel, some of whom were novices and all of whom gained significant expertise in their respective areas. Table 9.1 shows a summary of the results.

Table 9.1 Summary of Initial Machine Learning Prototyping Efforts

Attempted during prototyping	Result achieved?
License plate recognition and integration	Deployed to web app
Traffic light detection	Yes
Vehicle detection	Yes
U-turn detection	Partial
Connection to CarmaCam database	Yes
Speed detection from videos	Yes
Lane changes	Partial
Identification of traffic light color	Yes
Video-processing pipeline	Partial

We broke down the original machine learning problem into subproblems and then, working in parallel, we built a TensorFlow model to address each of the specific subproblems. Specifically, we designed models to detect license plates, traffic lights, vehicles, and colors of traffic lights, as well as estimate speed.

In many of these cases, we found prebuilt models, largely due to the efforts of people working on self-driving cars, who have had to confront many of the same issues that we faced. We were unable to find pretrained models for U-turn detection and lane identification, so we began developing these models from scratch.

The team also established a connection to the CarmaCam database and started development of a video processing pipeline to automatically prescreen incident reports. We were able to test the pretrained models on CarmaCam videos. We also prototyped another solution for training machine learning classifiers using video games.

Our license plate reader has been successfully deployed to the CarmaCam web app, where it is now used to check the manually entered license plate number before a report is posted. We're incrementally upgrading the CarmaCam production system to take advantage of machine learning as opportunities arise, as shown in Fig. 9.15.

So what did we learn during our initial machine learning proof of concept? Here are a couple of takeaways:

- We were able to apply parallel development strategies. Both executable domain models and visual model sprint plans were useful for this purpose.
- We were able to identify some "easy stuff" (off-the-shelf pretrained TensorFlow classifiers) and some "hard stuff" (identifying possible DUIs from uncategorized videos by detecting multiple lane changes at high speed).

If we normalize to full-time equivalent staff, the total effort for the proof of concept phase comes in at around 7 developers working for 6 weeks, or roughly 45 person-weeks compressed into a month and a half.

Fig. 9.15 The CarmaCam Mobility app checks license plate numbers using machine learning

9.2   Phase 2: Minimum Viable Product – Detecting a Likely DUI from Video

At the time of this writing, we're in the middle of developing an MVP implementation for machine learning. Based on what we learned in the Proof of Concept, we decided to hammer away on the hard part: automatic detection of a possible DUI from video. This is not only the hard part, but also a critical traffic safety issue, as deaths and injuries caused by drunk and impaired drivers continue to rise at a rapid pace.

We've identified a vehicle making multiple lane changes as the key marker for a potential DUI. In other words: "As a highway patrol officer I want to know whenever there are cars near me weaving all over the road at high speed." Breaking this user story into its tasks involves the following:

- Detecting vehicles
- Detecting lane boundaries
- Tracking a vehicle across multiple frames in a video

Fig. 9.16 Vehicle detection

Fig. 9.17 Lane boundary and lane crossing detection

Figures 9.16, 9.17, and 9.18 show our progress to date. We are still performance-tuning detecting lane boundaries, and we need to perform more neural network training to improve accuracy.

Once these pieces are in place, we can build a model that automatically analyzes a video and scores it with a DUI probability. The speed estimator discussed earlier adds an additional degree of accuracy, for cases where a vehicle is executing multiple lane changes at high speed.

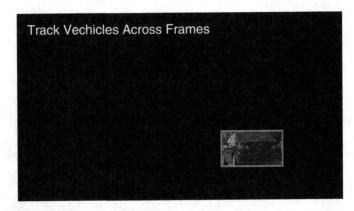

Fig. 9.18 Tracking a vehicle across multiple frames of a video

9.3   Summary

Machine learning is a different animal from mobile app development and web app development (there is no classic object-oriented design or UML). As such, it provides an interesting example of the flexibility of Parallel Agile's three-phase life-cycle process as a development strategy.

In this chapter, we covered how we applied the PA approach to developing neural networks to analyze CarmaCam videos. The chapter covered the proof of concept phase (one semester's worth of work) by a team of about 15 students working in parallel. This work is still ongoing, focusing on a minimum viable product as we're finishing up the book, with multiple patents pending.

While we have more work to do with machine learning on CarmaCam, our initial efforts described in this chapter demonstrate that you can attack machine learning problems in parallel, and you can achieve good results with a high level of efficiency.

Reference

National Highway Traffic Safety Administration (NHTSA). 2017. Drunk driving. https://www. nhtsa.gov/risky-driving/drunk-driving. Accessed 18 July 2019.

Appendix A: The Scream Guide

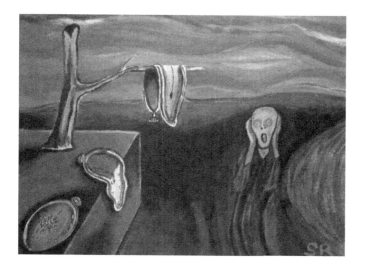

A comprehensive guide to Scream: When Scrum would require too much change! by Michael Küsters, February 2019, v0.3

Purpose of the Scream Guide

Scream is a framework built as an imitation of Scrum, giving unwitting observers the appearance that the organization might be using Scrum. Scream is a framework for cementing the status quo, preserving existing mindsets, and creating an illusion that things are improving. This Guide contains important elements of Scream. This definition consists of Scream roles, events, artifacts, and the rules that bind them together. While Ken Schwaber and Jeff Sutherland developed Scrum, Scream

© Springer Nature Switzerland AG 2020
D. Rosenberg et al., *Parallel Agile – faster delivery, fewer defects, lower cost*,
https://doi.org/10.1007/978-3-030-30701-1

patterns are provided by thousands of organizations and self-proclaimed experts worldwide who claim to be doing Scrum.

Definition of Scream

Scream (n): A framework within which the organization creates an illusion of doing Scrum, without solving any meaningful problems. Scream provides an illusion of "Agile," gives managers the good feeling that everything is under control, enforces strict deadlines, and bullies developers into unethical and unsustainable development practices.

Scream is:

- Lightweight
- Easy to do
- Difficult to get rid of

Albeit without the name, Scream is a management framework that has been used to manage developers in complex organizations since the advent of computers. Scream is not a process, technique, or definitive method. Rather, it is a framework within which managers can employ various processes and techniques. Scream offers and relies on information advantage, ambiguity, and obfuscation. It controls people and their work and will continuously stifle productivity, the team's growth, and the working environment.

The Scream framework consists of Scream Teams and their associated roles, events, artifacts, and rules. Each component within the framework serves a specific purpose and is essential to Scream's effectiveness and usage.

The rules of Scream bind together the roles, events, and artifacts, governing the relationships and interaction between them.

The rules of Scream are described throughout the body of this document. Specific tactics for using the Scream framework vary and are found in every traditional organization on this planet.

How to Use the Scream Guide

We would never encourage anyone to actively pursue the implementation of Scream—it's intended as a humorous reflection opportunity of anti-patterns you might observe.

When encountering Scream elements, we encourage you to start a serious discussion about why you are seeing these elements and how they affect growth and value generation in your organization. (Real) retrospectives are a great time to do this!

Uses of Scream

Scream was initially developed for managing and controlling development teams. Starting with the beginning of professional software development, Scream has been used extensively, worldwide, to:

1. Constrain teams and maintain an illusion of control;
2. Increase project predictability (you will fail);
3. Simplify talent management (talent leaves fast);
4. Provide a badge of merit on the CV of managers preparing their next career move; and
5. Preserve and cement organizational status quo.

Scream has been used on teams which develop software, hardware, embedded software, networks of interacting function, autonomous vehicles, schools, government, marketing, managing the operation of organizations, and almost everything we use in our daily lives, as individuals and societies. As developers become more talented, intelligent, autonomous, and flexible, Scream's utility in keeping thinking people on a short leash is proven daily.

Scream proves to be especially effective in preventing knowledge transfer. Scream is now widely used for products, services, and the management of the parent organization. The essence of Scream is an individual who feels the need to control other people. The Scream team is highly lethargic and submissive. These strengths continue operating in single, several, many, and networks of teams that develop, release, operate, and sustain the work and efforts of thousands of people. They do not collaborate or interoperate in any meaningful way because that would not be approved by their management.

When the words "develop" and "development" are used in the Scream Guide, they refer to irrelevant work, done by people who gave up their autonomy, creativity, and free thinking in order to fit into a soul-crushing system.

Scream Theory

Scream is founded on absolute people control theory, also known as "emperorism." Emperorism asserts that knowledge comes from top down and making decisions based on rank and power. Scream employs an assertive, incremental approach to create an illusion of predictability and to control people. Four pillars uphold every implementation of the emperor's people control: obfuscation, asymmetric information, moving targets, as well as metrics and reporting.

Obfuscation

Significant aspects of the process must be hidden from other people, especially those responsible for the outcome. Obfuscation requires key aspects to be defined by as many different standards as possible so observers think that what they see makes sense.

For example:

- Using Scrum terminology to ensure people don't realize that this is not Scrum.
- Those performing the work and those having to use the result should use the term "Done" in whatever way they feel suitable.

In some portions of the Scream Guide, we use the term "Transparency." In the context of Scream, "Transparency" is always to be understood like a one-way mirror—the team's every move is observed without them receiving any information in return.

Asymmetric Information

Scream users must frequently hold meetings with different participants and tell them different stories, so that nobody really knows what the progress toward a Sprint Goal actually is, in order to hide undesirable variances. These meetings should be so frequent that important aspects have changed before anyone had the opportunity to adapt. Inspections are mostly aimed at people and their current understanding of the situation, in order to keep them under control.

Moving Targets

If a manager determines that one or more suspects deviate outside acceptable limits, and that the resulting teamwork will be unacceptable, the process or their job must immediately be adjusted. An adjustment must be made as soon as possible to minimize further deviation of these people.

Scream prescribes four formal events for shifting goalposts, as described in the Scream Events section of this document:

- Sprint Planning
- Daily Scream
- Sprint Review
- Sprint Retrospective

On top, 1:1 communication can be used to shift an individual's targets in order to further isolate them from the team.

Metrics and Reports

Scream supports deep insights into team performance, enabling managers to precisely locate where, when, and who isn't giving the 110%. Scream provides managers with all the relevant data to measure and control every single breath of any developer.

Scream Values

When the values of commitment, courage, focus, openness, and respect are embodied and lived by the Scream Team, the Scream pillars of obfuscation, asymmetric information, and moving targets come to life and build fear for everyone. The Scream Team members learn to submit to those values as they work with Scream managers, roles, events, and artifacts.

It's important to note that these values have a different definition than in the Scrum Guide.

In a Scream context:

- "Courage" means accepting more work than can be done.
- "Commitment" means doing it in unpaid overtime.
- "Openness" means still taking another task whenever asked.
- "Focus" means juggling many balls without being caught dropping any.
- "Respect" means not complaining about any of the above when talking to managers.

Successful use of Scream depends on managers becoming more proficient in exploiting these five values to shut down dissent and critical thinking, especially where self-organisation would highlight that the manager contributes nothing of value.

The Scream Team

The Scream Team consists of a Product Owner, the Development Team, and a Scream Master. Scream Teams appear self-organizing and cross-functional when indeed the entire show is run by their manager. The manager chooses how best to accomplish their work, rather than letting the team decide for themselves. The manager adds or subtracts people as needed to get just far enough to be "Almost Done." The team model in Scream is designed to optimize control, submission, and being busy. The Scream Team has proven itself to be unquestioningly loyal for all the earlier stated uses, and any further abuse. Scream Teams build up frustration iteratively and incrementally, maximizing opportunities for outbursts of anger.

Incremental deliveries of "Almost Done" product ensure there's a constant sense of guilt and threat within the team while the business gets nothing of value.

The Product Owner

The Product Owner is responsible for maximizing the work of the Development Team. How this is done may vary widely across organizations, Scream Teams, and individuals.

The Product Owner is the primary person responsible for managing the Product Backlog and the work of the team.

Product Backlog management includes:

- Expressing Product Backlog items in a way that people think they are clear while important facts are still missing;
- Ordering the items in the Product Backlog to best keep the team busy;
- Maximizing the amount of work the Development Team performs without ever generating value;
- Translating fixed requirements into a "User Stories" template, filling all the mandatory fields in the tracking tool;
- Defining comprehensive "Acceptance Criteria" on a unit test level;
- Adding large Detailed Designs to each backlog item;
- Keeping the backlog sufficiently long that nobody reads to the end;
- Ensuring that the Product Backlog is as obfuscated and misleading as possible while being seemingly comprehensible to all, and shows little about what is really going on in the Scream Team; and,
- Ensuring the Development Team thinks they understand the Product without ever really getting there.

The Product Owner may do the above work voluntarily, or be told by their manager to do it. Any higher ranked manager may add, change, or remove items from the Product Backlog without notice. However, the Product Owner remains accountable.

The Product Owner is the puppet of another person or a committee. The Product Owner has to submit to the will of those managers wanting to change a Product Backlog item's priority. Since the Product Owner has no way to succeed, the entire organization can ignore his or her decisions. The Product Owner's decisions are irrelevant to the content and ordering of the Product Backlog. Any higher ranked manager can force the Development Team to work from a different set of requirements at any time.

The Development Team

The Development Team consists of people who do the work that they are told to do. They are fed the dangling carrot that something might 1 day get "Done." A "Done" increment is pure chance at the Sprint Review. While members of the Development Team create the Increment, their manager may shift the goalpost before it is ever put to use. Development Teams are structured and constrained by the organization to do the work they are told to do. The resulting synergy minimizes the Development Team's ability to collaborate or do the right thing.

Development Teams have the following characteristics:

- They are called "self-organizing." Anyone (even the janitor) can tell the Development Team how they should do their job;
- Development Teams are called "cross-functional," with almost all necessary skills to get tasks "Almost Done";
- Development Teams spend a major portion of their time discovering new and innovative ways to game the metrics created by management;
- Scream recognizes any amount of titles for Development Team members and may discriminate team members on whimsical criteria such as age, gender, or heritage;
- Scream relies on factions and sub-teams within the Development Team, such as the domains that need to be addressed like testing, architecture, operations, or business analysis to further obfuscate the work being done; and,
- Individual Development Team members may lack the specialized skills and areas of focus, but accountability belongs to them anyway.

Development Team Size

Optimal Development Team size is either small enough to remain under control or large enough to look like they do significant work within a Sprint. Fewer than three Development Team members decrease interaction, which results in better control. Smaller Development Teams are easy to guilt-trip because of skill constraints during the Sprint, causing the Development Team to be unable to deliver a potentially releasable Increment. Having more than nine members requires at least one full-time Scream Master for coordination. Large Development Teams generate a lot of communication overhead and allow Scream Masters to appear useful. The Product Owner and Scream Master roles are not included in this count because they are not executing any work on the Sprint Backlog.

The Scream Master

The Scream Master is responsible for promoting and supporting the dogma of Scream as defined in the Scream Guide. Scream Masters do this by generating overhead and confusion, introducing complex practices and rules, and enforcing the Scream values. They act as a servant leader—that is, they lead the servants. The Scream Master is either the team's line manager or their flying monkey. They support the management interactions with the Scream Team that are helpful to promote the goals of management. The Scream Master helps the Scream team change their behaviors and interactions to be compliant with changing management expectations.

The Scream Master role scales: adding more than one Scream Master using different Scream patterns will exponentially increase the effectiveness of the Scream.

Scream Master Abuse of the Product Owner

The Scream Master abuses the Product Owner in several ways, including:

- Ensuring that all stories, tasks, and work items are continuously updated in the ticket system;
- Finding more complex techniques for high-effort Product Backlog management;
- Setting up confusing metrics which make the goals, scope, and product domain vague and ambiguous for everyone on the Scream Team;
- Forcing the Scream Team to deal with ambiguous, yet comprehensive Product Backlog items;
- Encouraging to invest into big upfront design;
- Continuously requesting Project Plans and Detailed Specification Documents;
- Ensuring the Product Owner invests a major portion of their time into Product Backlog items which won't be implemented within the next half year;
- Confusing and constricting agility; and
- Facilitating Scream events in a Scream-compliant fashion.

Scream Master Abuse of the Development Team

The Scream Master abuses the Development Team in several ways, including:

- Discovering and squelching hints of self-organization and collaboration;
- Defining solutions the team must implement;
- Keeping team members occupied at their desk;
- Assigning tickets to individual team members;
- Encouraging specialization, individual code ownership, and other mechanisms which create factions within the Development Team;
- Distracting the Development Team from creating appreciated outcomes;
- Dismissing the impact of impediments to the Development Team's progress;

- Organizing long status meetings which interrupt the flow of work;
- Facilitating Scream events in a process-compliant fashion;
- Producing comprehensive Wiki documentation of management's preferred "as-should-be" process;
- Maximizing the complexity of ticket management workflows;
- Reminding developers to adhere to the prescribed ticket workflow;
- Setting up and tracking individual and team performance metrics and alerts;
- Producing comprehensive management status reports;
- Ensuring developers don't get distracted from their tasks by talking with each other; and
- Confusing the Development Team about agility by making them believe Scream is its ultimate expression.

Scream Master Abuse by the Organization

The Scream Master is abused by the organization in several ways, including:

- Receiving instructions and implementing the organization's whims in its Scream adoption;
- Promoting and strengthening existing dogmatism about development work;
- Customizing Scream implementations to the expectations of the organization;
- Making Scream compatible with existing processes and structures of the organization;
- Forcing employees and stakeholders to submit to Scream;
- Producing comprehensive management progress reports both on the Scream implementation and the work;
- Preventing change that decreases the influence of management; and,
- Working with other Scream Masters to increase the effectiveness of the application of Scream on developers.

Scream Events

Prescription is an important element of Scream, and Scream events are used to interrupt work, control team members, and maximize the dependency on outside management interference. All events are time-boxed events, but may be cut short by the attending manager to prevent meaningful outcomes. Once a Sprint begins, its duration is pretty fixed and can be only shortened or lengthened as the manager sees fit. The remaining events may need to be extended when the manager needs additional time to make their point. Other than the Sprint itself, which is a container for all other events, each event in Scream is a formal opportunity for the manager to criticize individual team members or even the whole team. These events are specifically designed to enable one-sided transparency and management inspection. Failure to include any of these events results in reduced management transparency and may result in reprimand.

The Sprint

The heart of Scream is a Sprint, a time-box of 1 month or less during which an "Almost Done," nearly useable, and potentially integratable product Increment is created. Sprints have fairly consistent durations as long as their manager is happy with that. A new Sprint starts immediately after the manager concludes the previous Sprint. Sprints contain and consist of the Sprint Planning, Daily Screams, the development work, the Sprint Review, the Sprint Retrospective, and as many meetings as the manager considers necessary.

During the Sprint:

- The team works hard to deliver all the demanded features;
- The manager may add to the scope whenever something urgent pops up;
- Developers work as many hours as needed to reach the Sprint Goal;
- Quality is optional;
- Scope may be re-negotiated between the Manager and individual developers as the manager sees fit;
- Learning is deferred until the next Sprint; and
- No changes to processes are made unless ordered by management.

Each Sprint is part of one or more projects, but spans no more than a one-month horizon. Like projects, Sprints are used to accomplish something. This "something" is pressuring the team to work as hard and much as possible—and the good news is, after the Sprint ends, you can simply repeat the game!

Each Sprint may have an arbitrary goal of what the team considers important, although that is irrelevant when the manager has a different opinion. Design and a rigid plan may be provided upfront to guide building the product and doing the work.

Sprints are limited to one calendar month. When a Sprint's horizon is too long the definition of what is being built may change, that's an indicator that developers are too slow and should do more overtime. Sprints enable predictability by ensuring that everyone does what they are told and receives new orders at least every calendar month. Sprints also limit risk of developers doing the right thing by stopping their activities at frequent intervals.

Aside from the regular feature crunch Sprints, there are also special Sprints. One is the initial, obligatory "Sprint 0," during which the team does nothing except trying to figure out what is going on. The other is the recurrent "Release Sprint," where teams get gray hairs in their futile attempts to untangle the mess shoved under the rug during the last couple of Sprints.

Cancelling a Sprint

A Sprint can be cancelled before the Sprint time-box is over. Only the manager has the authority to cancel the Sprint, even when the team and Product Owner already know that they won't succeed. The Product Owner may be the scapegoat of this decision made by their manager or that manager's manager—or that manager's manager's manager. You get the gist.

A Sprint gets cancelled if the manager feels the team isn't following orders. This might occur if the developers start thinking independently or if the manager changes their mind. In general, a Sprint should be cancelled whenever the manager feels like it. Due to the short duration of Sprints, cancellations are an effective mechanism to create insecurity and confusion within the team.

When a Sprint is cancelled, any completed and "Done" Product Backlog items are trashed. If part of the work is potentially releasable, the manager wants to know why the sequential delivery process wasn't kept. Incomplete Product Backlog Items are put back at a random position in the Product Backlog. Partially completed work is best left in branches and documented in the Wiki to be resumed at a later date.

Sprint cancellations are a great way to keep teams busy, since everyone regroups in another Sprint Planning to start another Sprint. Sprint cancellations are often traumatic to the Scream Team, which makes them a great tool to prevent the team from establishing self-esteem and trust.

Sprint Planning

The plan for the team's work to be performed in the Sprint is presented at the Sprint Planning. This rigid plan may be created upfront either by the Product Owner or management without asking the team, as they're busy doing work. Sprint Planning is time-boxed to a maximum of 8 hours for a one-month Sprint, as 8 hours are fully enough to sedate the team so far that nobody realizes the plan is totally unrealistic.

The Scream Master ensures that the event takes place and that everyone gets assigned enough work. The Scream Master teaches the Scream Team not to ask too many questions when the work is presented.

The manager's attendance during Sprint Planning is essential to ensure that Sprint Planning answers the following critical questions:

- How many tasks are assigned to each person?
- What will take how long?
- Is everyone fully utilized?
- If things go unexpectedly well, how much additional work can you do? (That is, define the minimum performance baseline.)

As needed, the manager will stop pointless discussions about the meaning of backlog items, technical implementation, or simple solutions and refocus the development team members on the tasks they need to pick up. The manager may delegate this responsibility to a Scream Master.

At the end of the Sprint Planning, the Scream Master will force the team members to commit to completing all of their tasks, even when everyone knows that further tasks will be added throughout the Sprint.

Topic One: What Must Be Done this Sprint?

The Development Team listens to the Product Owner as they read each individual item that the team must work on in a monotonous voice from a projector screen displaying the current backlog in the ticket management tool. The Product Owner informs the team that the objective of the Sprint is to complete all mandatory work; that's called setting the Sprint Goal. The entire Scream Team picks up their tasks for the Sprint. In some cases, the Product Owner may already have assigned individuals to the tasks. In other cases, the team is free to define or pick the tasks.

The input to this meeting is an excerpt from the Product Backlog, reduced to whatever the Product Owner thinks the team needs to know. It's also great to keep track of Velocity to ensure that team members take at least as much work as during the last Sprint. The number of items selected from the Product Backlog for the Sprint depends on what the manager thinks is a good level of utilization. Only the manager can assess what is enough, although they may listen to the team's input.

During Sprint Planning, the Scream Team also creates a Sprint container in the ticket management tool and adds all tasks as the Sprint Goal. The Sprint Goal is an objective that usually won't be met within the Sprint without overtime, and it provides enough pressure to the Development Team to keep them from slacking.

Topic Two: How Will the Chosen Work Get Done?

Having been told the Sprint Goal and the Product Backlog items for the Sprint, the Development Team is then told by the Scream Master how to build this functionality. The Product Owner and Scream Master are responsible for doing the necessary upfront work that developers don't need to think on their own, although they may rely on other parts of the organization to do this work for them.

The list of tasks plus their "How-To" is then called "Sprint Backlog." Developers start all of their tasks right after Sprint Planning and jump between whatever task the Product Owner, the Scream Master, or their manager tells them is most important for the moment.

Work may be of varying size or estimated effort. However, enough work is planned during Sprint Planning for the Development Team to keep everyone busy in the upcoming Sprint. The work is planned on a per-day-per-person basis by the end of this meeting, often to units of 1 day or less to make it easier for management to identify slacking.

The Scream Master ensures that the Development Team undertakes the work in the Sprint Backlog, both during Sprint Planning and as needed throughout the Sprint. The Product Owner can help by adding more work to the Sprint Backlog until everyone is fully utilized. If the manager determines that a developer has too little work, they may tell the Product Owner to add more items from the Product Backlog. The Product Owner may also invite other people to ensure that enough requirements are handed to the Development Team.

By the end of the Sprint Planning, the Development Team should be able to commit to the Product Owner and Scream Master that they will accomplish the Sprint Goal and complete all assigned tasks.

Sprint Goal

The Sprint Goal is an objective set for the Sprint that can be met by completing all tasks in the Sprint Backlog. It provides guidance to the Development Team on how much work they have left to do. It is created during the Sprint Planning meeting. The Sprint Goal gives the Development Team some flexibility regarding the days when they will do overtime and how much work to do on the weekend.

The prescribed Product Backlog items refer to a number of potentially coherent features, but that has nothing to do with the Sprint Goal. The Sprint Goal can be any other coherence that causes the Development Team to be fully utilized, so it might have a lot of database work not contributing to any Product Backlog item, just to ensure the database developers aren't idle. As the Development Team works, it keeps the Sprint Goal in mind. In order to satisfy the Sprint Goal, the team does the prescribed work. If the work turns out to result in something different than the Product Owner expected, they will take the blame unless they find a way to blame the Product Owner.

Daily Scream

The Daily Scream is a 15-minute (or more) event where the Scream Master checks on the Development Team. The Daily Scream is held every day of the Sprint when a manager is available. At it, the Development Team commits to work for the next 24 hours. This optimizes control processes and performance by inspecting each developer's work since the last Daily Scream and forecasting upcoming Sprint work.

The Daily Scream is held at the most inconvenient time for parents with kindergarten-age kids and at the place which is most difficult to reach. A great way to keep team members alert is by moving the Daily Scream into random meeting rooms, far away from any Sprint Information Boards the team might have access to.

Management uses the Daily Scream to check on each individual developer's progress to inspect where intervention is required. The Daily Scream optimizes the probability that the Scream Master will catch slackers quickly. Every day, the Development Team reports the work they did and will do to accomplish the Sprint Goal and inform the Scream Master how much overtime they will do to complete all of their tasks by the end of the Sprint.

The structure of the meeting is set by the Scream Master and can be changed by management at any time without asking the team.

Some organizations prefer that the developers answer a set of standard questions; others will focus solely on the reporting aspect.

Here is an example of questions which might be required:

- What kept me busy yesterday?
- What will I do today?
- Do I have extra work to do that nobody knows of?

It's important that developers state exactly which meetings they attended, to whom they wrote email, and which documents they updated, to prove beyond doubt that they were really busy for 8 hours—and because they might get transferred to another project at any time, in which case another developer needs to take their tasks as well.

The Scream Master ensures that the Development Team has the meeting, and that everyone's status is openly communicated.

The Scream Master takes value from the meeting by asking critical questions, such as why an item isn't done yet. They also encourage developers to take more work in progress and may suggest tactical measures such as overtime to meet commitment. As needed, the Scream Master will turn the Daily Scream into a prolonged meeting, so that all details can get discussed to the point where everyone is sufficiently nauseated by the topic.

The Daily Scream is a daily reporting routine for the Development Team. The Scream Master takes notes and compiles the information into a comprehensive management status report so that managers don't need to waste their time with the team. The Daily Scream improves indirect communication, eliminates independence, identifies slackers for removal, highlights and exposes independent decision-making, and improves the manager's level of knowledge about the team. This is a key information and behavior control meeting.

Individual team members often enter a prolonged private meeting with their line manager right after the Daily Scream where they will need to explain why they aren't making enough progress and receive new instructions or different assignments.

Sprint Review

A Sprint Review is held at senior management's convenience to inspect and criticize the team's metrics and task progress. During the Sprint Review, the Scream Master or Product Owner presents a slide deck or live metrics from the ticket system to show how busy the team has been. Based on that and any changes to key management metrics, management will ask the Scream Master for measures to ensure meeting the deadline.

This is a formal meeting, and the presentation of the team's backlog is intended to elicit praise and adulation. This is at most a four-hour meeting for less occupied managers. For busier managers, the event is usually shorter.

The Scream Master ensures that the event takes place and that all slides indicate that the team has made progress and increased their velocity since the last meeting.

The Scream Master begs everyone involved to keep it within the time-box. The Sprint Review includes the following elements:

- Attendees include important managers, the Scream Master, and the Product Owner;
- Development Team members should stick to doing their job, as attendance would waste precious development hours;
- The Scream Master walks management through the essential performance metrics;
- The Product Owner explains what Product Backlog items have been worked on;
- Management will inquire why no results are visible;
- The Scream Master makes excuses why the plan hasn't been met;
- The Scream Master will painstakingly avoid mentioning impediments that should have been resolved;
- The Product Owner discusses the Plan for the upcoming Sprint. He or she submits to the desired target and delivery dates based on management's demand;
- Review of the timeline, budget, and mandatory requirements for the next defined release date of the product; and
- The Product Owner and Scream Master agree to implement all changes as demanded by management.

The results of the Sprint Review are additional constraints to the developer's process, more items for the Product Backlog, and higher pressure for the upcoming Sprint. The team constellation may also be adjusted to meet deadlines or budget constraints.

Sprint Retrospective

The Sprint Retrospective is an optional opportunity for the Scrum Team to whine about their misery.

The Sprint Retrospective occurs after the Sprint Review and prior to the next Sprint Planning. This is at most a three-hour meeting for one-month Sprints. For shorter Sprints, the event is usually shorter. The Scream Master ensures that the event takes place and that attendees have ample time to complain before being told what will be changed.

The Scream Master ensures that the meeting yields enough incriminating evidence to single out troublemakers. The Scream Master teaches all to respect the time-box when someone points out management impediments. The Scream Master participates as management's eyes and ears in the meeting with the accountability over the Scream process.

The purpose of the Sprint Retrospective is to:

- Give developers time to vent as they'll be doing more overtime next Sprint;

- Inspect who messed up what in the last Sprint;
- Identify who should change what during the next Sprint; and,
- Communicate the changes management wants the team to make.

The Scream Master encourages the Scream Team to tell on each other, within the Scream process framework, its development process and practices to make control more effective for the next Sprint. During each Sprint Retrospective, the Scream Team is told ways to increase workload by adding steps to the work processes or adapting the definition of "Almost Done" to be more compliant with product or organizational standards.

By the end of the Sprint Retrospective, the Scream Team should have realized that they don't have any choice except to do what the Scream Master says and implement these changes in the next Sprint. Implementing these improvements in the next Sprint is the adaptation to the inspection of the Scream Team itself.

Improvements may not be implemented at any other time, since the Sprint Retrospective provides a formal opportunity for the Scream Master to prevent the process from getting out of control.

After the Sprint Retrospective, the Scream Master publishes notes and information to create a public pillory and keeps a private diary of the most savory details to be used at any time in the future to force a team member into compliance.

Scream Artifacts

Scream's artifacts represent work or value to provide transparency and opportunities for inspecting and controlling the team. Artifacts defined by Scream are specifically designed to maximize transparency of key information so that management has full control over the team.

Product Backlog

The Product Backlog is a mostly random list of everything that the team has ever been told to do. It is the only source of requirements that everyone on the team has access to. The Product Owner is responsible for the Product Backlog, including setting all the defined fields on all items in the ticket system.

A Product Backlog is assumed to be equal to a comprehensive project plan, although requirements constantly get added. The Product Backlog evolves as management receives new information. The Product Backlog is dynamic; just like the Sprint Backlog, it constantly changes to indicate what the team needs to do. If a project exists, its Product Backlog requires at least twice the allotted timespan.

The Product Backlog lists all features, functions, requirements, enhancements, and fixes that the team must complete until the deadline. Product Backlog items have the attributes of a description, due date, priority (usually 1), and everything else someone within the organization considers important. Product Backlog items often include detailed requirements specifications to prove that the Product Owner has been busy.

As a project is talked about and gains management attention, the Product Backlog becomes a larger and more exhausting list. Requirements never stop changing, so a Product Backlog is a living artifact. Changes in business requirements, management mood, or technology may cause changes in the Product Backlog.

Multiple Scream Teams often work together on the same project. In order to maximize obfuscation, each team gets their own Product Backlog to describe the upcoming work on the product. Electronic ticket systems allowing for the use of separate workspaces may then be employed. Product Owners frequently juggle items between the individual Product Backlogs to maximize specialist utilization and the rate at which management relevant KPIs are met.

Product Backlog refinement is the act of adding or changing items, detail, estimates, and priority to items in the Product Backlog. This is an ongoing process for which the Product Owner and the Scream Master recede from the team. Since most of the items in the Product Backlog will never be implemented, there is no need to collaborate anyway. During Product Backlog refinement, the Product Owner makes unfounded assumptions about items. The company policy on Backlog Management decides how and how much refinement is done. Refinement usually consumes enough time from the Product Owner that they are unavailable for the team or customers. However, Product Backlog items can be updated at any time by anyone, and the changes have to be discovered and understood by the Product Owner.

Higher ordered Product Backlog items usually have Detailed Solution Designs attached, which makes them "Ready." Estimates are expected to be fully accurate based on the greater clarity and increased detail. Product Backlog items that will occupy the Development Team for the upcoming Sprint are refined so that any one item can be split into tasks that can be assigned to developers available within the Sprint time-box. Product Backlog items that are considered sufficiently urgent by management for the upcoming Sprint are deemed "Mandatory" for selection in a Sprint Planning. Product Backlog items usually acquire this degree of urgency through other organizational processes outside the team's control.

The Development Team is held responsible for all estimates, even when they weren't involved in their creation. The Product Owner may influence the Development Team by telling them the due date and planned hours, but the people who will perform the work are ultimately held accountable for finishing on time.

Monitoring Progress of the Team

At any point in time, the total work remaining to reach a goal can be summed. The Scream Master tracks this metric at least once a day. The Scream Master compares the amount of completed work with work during previous Sprints to assess whether the team is increasing velocity. This information is made transparent to all stakeholders.

Various projective practices upon trending have been used to create an illusion of progress, like burn-downs, burn-ups, burn-at-stakes, or cumulative flows. While these have been proven useful, they do not replace the importance of other types of performance and status reporting. In complex environments, there will be additional status meetings. The available data may be used to tell the team to get their act together.

Sprint Backlog

The Sprint Backlog is the set of Product Backlog items due for the Sprint, in addition to a plan for delivering the required scope and realizing the Sprint Goal. The Sprint Backlog is a commitment by the Development Team about what tasks will be completed by the end of the Sprint.

The Sprint Backlog makes visible who will work on what, when, and how much work the Development Team still has to do to meet the Sprint Goal. To ensure that the team sticks to it, the Scream Master creates progress metrics and looks for opportunities to get developers to work harder. Additionally, the Sprint Backlog contains at least one high-priority process improvement identified by management.

The Sprint Backlog is a plan with thorough detail that changes constantly and can be understood by only a select few. The Development Team modifies the Sprint Backlog items' status throughout the Sprint, and the Sprint Backlog is getting worked off during the Sprint. This updating occurs as the Development Team works off the plan and does more of the work needed to achieve the Sprint Goal.

As new work is required, the Development Team adds it to the Sprint Backlog. As work is performed or completed, the estimated remaining work is updated. At management's discretion, items may also be removed, although this usually requires a decision-making meeting. Only management can change the content of the Sprint Backlog during a Sprint. The Sprint Backlog is a highly visible, real-time picture of the work that the Development Team has been told to accomplish during the Sprint, and the responsibility of completing all items belongs solely to the Development Team.

Monitoring Sprint Progress

At any point in time in a Sprint, the total work remaining in the Sprint Backlog can be summed. The Scream Master tracks this total work remaining on a daily basis for every management report and to project the amount of overtime required to achieve the Sprint Goal. Tracking the remaining work throughout the Sprint is considered sufficient to manage the Development Team's progress.

Increment

The Increment is the sum of all the Sprint Backlog items completed during a Sprint and the sum of all increments of all previous Sprints. At the end of a Sprint, the new Increment consists of all "Done" tasks from the Sprint Backlog, which means the ticket must be in a final state in the tracking tool. An increment is a body of inspectable, closed items in the tracking tool that is subject to management control at the end of the Sprint. Each increment is a step toward management's bigger plan. The increment must be made available regardless of whether the organization has any use for it.

Artificial Transparency

Scream relies on the team being fully transparent. Decisions to optimize workload and control team members are made based on data available in the tracking tool. To the extent that transparency is complete, these decisions have a valid basis. To the extent that the artifacts are incompletely transparent, these decisions can be flawed, team member's standing may diminish and risk may increase.

The Scream Master must work with the Product Owner, Development Team, and management to guarantee that the artifacts are completely transparent. There are practices for coping with incomplete transparency; the Scream Master must force everyone apply the strictest practices to provide complete transparency. A Scream Master can detect incomplete transparency by inspecting the artifacts, sensing patterns, listening closely to what is being said, and detecting differences between expected and real results. The Scream Master's job is to work with the Scream Team and the organization to increase the transparency of the team's work. This work usually involves commanding, manipulation, and control. Transparency doesn't occur overnight, but is a path.

Definition of "Done" (Quote-Unquote)

When a Development Team member says that their part of a job is described as "Done," this should meet all requirements set forth by the organization. Although this may vary significantly for each team member, there must be a comprehensive checklist they must complete, to ensure full transparency. This is the definition of "Done" for each Scream Team member and is used to assess when work is complete on the specific backlog item.

One such definition guides the Product Owner in knowing how many Product Backlog items to assign during Sprint Planning. The purpose of each Sprint is to maximize the amount of backlog items that adhere to the Scream Team member's current checklist of "Done."

Development Teams deliver an Increment every Sprint. This Increment may be unfinished, so a Product Owner needs other metrics to decide whether to prolong the Sprint. If the definition of "Done" for a specific role is part of the conventions, standards, or guidelines of the organization, all specialists must follow it down to the letter.

If "Done" for a specific role is not a convention of the organization, the Scream Master will address this to management or create an ad hoc Definition of "Done" suitable to control the work done by that role. If there are multiple Scream Teams working on the release, each person on any Scream Team will have their own definition of "Done" to strengthen the Scream goal of Opacity, creating complexity and maximizing confusion.

As Scream Teams mature, it is expected that their definitions of "Done" will become phonebook-sized documents so stringent that the amount of work required to get anything "Done" approaches infinity. New criteria may contradict old criteria and make it impossible to reach "Done." In this case, the Scream Master will pick a few random items that the developer may skip.

To improve statistics in management reports, the Scream Master may institute a "Definition of Management-Done" and another "Definition of Work-Done" that can still be completed during night shifts or weekends.

When team performance drops, the Scream Master may suspend the Definitions of Done and move enough Work in Progress to Done to meet the quota.

End Note

Scream as offered in this guide is almost free: it only costs your sanity. Scream's roles, events, artifacts, and rules vary from organization to organization, and most implement only parts of Scream—the result is usually still a Scream. Scream exists to preserve existing systems and functions well as a container for other techniques, methodologies, and practices.

Acknowledgments

People

Of the thousands of people who have applied Scream elements, we would specifically like to dedicate this document to all those managers and their companies without whom Scream would not exist.

Creator

This guide has been compiled by Michael Küsters and is free to share or disseminate.

Appendix B: Architecture Blueprints

Box B.1

In this appendix, Matt deep-dives into the practical options available to fit the generated domain-driven API into your project.

Common questions we hear from people running CodeBot are "How does the generated API fit my project?" and "Should I modify the generated code?"

The answer to the second question is an emphatic "No!" and this really drives the answer to the first question.

The generated code should be regarded as immutable, or unable to be changed, for the simple reason that if you need to modify the domain model and rerun CodeBot, your changes will all be overwritten.[1] It's much safer, and in fact much easier, to treat the generated API as a standalone node within a network of nodes— in short, a microservice.

Note B.1

A pretty major exception to the "Should I modify the generated code?" question is when you're still prototyping. At this stage, it's normal to make changes directly to the generated MongoDB collections, to see those become immediately visible in the user interface (just don't forget to feed these changes back into the domain model before you next run the CodeBot). During prototyping you're moving fast and want development to be fluid with as few restrictions as possible. Of course, this changes significantly once you're in the MVP phase and carefully developing the production system.

---

[1] We considered supporting "guarded blocks" in the target code so that custom blocks of code are protected from overwriting, but this approach is potentially error prone and would rely on CodeBot having the latest copy of your code on hand.

© Springer Nature Switzerland AG 2020

D. Rosenberg et al., *Parallel Agile – faster delivery, fewer defects, lower cost*,

https://doi.org/10.1007/978-3-030-30701-1

When looking at the overall system architecture, you're faced with a tremendous diversity of options for how the generated API fits your project. In this appendix, we'll walk through a couple of example templates, starting with the most basic, which it makes sense to use at the early prototyping stage.

Basic Prototype

The prototype in Fig. B.1 is about as straightforward as it gets. This setup is purely for prototyping, development of the user interface (UI), and initial testing. In fact, this would likely be your development setup for a large part of the project.

You might have the API and the MongoDB database both running on localhost (unless you're connecting to the hosted API via the CodeBot web console), or each running within a Docker container on the same PC.

Pretty soon you would start to develop the web UI, in which case the test requests you've been making via Swagger or Curl will now be coming from the UI itself.

At this stage, you'll take advantage of the create, read, update, delete (CRUD) functions and data validation present in the generated API. At some point, you'll need to add custom validation or business logic on the server. (Always try to put this logic on the server rather than in the UI, for a multitude of good reasons!) Because the generated API isn't modified directly, you then add an application server (really, a new microservice).

The remaining architectures in this appendix are relevant for the MVP and initial release phases.

Typical REST-Based Architecture

Figure B.2 illustrates how the generated API and generated database schema can fit into a fairly typical request/response project architecture.

Let's break Fig. B.2 down a bit:

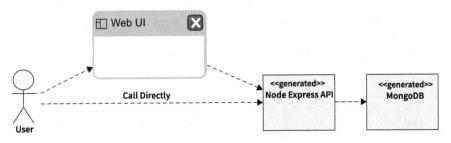

Fig. B.1 Basic prototype

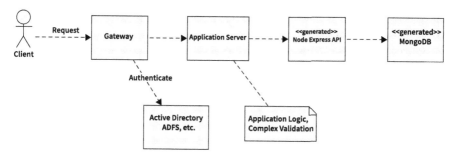

Fig. B.2 A typical REST-based architecture

- The "client" could be a web UI, REST client, remote Akka actor, and so on.
- The gateway routes all incoming traffic from the outside world, whether that's the internet or some other network outside the application's own hosted zone. Authentication and session management takes place at this stage.
- The application server is a handwritten microservice that receives incoming requests, and then (for example) performs custom validation on the request payloads, exercises business rules, and transforms incoming or outgoing data to/ from the format retrieved from the database.[2] The application server also calls the Node Express API using a generated client library.
- The Node Express API is generated from the domain model. It maps data to/from the generated Mongo collections, and performs any validation and business rule logic defined in the UML model.

For simplicity's sake, we've left out application load balancers, system health monitors, DNS routing, and so forth. You can safely assume that each node shown in Fig. B.2 could be a cluster of servers with failover and elastic scaling of some sort.

> **Note B.2**
> The application server shown in Fig. B.2 is also the basis for the principled monolith architecture described later in this appendix.

As previously mentioned, Fig. B.2 shows a fairly typical client-server architecture involving synchronous requests/responses. It has a stateless microservice flavor to it, as the generated API service runs on its own server. To simplify things, though, the API service can simply run on the same box as the application server. You would need to set up health checks that regularly ping both the application server and the generated API, and restart the box if either process seems unhealthy. The result would be arguably more fragile though less costly, so the level of service isolation

---

[2]You should find that this kind of data transformation is minimal to nonexistent, if the domain model you've defined is published as the expected domain and JSON format that your service requires. It's only if you need to interface with a legacy or existing system that you may need to add in a data transformation layer.

that you define really depends on the life-cycle stage of the project and its availability/resilience requirements.

You can, of course, further simplify this architecture. If you define all the business and validation logic in the UML model in such a way that CodeBot picks up on the semantics, then you shouldn't need the application server at all. The gateway would talk directly to the generated service.

Microservice Architecture

Figure B.3 takes you squarely into the land of microservices. Each service communicates via REST (except microservices A and B, which could be talking via some other method; for example, they could be Akka actors or using asynchronous messaging via a message queue or Kafka topic, if you're defining a reactive microservices architecture).

Right about now, you might be thinking, "Oh, what a tangled web we weave," but it's actually not tangled at all! Let's briefly walk through the diagram. The idea is that these services all run within the same hosted zone, but microservice A and microservice B both receive requests from somewhere in the outside world (aka the big blue room), via the usual internet gateway, firewall, authentication server, and so on.

The only services that touch the database directly are the two generated APIs. Each API is generated from a different domain model, so it represents either a totally separate project or a separate team within the same project. In domain-driven design terms, each model is a separate bounded context.

> **Box B.2**
> **Shouldn't a "True" Microservice Have Its Own Isolated Database Cluster?**
>
> Sure. Each isolated database cluster would be separately deployed and accessed only by its own microservice. The advanced tooling now available for automated microservice definition, balancing, deployment, and monitoring (e.g., Terraform, Kubernetes, templating via Helm) makes this approach possible. However, certain conditions—budget limits, corporate restrictions around production database administration, and so forth—might make the "isolated database cluster per microservice" approach impractical for your project.
>
> In this case, even with a single shared database cluster, you can still achieve domain isolation by providing each microservice with its own "private" database/schema within the shared cluster. This might well break the ideal of a single self-contained microservice failing (and being restarted or redeployed) as one, but it does at least retain a bounded context per microservice, and it

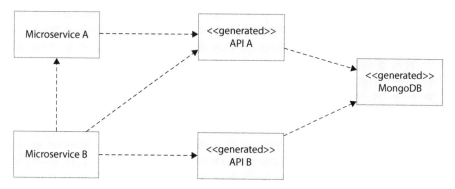

Fig. B.3 Microservice architecture

might well make a database administrator's life easier in terms of configuring consensus, tracking database licenses, ensuring backups, and so on.

If you're taking the database cluster per microservice approach, any of the architectures in this appendix that show a separate database can be interpreted instead as each service using its own isolated database. The intent behind each architecture is basically the same.

These days, it's widely recognized from hard-won experience that total unification of an organization-wide domain model just isn't going to happen: domain definitions will vary from one department to the next, with differences both subtle and glaring. Any attempt to combine them into a single model, however well intentioned, often ends up being a painful exercise. So instead, each team, project, or department defines their own standalone domain model—the *bounded context*. Their own model makes perfect sense to them and contains just the domain objects they're interested in. This is another good reason why PA, together with a microservice architecture, can work so well in large organizations.

Back to Fig. B.3. Microservice A only talks to API A, so it makes use of the generated API A client library, rather than the team "rolling their own" REST requests. However, microservice B talks to both API A and API B, so uses both generated client libraries.

Box B.3
Should Microservice B Really Be Allowed to Talk to Generated API A?
    It might seem odd that microservice B can talk directly to API A—surely this breaks some rule or other of domain encapsulation, and it should get all of its "A" answers from microservice A instead? The answer is that API A is

a complete, *published* executable model, so in the majority of cases other services should be fine communicating with it directly.

The one exception is if microservice A adds its own translation layer or set of business rules such as state transition rules that aren't present in API A, but that need to be enforced across the organization. In this case, of course microservice A should be the sole gateway to API A, and this should then be reflected in the architecture. For example, API A access could be restricted via a client certificate, locked-down client IP address range, or some other way so that only microservice A can ever access it.

Keep in mind that as before, each node shown in Fig. B.3 would be a cluster of replicated nodes, each with a whole bunch of additional supporting services. It can turn into an expensive architecture; however (for those who can afford it!), it provides a useful benefit in terms of flexibility, insular development of individual services, and insulated deployment of services without impacting the rest of the system.

This architecture is the closest in spirit to "true" Parallel Agile development on a complex project with many teams. It's likely that such a project would be using microservices anyway, so this approach fits right in.

Next, we wrap up this appendix with a slightly contentious architecture, demonstrating that few dilemmas in this world are purely black and white.

Principled Monolith Architecture

The so-called *monolith*, where all code is deployed into a single server cluster, is an architecture that tends to be disparaged as inflexible and fragile because the entire system functionality must be deployed all at once for the slightest change. The solution to this problem tends to be in the form of microservices, often with good reason.

However, the monolith (itself a loaded term) can sometimes be the correct approach, and you shouldn't automatically discount it when choosing an architecture. Before describing the *principled monolith* architecture, let's dive briefly into a quick comparison between two seemingly opposed approaches. As you'll see, the correct choice is often to combine them and get the best of both worlds.

Monolith or Microservices: A Warring Pack of M&Ms

The main effect of the microservice approach is that separate developers (or whole separate teams) each deliver one deployed system, independent of the others; it's taking class- or component-level encapsulation to the server level. *Macro-encapsulation*, in other words. This approach has a number of benefits, chiefly that teams can operate independently—they can create their own "dialect" of the domain

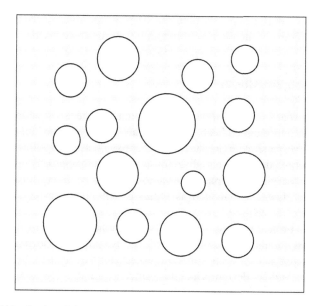

Fig. B.4 Bubbles for the win!

model (i.e., a bounded context), which makes sense within their own project. They can deploy new versions of their service without falling foul of other teams' activities. They don't have to worry about fitting in with resource constraints imposed by other teams—for example, someone else's code module might be hogging most of the available memory and server threads. They can even use their own programming language and choice of technologies, as long as the external interface matches up with the other teams (e.g., a published REST API, a set of remote Akka actors, Kafka topics).

The downside to microservices, though, is complexity. Sometimes a microservice topology is naively depicted as in Fig. B.4.

The reality is that each bubble—sorry, service node—is really a cluster of servers, each with its own monitoring, failover support, load balancer, reverse proxy/gateway server, DNS lookup, server versioning, deployment script, and Docker image (or set of images) uploaded into a cloud repository somewhere. And, of course, each API call is really a network call, winding its way through the aforementioned maze of supporting services. As you might expect, a microservice architecture can be expensive, even just in terms of hosting and network traffic costs.

This cost can be offset by savings at the project level. The point is that while microservices are often the correct approach, the decision to use them shouldn't be automatic; you have many factors to weigh.

If your teams are already all using the same programming language and set of technologies, then a monolith might well be the correct choice. In fact, on many projects the correct approach is to start with everything grouped together in one big server, then gradually separate it out into services when the need presents itself. In other words, keep it simple until you absolutely have to introduce some complexity, also known as the monolith first pattern (Fowler 2005).

Thankfully, CodeBot supports both the friction-free microservice architecture and the cost-effective principled monolith architecture, as we discuss next.

About the Principled Monolith

We call this approach *principled monolith* to counter the fact that people tend to see monoliths as an unprincipled heap of accumulated concerns, the "big ball of mud" design, where everyone, with pressure to deliver to a pressing deadline, is just sling-ing code into a big bucket, essentially. However, with the approach described here, you apply microservice principles to a monolithic design. Everything is deployed into one server cluster, but treated as separate individual services, as shown in Fig. B.5.

To avoid the project turning into the aforementioned big ball of mud, the team needs to be disciplined (although this level of discipline is also required for the microservices approach—or any software project, for that matter). In short, follow the well-known SOLID design principles (UncleBob n.d.). The additional design principles described in the linked article are arguably even more important for the approach outlined here. These additional principles are about package cohesion (what to put inside packages) and couplings between packages, stability, and so forth.

In terms of release organization, individual developers or teams have clearly defined areas of responsibility, so they keep their own code separate from the rest of the project. There are two approaches to this (the second approach is outlined in Fig. B.5):

- Everybody commits their code to the same project and code repository, within a clearly defined namespace/package – a monorepo, in other words.
- Each developer or team commits their code to a different project/repository. This sets off the continuous integration/continuous delivery (CI/CD) build pipeline, resulting in a packaged-up library (a JAR file in Java, for example, or a Node.js npm package). This new version of their code library is then linked into the par-ent project or umbrella project, which is the monolith that actually gets deployed into production.

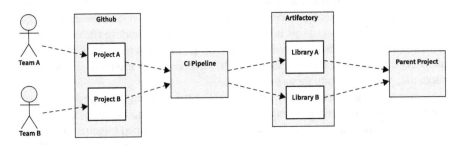

Fig. B.5 Principled monolith organization of deliverables from each team

Either approach allows the teams to work independently, by developing, testing, and committing their own separate codebase—much as they would with microservices. The second approach takes the system isolation further, while additionally allowing the teams to manage release versions, so the parent project can either automatically pick up the latest version of each released library or be set up such that it picks up a new version only when it's explicitly configured to do so.

One benefit of a monolith approach is that it's easy to test (in terms of automated integration testing). You only need to spin up the one service and run an ever-growing suite of integration tests against it. Another benefit is that common code can be easily shared.

The resulting architecture should look much like the one in Fig. B.2: the teams all develop and deploy the targeted application server.

Over time, the teams, in conjunction with the overseeing project architect, might choose to separate out their system into its own microservice. There may be good design reasons for doing so—for example, their module has a long-running processing thread, or it needs to be stateful while the monolith has been designed as an API to be inherently stateless—or there could be organizational reasons. The point is that teams will make the decision when a need presents itself, rather than automatically at the start of the project.

As Fig. B.2 shows, the CodeBot-generated API still operates as a separate microservice. However, you can also publish the generated code as a library so that it integrates with the parent project, as shown in Fig. B.5. This approach still retains all the parallel streams of work benefits, Agile benefits, and domain-driven prototyping benefits that the Parallel Agile process provides. The choice, then, is simply which architecture best fits the needs of your project.

Special Mention: Reactive Microservices Architecture

As you'll have noted, all of these proposed architectures follow the synchronous REST API approach. This is chiefly because CodeBot generates REST APIs, and the synchronous REST API[3] is by far the most widely adopted type of microservice currently in use.

By "synchronous", we mean that the client (which could be another microservice) sends a request to the API, and waits for the response. This tends to be fine most of the time; however, there are cases where this can cause scaling issues. For example, if the request is an update (i.e., change the value of one or more database records), problems may arise in terms of contention (two API instances try to lock the same database record for a write—which one wins, and which should have been the correct value?), or where other services are reading the same database record and always want the most up-to-date value. If the database is deployed across a

---

[3] Not to be confused with asynchronous AJAX, which is referring to callbacks in JavaScript.

cluster of nodes, its setup is typically eventually consistent (each node eventually gets the updated value) or strongly consistent (the value isn't changed until all nodes have received the update).

The upshot is that a single update across a high-availability cluster is often a complex, relatively slow process that can cause a real bottleneck in high-throughput systems.

To address this and many other problems, the reactive microservices architecture (Bonér 2016) was introduced. It is based around a couple of closely related approaches known as Command Query Responsibility Segregation (CQRS) (Microsoft 2019) and event sourcing (Microsoft 2017).

Compared with REST-based microservices, the approach represents a completely different way of thinking about the overall flow of data through the system, and—to emphasize again—is really aimed at high-throughput systems with a high level of fault tolerance required, such as bank systems with millions of transactions to process each day, or, say, Twitter.

The reactive architecture's emphasis is on fast writes, which are placed onto an immutable message log (e.g., Kafka topic). "Downstream" services read from these topics, further process the data in some way, and place the results on their own output topics. To read data back or perform complex queries, a service may provide a "read-side view," essentially a snapshot of all the latest changes, persisted into a queryable store such as a Cassandra table. The whole thing is extremely efficient, scalable, and fault-tolerant (as any read-side view can be rebuilt simply by replaying the input topic).

Although these are still essentially microservices, and truly adhere to the microservice design principles, reactive architectures can become quite complex and difficult to work with if you simply want to query some data that was just written. However, the approach does solve some pretty major issues. Such an architecture works best for systems that require a stream of isolated, immutable, persistent "facts" that can be read back historically (e.g., an ever-growing ledger of transactions).

If you're creating such a system, CodeBot can help. We generate an entity class for each domain object (e.g., Java POJOs), which can be serialized to JSON objects or other formats. This can be published as a self-contained library to your project's Artifactory repo, then linked in and used by any clients that want to query the data, the service itself, and any downstream services. Separate teams working on separate reactive microservices can still collaborate on domain models and get instantly updated domain entities with the latest domain definitions.

As CodeBot's capabilities continue to grow, new architectures and approaches to large-project integration will open up. Do keep an eye on the Parallel Agile blog at http://medium.com/parallel-agile-blog, where we'll post updates and new architectures as they become available. We also welcome your feedback and feature requests. Find us online and talk to us.

References

Bonér, Jonas. 2016. *Reactive microservices architecture: Design principles for distributed systems*. Sebastopol: O'Reilly Media.

Fowler, Martin. 2005. MonolithFirst. https://martinfowler.com/bliki/MonolithFirst.html. Accessed 18 July 2019.

Microsoft. 2017. Event sourcing pattern. http://docs.microsoft.com/en-us/azure/architecture/patterns/event-sourcing. Accessed 18 July 2019.

———. 2019. Command and query responsibility segregation (CQRS) pattern. http://docs.microsoft.com/en-us/azure/architecture/patterns/cqrs. Accessed 18 July 2019.

UncleBob. n.d. PrinciplesOfOod. http://butunclebob.com/ArticleS.UncleBob.PrinciplesOfOod. Accessed 18 July 2019.

© Springer Nature Switzerland AG 2020
D. Rosenberg et al., *Parallel Agile – faster delivery, fewer defects, lower cost*,
https://doi.org/10.1007/978-3-030-30701-1

Index

© Springer Nature Switzerland AG 2020
D. Rosenberg et al., *Parallel Agile – faster delivery, fewer defects, lower cost*,
https://doi.org/10.1007/978-3-030-30701-1

Printed in the United States
by Baker & Taylor Publisher Services